SAS® Programming I: Essentials

Course Notes

SAS® Programming I: Essentials Course Notes was developed by Deborah Blank and Christine Vitron. Additional contributions were made by Larry Stewart, Amy Peters, Betsy McDowell, and Gina Rayman. Editing and Production support was provided by the Curriculum Development and Support Department.

SAS® Programming I: Essentials Course Notes

Book code 57690, course code PROGI, prepared date 24JUL00.

Table of Contents

Course Description

This course is designed for those who want to learn to write SAS programs to accomplish typical data-processing tasks. This course is a prerequisite to many other SAS courses.

After completing this course, you should be able to

- read a SAS data set

- read a raw data file

- combine SAS data sets through concatenation and merging

- create a SAS variable through the assignment statement and conditional logic

- investigate and summarize your data

- calculate simple statistics

- create list, summary, HTML, and graph reports.

To learn more...

A full curriculum of general and statistical instructor-based training is available at any of the Institute's training facilities. Institute instructors can also provide on-site training.

For information on other courses in the curriculum, contact the Professional Services Division at 1-919-677-8000, then press 1-7321, or send email to saspsd@vm.sas.com. You can also find this information on the Web at www.sas.com/training/ as well as in the Training Course Catalog.

For a list of other SAS books that relate to the topics covered in this Course Notes, USA customers can contact our Book Sales Department at 1-800-727-3228 or send email to sasbook@sas.com. Customers outside the USA, please contact your local SAS Institute office.

Also, see the Publications Catalog on the Web at www.sas.com/pubs/ for a complete list of books and a convenient order form.

Prerequisites

Before attending this course, you should have completed the Introduction to Programming Concepts Using SAS® Software course or have at least six months of programming experience.

Specifically, you should be able to

- understand file structures and system commands on your operating systems

- use a full-screen text editor

- write system commands to create and access system files

- understand programming logic.

General Conventions

This section explains the various conventions used in presenting text, SAS language syntax, and examples in this book.

Typographical Conventions

You will see several type styles in this book. This list explains the meaning of each style:

UPPERCASE ROMAN is used for SAS statements, variable names, and other SAS language elements when they appear in the text.

italic identifies terms or concepts that are defined in text. Italic is also used for book titles when they are referenced in text, as well as for various syntax and mathematical elements.

bold is used for emphasis within text.

monospace is used for examples of SAS programming statements and for SAS character strings. Monospace is also used to refer to field names in windows, information in fields, and user-supplied information.

<u>select</u> indicates selectable items in windows and menus. This book also uses icons to represent selectable items.

Syntax Conventions

The general forms of SAS statements and commands shown in this book include only that part of the syntax actually taught in the course. For complete syntax, see the appropriate SAS reference guide.

> **PROC CHART** DATA=*SAS-data-set*;
>   **HBAR | VBAR** *chart-variables </ options>*;
> **RUN**;

This is an example of how SAS syntax is shown in text:

- **PROC** and **CHART** are in uppercase bold because they are SAS keywords.
- DATA= is in uppercase to indicate that it must be spelled as shown.
- *SAS-data-set* is in italic because it represents a value that you supply. In this case, the value must be the name of a SAS data set.
- **HBAR** and **VBAR** are in uppercase bold because they are SAS keywords. They are separated by a vertical bar to indicate they are mutually exclusive; you can choose one or the other.
- *chart-variables* is in italic because it represents a value or values that you supply.
- *</ options>* represents optional syntax specific to the HBAR and VBAR statements. The angle brackets enclose the slash as well as *options* because if no options are specified you do not include the slash.
- **RUN** is in uppercase bold because it is a SAS keyword.

Chapter 1   A Tour of the SAS® System

1.1 An Overview of the SAS System

Objectives

- Learn the origin of the SAS System.
- Understand the structure and design of SAS.

3

Origin of SAS

- The early 1960s
- Agricultural research at Land Grant Universities
- Business need: general purpose statistical software to manage and manipulate large volumes of data and perform statistical analysis.

4

In the early 1960s, the Statistics Department at North Carolina State University was awarded an agricultural research project. The people working on the project needed computer software for the IBM mainframe that could access and manipulate large volumes of data and perform statistical analysis on the data. There was no package available that met their needs, so they started designing a solution.

Turning Data Into Information

Process of delivering meaningful information:

- 80% Data-related:
  - Access
  - Scrub
  - Transform
  - Manage
  - Store and retrieve
- 20% Analysis

5

The team soon realized that in order to do analysis, they would first have to perform many data-specific tasks. They needed to

- access data
- scrub the data by deleting, modifying, and correcting data values
- transform the data by subsetting, converting, or summarizing it
- store and retrieve the data.

The team's software design was the basis for the SAS System.

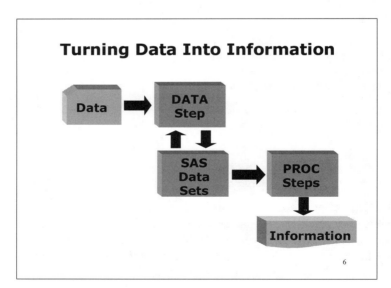

Turning Data Into Information

6

SAS software reads data from multiple sources and, through a step known as the *DATA step*, converts the data into a SAS data set. (A *SAS data set* is a file that is created by SAS and read by SAS software.)

When data is in the form of a SAS data set, steps known as *procedure steps*, or *PROC steps*, manipulate, analyze, and produce reports from the data. The PROC steps enable users to turn data into useful, meaningful information.

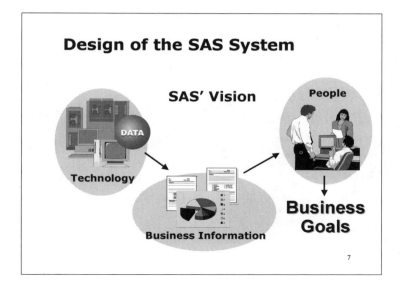

Since its inception, SAS' vision has been to help organizations make better business decisions. Its goal is to help companies use their technology resources to turn data into useful business information.

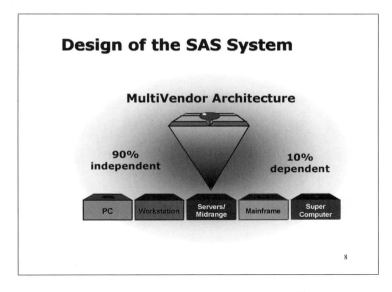

One of the key technologies of SAS is MultiVendor Architecture (MVA). SAS is designed so that 90% of the code is completely hardware-independent. The software looks and behaves the same on any supported operating system. If you learn to use SAS on a Windows personal computer but later need to run SAS applications on a mainframe, you do not have to relearn the software or make major modifications to your program.

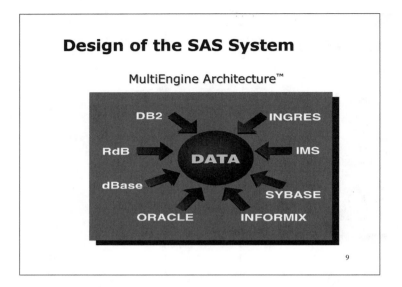

Another key technology is data access and integration. SAS enables users to work with and integrate data from a variety of sources through its MultiEngine Architecture (MEA).

SAS is able to read data from a variety of sources, including most relational databases. This means that your organization does not have to rewrite large DB2 tables, for example, into SAS data sets. SAS is able to work directly with the data as it exists in the database.

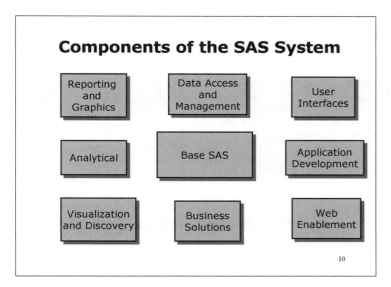

SAS has developed numerous system components to address key technologies and the primary steps of any application. The nucleus of the entire SAS System is base SAS. It includes the functionality to create SAS data sets and perform data manipulation.

In addition to base SAS, SAS Institute created solutions for

- accessing and managing data from multiple sources
- analyzing data
- producing reports and presentation-quality graphics
- using visualization methods to explore and understand data.

1.2   Introduction to the Course Scenario

Objectives

- Learn about the course scenario.

12

Course Scenario

Throughout this course, you have the opportunity to apply your new programming skills to a business case study.

13

Course Scenario

In this course, you will be working with business data from International Airlines (IA).

14

Course Scenario

International Airlines is a fictitious airline that transports people and cargo from city to city around the world.

15

Course Scenario

International Airlines maintains various kinds of data:

- flight data
- passenger data
- cargo data
- employee data
- revenue data.

16

Here are some of the tasks you will perform using data from IA:

- IA currently has all its flight crew employee data stored in a fixed column raw data file. You will import the data into a SAS data set in order to create list reports and frequency tables.

- IA needs a list of all its flight crew employees in order to perform an annual employee review. You will print out the SAS data set containing all the employee data.

- You need to create some frequency tables in order to complete the annual employee review.

- The flight crew employees receive a wide range of salaries based on several different job codes. You want to summarize the employee data so the airline can recode the salaries and job codes.

- You want to produce a report with the employee salary information formatted like currency.

- IA wants an accurate picture of the passenger capacity of its planes. You need to create two reports: a summary statistic report and a detailed list. The aircraft data are stored in a SAS data set containing more variables than you need for the reports. You will create a new SAS data set containing only those variables you need for your reports.

- IA wants to determine whether or not actual revenue exceeded budgeted goals for each month of the year. The goals and actual sales are stored in two separate data sets. In order to do the comparison, you will need to merge the two SAS data sets.

Course Scenario

The tasks you will perform with the data are common to all businesses.

The solutions are easy to apply to your own business problems.

17

1.3 Introduction to the Course Tools

Objectives

- Describe tools used throughout the course.

19

Report Writing

You learn to produce list reports using
- the REPORT procedure
- the PRINT procedure.

20

Frequency Reports

You learn to produce frequency reports using the FREQ procedure.

21

Examining Data Sets

You learn to use the CONTENTS procedure to examine the structure of a SAS data set.

22

Sorting Data

You learn to use the SORT procedure to rearrange your data in alphabetical or numeric order.

23

Subsetting Data

You learn to subset your data using
- the WHERE statement
- the subsetting IF statement.

24

Combining Data Sets

You learn to merge and concatenate data sets using
- the MERGE statement
- the SET statement.

25

Producing Web-Ready Reports

You learn to produce Web-ready HTML reports using Output Delivery System (ODS) statements.

26

Chapter 2   Getting Started with the SAS® System

2.1 Introduction to SAS Programs

Objectives

- State the components of a SAS program.
- State the modes in which you can run a SAS program.

3

SAS Programs

A SAS program is a sequence of steps that the user submits for execution.

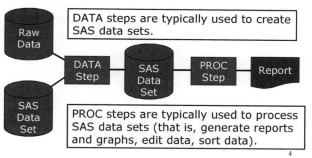

DATA steps are typically used to create SAS data sets.

PROC steps are typically used to process SAS data sets (that is, generate reports and graphs, edit data, sort data).

4

SAS Programs

```
data work.staff;
   infile 'emplist.dat';
   input LastName $ 1-20 FirstName $ 21-30
         JobTitle $ 36-43 Salary 54-59;      } DATA
                                                STEP
run;

proc print data=work.staff;
run;                                          }
                                                PROC
proc means data=work.staff mean max;          } STEPS
   class JobTitle;
   var Salary;
run;
```

5

The DATA step creates a new temporary SAS data set named WORK.STAFF by reading variables described in the INPUT statement from the EMPLIST.DAT raw data file.

The PROC PRINT step creates a listing report of the WORK.STAFF data set.

The PROC MEANS step creates a report summarizing the average (MEAN) and maximum (MAX) SALARY for each value of JOBTITLE.

To run this program in the OS/390 environment, only the raw data file name must be changed, for example:

```
infile '.prog1.rawdata(emplist)';
```

Running a SAS Program

You can invoke SAS in

- interactive windowing mode (SAS windowing environment)
- interactive menu-driven mode (SAS/ASSIST, SAS/AF, or SAS/EIS software)
- interactive line mode
- batch mode
- noninteractive mode.

6

SAS Windowing Environment

Interactive windows enable you to interface with SAS.

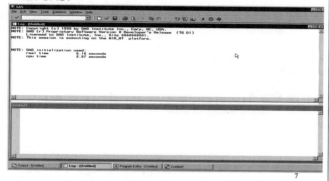

7

OS/390 (MVS) Batch Execution

Place the JCL appropriate for your location before your SAS statements.

```
//jobname JOB accounting info,name …
// EXEC SAS
//SYSIN DD *
data work.staff;
    infile '.prog1.rawdata(emplist)';
    input LastName $ 1-20 FirstName $ 21-30
          JobTitle $ 36-43 Salary 54-59;
run;

proc means data=work.staff mean max;
    class JobTitle;
    var Salary;
run;
```

8

Noninteractive Execution

To execute a SAS program in noninteractive mode,

- use an editor to store the program in a file. (CMS and directory-based users should use a filetype or extension of SAS.)

- identify the file when you invoke SAS.

CMS and directory-based:

> **SAS** *filename*

OS/390 (TSO):

> **SAS INPUT**(*filename*)

9

2.2 Running SAS Programs

Objectives

- Invoke the SAS System and include a SAS program into your SAS session.
- Submit a program and browse the results.
- Navigate the SAS windowing environment.

11

Submitting a SAS Program

When you execute a SAS program, the output generated by SAS is divided into two major parts:

SAS log   contains information about the processing of the SAS program, including any warning and error messages

output   contains reports generated by SAS procedures and DATA steps.

12

SAS Log

```
1      data work.staff;
2          infile 'emplist.dat';
3          input LastName $ 1-20 FirstName $ 21-30
4               JobTitle $ 36-43 Salary 54-59;
5      run;
NOTE: The infile 'emplist.dat' is:
      File Name=emplist.dat,
      RECFM=V,LRECL=256
NOTE: 18 records were read from the infile 'emplist.dat'.
      The minimum record length was 59.
      The maximum record length was 59.
NOTE: The data set WORK.STAFF has 18 observations and 4 variables.

6      proc print data=work.staff;
7      run;
NOTE: There were 18 observations read from the dataset WORK.STAFF.

8      proc means data=work.staff mean max;
9          class JobTitle;
10         var Salary;
11     run;
NOTE: There were 18 observations read from the dataset WORK.STAFF.
```

The SAS log contains a record of your SAS session. It displays SAS programming statements as well as error messages and informational notes.

SAS Output

```
                        The SAS System

                             First
        Obs    LastName      Name        JobTitle    Salary

         1     TORRES        JAN         Pilot       50000
         2     LANGKAMM      SARAH       Mechanic    80000
         3     SMITH         MICHAEL     Mechanic    40000
         .        .            .            .          .
         .        .            .            .          .
         .        .            .            .          .
        17     WAGSCHAL      NADJA       Pilot       77500
        18     TOERMOEN      JOCHEN      Pilot       65000
```

```
                     The SAS System

                    The MEANS Procedure

                 Analysis Variable : Salary

                     N
        JobTitle    Obs       Mean        Maximum

        Mechanic     8      58750.00     80000.00

        Pilot       10      73750.00    105000.00
```

SAS output includes any reports that your SAS program created. In this example, the PRINT procedure and the MEANS procedure created output.

Running a SAS Program - Windows

File: c2s2d1.sas

- Start a SAS session.
- Include and submit a program.
- Browse the results.

Starting a SAS Session

1. Double-click the SAS icon to start your SAS session.

🖉   How you invoke the SAS System varies by your operating
       environment and any customizations in effect at your site.

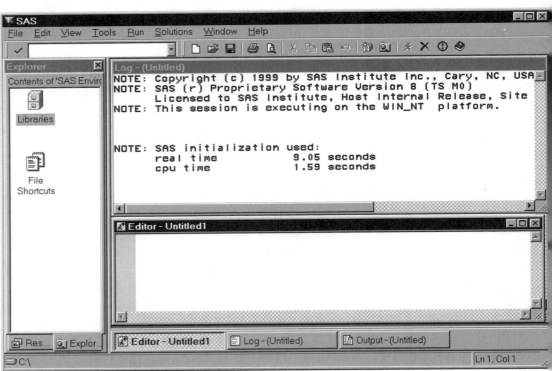

The Enhanced Editor, the default editor on Windows, provides many helpful
features including color coding. Because the Enhanced Editor is not available
in all operating environments, the demonstrations in this course may use the
Program Editor, an alternative editing window. Refer to the end of this
chapter for a discussion of the Enhanced Editor.

2. To close the Enhanced Editor, select ☒. To open the Program Editor, select **View** ⇨ **Program Editor**.

✎ The Results window and Explorer window have slightly different functionality in different operating environments. Refer to the end of this chapter for a discussion of these windows.

3. To close the Explorer window, click in the window and select ☒. To close the Results window, click in the window and select ☒.

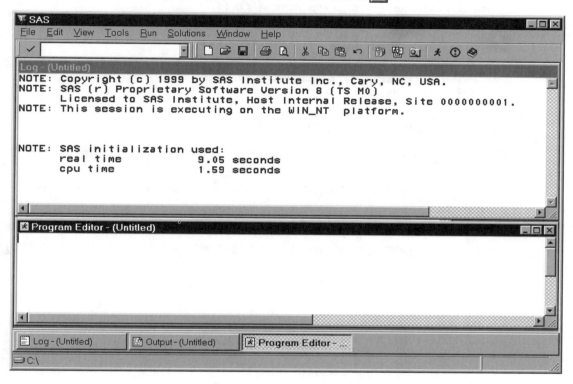

Including and Submitting a SAS Program

1. To include (copy) a SAS program into your SAS session, issue the INCLUDE command.
   a) Type **include** and the name of the file containing the program in the command bar.
   b) Press Enter.

You can also select **File** ⇨ **Open** or click on 📂 and then select the file you want to include.

The program is included into the Program Editor window.

You can use the Program Editor window to

- access and edit existing SAS programs
- write new SAS programs
- submit SAS programs
- save programming statements in a file.

```
Program Editor - c2s2d1.sas
data work.staff;
    infile 'emplist.dat';
    input LastName $ 1-20 FirstName $ 21-30
          JobTitle $ 36-43 Salary 54-59;
run;

proc print data=work.staff;
run;

proc means data=work.staff mean max;
    class JobTitle;
    var Salary;
run;
```

✐   The program contains three steps: a DATA step and two PROC steps.

2. Issue the SUBMIT command or click on 🏃 or select **Run** ⇨ **Submit** to submit the program for execution. The output from the program is displayed in the Output window.

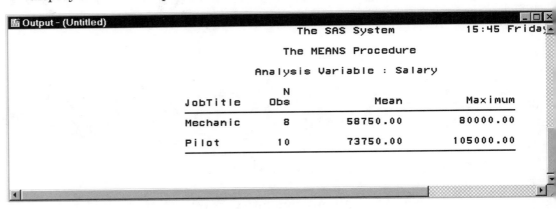

```
Output - (Untitled)
                                The SAS System            15:45 Friday

                              The MEANS Procedure

                          Analysis Variable : Salary

                             N
        JobTitle            Obs              Mean           Maximum

        Mechanic             8          58750.00          80000.00

        Pilot               10          73750.00         105000.00
```

Examining Your Program Results

The Output window

- is one of the primary windows and is open by default.
- becomes the active window each time it receives output.
- automatically accumulates output in the order in which it is generated. You can issue the CLEAR command or select **Edit** ⇨ **Clear All** to clear the contents of the window.

To scroll horizontally within the Output window, use the horizontal scrollbar or issue the RIGHT and LEFT commands.

To scroll vertically within the Output window, use the vertical scrollbar or issue the FORWARD and BACKWARD commands.

✎   You can also use the TOP and BOTTOM commands to scroll vertically within the Output window.

1. Scroll to the top to view the output from the PRINT procedure.

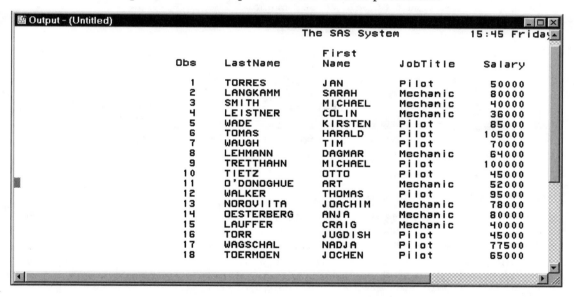

2. Issue the LOG command or select **Window** ⇨ **Log** to display the Log window and browse the messages that the program generated.

The Log window

- is one of the primary windows and is open by default.
- acts as a record of your SAS session; messages are written to the log in the order in which they are generated by the program. You can issue the CLEAR command or select **Edit** ⇨ **Clear All** to clear the contents of the window.

Partial Log

```
 Log - (Untitled)                                                              _□×
NOTE: 18 records were read from the infile 'emplist.dat'.
      The minimum record length was 59.
      The maximum record length was 59.
NOTE: The data set WORK.STAFF has 18 observations and 4 variables.
NOTE: DATA statement used:
      real time               0.90 seconds
      cpu time                0.19 seconds


96
97    proc print data=work.staff;
98    run;

NOTE: There were 18 observations read from the dataset WORK.STAFF.
NOTE: PROCEDURE PRINT used:
      real time               0.65 seconds
      cpu time                0.12 seconds


99
100   proc means data=work.staff mean max;
101      class JobTitle;
102      var Salary;
103   run;

NOTE: There were 18 observations read from the dataset WORK.STAFF.
```

The Log window contains the programming statements that were most recently submitted, as well as notes about

- any files that were read
- the records that were read
- the program execution and results.

In this example, the Log window contains no warning or error messages. If the program contains errors, relevant warning and error messages are also written to the SAS log.

3. Issue the END command or select **Window** ⇨ **Program Editor** to return to the Program Editor window.

Running a SAS Program - UNIX (Optional)

File: c2s2d1.sas

- Start a SAS session.
- Include and submit a program.
- Browse the results.

Starting a SAS Session

1. Double-click the SAS icon or type in the appropriate command to start a SAS session.

   ✎ How you invoke the SAS System varies by your operating environment and any customizations in effect at your site.

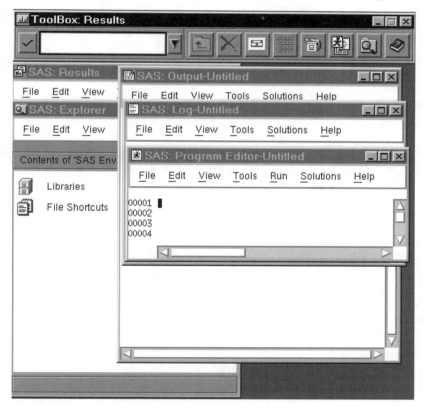

   The Results Window and Explorer window have slightly different functionality in different operating environments. Refer to the end of this chapter for a discussion of these windows.

2. To close the Explorer window, click in the window and select ☒. To close the Results window, click in the window and select ☒.

Including and Submitting a SAS Program

1. To include (copy) a SAS program into your SAS session, issue the INCLUDE command.

    a. Type **include** and the name of the file containing your program in the command bar.

    b. Press Enter.

You can also select **File** ⇨ **Open** or click on 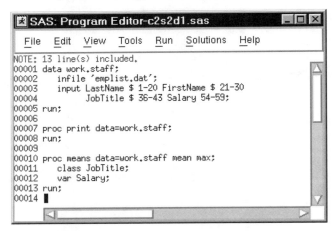 and then select the file you want to include.

The program is included into the Program Editor window.

You can use the Program Editor window to

- access and edit existing SAS programs
- write new SAS programs
- submit SAS programs
- save programming statements in a file.

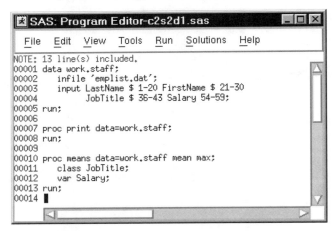

🖉   The program contains three steps: a DATA step and two PROC steps.

2. Issue the SUBMIT command or click on 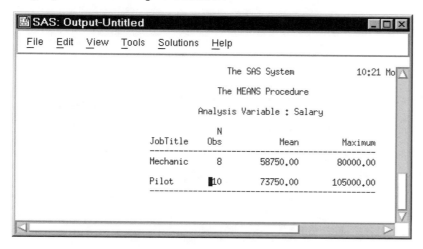 or select **Run** ⇨ **Submit** to submit your program for execution. The output from your program is displayed in the Output window.

```
SAS: Output-Untitled                                    _ □ ×

 File   Edit   View   Tools   Solutions   Help

                              The SAS System              10:21 Mo

                           The MEANS Procedure

                      Analysis Variable : Salary
                          N
             JobTitle    Obs          Mean          Maximum
             ---------------------------------------------------
             Mechanic     8        58750.00        80000.00

             Pilot       10        73750.00       105000.00
             ---------------------------------------------------
```

Examining Your Program Results

The Output window

- is one of the primary windows and is open by default.
- becomes the active window each time it receives output.
- automatically accumulates output in the order in which it is generated. You can issue the CLEAR command or select **Edit** ⇨ **Clear All** to clear the contents of the window.

To scroll horizontally within the Output window, use the horizontal scrollbar or issue the RIGHT and LEFT commands.

To scroll vertically within the Output window, use the vertical scrollbar or issue the FORWARD and BACKWARD commands.

✎   You can also use the TOP and BOTTOM commands to scroll vertically within the Output window.

1. Scroll to the top to view the output from the PRINT procedure.

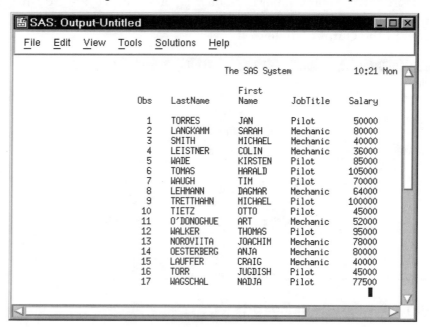

2. Issue the LOG command or select **Window** ⇨ **Log** to display the Log window and browse the messages that the program generated.

   The Log window

   • is one of the primary windows and is open by default.

   • acts as a record of your SAS session; messages are written to the log in the order in which they are generated by the program. You can issue the CLEAR command or select **Edit** ⇨ **Clear All** to clear the contents of the window.

   Partial Log

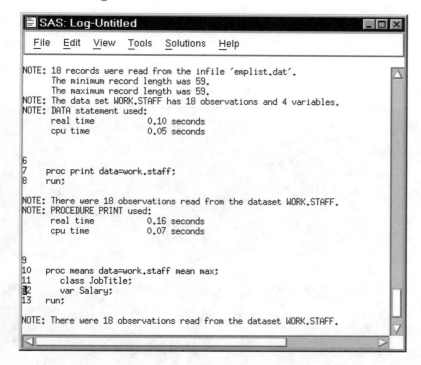

   The Log window contains the programming statements that were most recently submitted, as well as notes about

   • any files that were read

   • the records that were read

   • the program execution and results.

   In this example, the Log window contains no warning or error messages. If your program contains errors, relevant warning and error messages are also written to the SAS log.

3. Issue the END command or select **Window** ⇨ **Program Editor** to return to the Program Editor window.

Running a SAS Program - OS/390 (Optional)

File: *userid*.prog1.sascode(c2s2d1)

- Start a SAS session.
- Include and submit a program.
- Browse the results.

Starting a SAS Session

Type in the appropriate command to start your SAS session.

    How you invoke the SAS System varies by your operating environment and any customizations in effect at your site.

```
+Log-------------------------------------------------------------------------
| Command ===>
|
| NOTE: Copyright (c) 1999 by SAS Institute Inc., Cary, NC, USA.
| NOTE: SAS (r) Proprietary Software Version 8 (TS M0)
|       Licensed to SAS INSTITUTE DATA CENTER, Site 0001000014.
| NOTE: This session is executing on the OS/390 V02R06M00 platform.
|
| NOTE: Running on IBM Model 9672 Serial Number 005599,
|               IBM Model 9672 Serial Number 105599,
|               IBM Model 9672 Serial Number 205599.
|
|
|     888       Welcome to the SAS Information Delivery System
+
+Program Editor--------------------------------------------------------------
| Command ===> █
|
| 00001
| 00002
| 00003
| 00004
| 00005
| 00006
| 00007
| 00008
| 00009
| 00010
| 00011
| 00012
| 00013
+
S▇                        LOG                                    +Cr
```

Including and Submitting a SAS Program

1. To include (copy) a SAS program into your SAS session, issue the
    INCLUDE command.

    a. Type **include** and the name of the file containing your program on
        the command line of the Program Editor.

    b. Press Enter.

```
-Program Editor------------------------------------------------------------+
 Command ===> include '.prog1.sascode(c2s2d1)'█

 00001
 00002
 00003
 00004
 00005
 00006
```

The program is included into the Program Editor window.

You can use the Program Editor window to

• access and edit existing SAS programs

• write new SAS programs

• submit SAS programs

• save programming statements in a file.

The program contains three steps: a DATA step and two PROC steps.

```
+Program Editor------------------------------------------------------------+
 Command ===>

 00001 data work.staff;
 00002    infile '.prog1.rawdata(emplist)';
 00003    input LastName $ 1-20 FirstName $ 21-30
 00004          JobTitle $ 36-43 Salary 54-59;
 00005 run;
 00006
 00007 proc print data=work.staff;
 00008 run;
 00009
 00010 proc means data=work.staff mean max;
 00011    class JobTitle;
 00012    var Salary;
 00013 run;
```

2. Issue the SUBMIT command to submit your program for execution. The first page of the output from your program is displayed in the Output window.

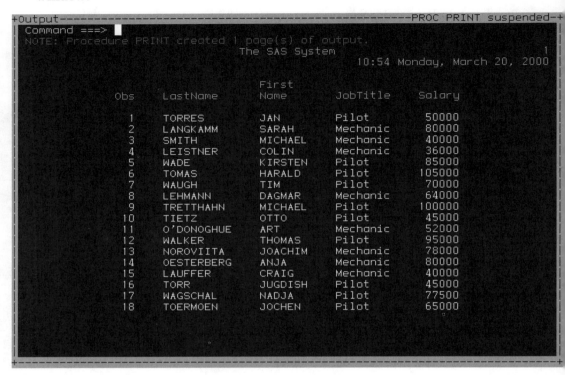

```
+Output----------------------------------------------+--PROC PRINT suspended-+
|Command ===>                                                                 |
|NOTE: Procedure PRINT created 1 page(s) of output.                           |
|                           The SAS System                                   1|
|                                             10:54 Monday, March 20, 2000    |
|                                                                             |
|                                  First                                      |
|                Obs    LastName    Name        JobTitle     Salary           |
|                                                                             |
|                  1    TORRES      JAN         Pilot         50000           |
|                  2    LANGKAMM    SARAH       Mechanic      80000           |
|                  3    SMITH       MICHAEL     Mechanic      40000           |
|                  4    LEISTNER    COLIN       Mechanic      36000           |
|                  5    WADE        KIRSTEN     Pilot         85000           |
|                  6    TOMAS       HARALD      Pilot        105000           |
|                  7    WAUGH       TIM         Pilot         70000           |
|                  8    LEHMANN     DAGMAR      Mechanic      64000           |
|                  9    TRETTHAHN   MICHAEL     Pilot        100000           |
|                 10    TIETZ       OTTO        Pilot         45000           |
|                 11    O'DONOGHUE  ART         Mechanic      52000           |
|                 12    WALKER      THOMAS      Pilot         95000           |
|                 13    NOROVIITA   JOACHIM     Mechanic      78000           |
|                 14    OESTERBERG  ANJA        Mechanic      80000           |
|                 15    LAUFFER     CRAIG       Mechanic      40000           |
|                 16    TORR        JUGDISH     Pilot         45000           |
|                 17    WAGSCHAL    NADJA       Pilot         77500           |
|                 18    TOERMOEN    JOCHEN      Pilot         65000           |
|                                                                             |
+-----------------------------------------------------------------------------+
```

Examining Your Program Results

The Output window

- is one of the primary windows and is open by default.
- becomes the active window each time it receives output.
- automatically accumulates output in the order in which it is generated. You can issue the CLEAR command or select **Edit** ⇨ **Clear All** to clear the contents of the window.

To scroll horizontally within the Output window, use the horizontal scrollbar or issue the RIGHT and LEFT commands.

To scroll vertically within the Output window, use the vertical scrollbar or issue the FORWARD and BACKWARD commands.

 You can also use the TOP and BOTTOM commands to scroll vertically within the Output window.

1. Issue the END command. If the PRINT procedure produced more than one page of output, you are taken to the last page of output. If the PRINT procedure produced only one page of output, the END command allows the MEANS procedure to execute and produce its output.

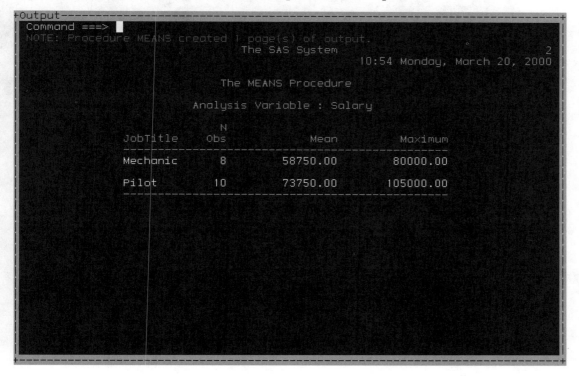

```
+Output————————————————————————————————————————————————————————————————————+
|Command ===>                                                                |
|NOTE: Procedure MEANS created 1 page(s) of output.                          |
|                         The SAS System                                   2 |
|                                       10:54 Monday, March 20, 2000         |
|                                                                            |
|                      The MEANS Procedure                                   |
|                                                                            |
|                  Analysis Variable : Salary                                |
|                                                                            |
|                        N                                                   |
|           JobTitle    Obs          Mean            Maximum                 |
|           ---------------------------------------------------              |
|           Mechanic      8        58750.00          80000.00                |
|                                                                            |
|           Pilot        10        73750.00         105000.00                |
|                                                                            |
+————————————————————————————————————————————————————————————————————————————+
```

You can issue an **AUTOSCROLL 0** command on the command line of the Output window to have all of your SAS output from one submission placed in the Output window at one time. This eliminates the need to issue an END command to run each step separately.

The AUTOSCROLL command will be in effect for the duration of your SAS session. If you would like to have the Output window behave this way every time you invoke SAS, you can save this setting by typing **AUTOSCROLL 0; WSAVE** on the command line of the Output window.

2. Issue the END command to return to the Program Editor window.

```
+Log--------------------------------------------------------------------------
  Command ===>

  7     proc print data=work.staff;
  8     run;

  NOTE: There were 18 observations read from the dataset WORK.STAFF.
  NOTE: The PROCEDURE PRINT used 0.05 CPU seconds and 4428K.

  9
  10    proc means data=work.staff mean max;
  11        class JobTitle;
  12        var Salary;
  13    run;

  NOTE: There were 18 observations read from the dataset WORK.STAFF.
  NOTE: The PROCEDURE MEANS used 0.04 CPU seconds and 4890K.


+--------------------------------------------------------------------------
+Program Editor-----------------------------------------------------------
  Command ===>

  00001
  00002
  00003
  00004
  00005
  00006
+--------------------------------------------------------------------------
```

After the program executes, you can view messages in the LOG window.

The Log window

- is one of the primary windows and is open by default.
- acts as a record of your SAS session; messages are written to the log in the order in which they are generated by the program. You can issue the CLEAR command to clear the contents of the window.

The Log window contains the programming statements that were recently submitted, as well as notes about

- any files that were read
- the records that were read
- the program execution and results.

In this example, the Log window contains no warning or error messages. If your program contains errors, relevant warning and error messages are also written to the SAS log.

Running a SAS Program - OS/390 Batch (Optional)

File: *userid*.prog1.sascode(jcl)

- Submit a program.
- Browse the results.

Submitting a SAS Program

1. To submit a SAS program,
   a. use an editor to create a file containing the necessary JCL and your SAS program
   b. issue a SUBMIT command or perform the steps necessary to submit your program for execution.

```
Command ===>                                              Scroll ===> PAGE
****** ********************* Top of Data ********************************
000001 //SASCLASS JOB (,1234),XXXXXX,MSGCLASS=H,NOTIFY=,TIME=(,4)
000002 // EXEC SAS8
000003 //SYSIN DD *
000004 data work.staff;
000005     infile '.prog1.rawdata(emplist)';
000006     input LastName $ 1-20 FirstName $ 21-30
000007          JobTitle $ 36-43 Salary 54-59;
000008 run;
000009 proc print data=work.staff;
000010 run;
000011 proc means data=work.staff mean max;
000012     class JobTitle;
000013     var Salary;
000014 run;
000015 /*
****** ********************* Bottom of Data *****************************
```

The program contains three steps: a DATA step and two PROC steps.

Examining Your Program Results

1. View the results of your batch job.

```
-------------------------------- IOF Job Summary -----------------------------
COMMAND ===>                                              SCROLL ===> SCREEN
--JOBNAME----JOBID--STATUS---RAN/RECEIVED------DAY--------DEST----------------
   SASCLASS J21333  OUTPUT   14:29   3/20/2000 TODAY      C4213H21
--RC--PGM---------STEP-----PRSTEP---PROC-----COMMENTS------------------------
   0  SASXALV     SAS               SAS8
--------DDNAME---STEP-----STAT-ACT-C-GRP-D-SIZE-U--DEST--------------UCS------
_    1  LOG      *         HELD      H   1 H    17 L  C4213H21
_    2  JCL      *         HELD      H   1 H    69 L  C4213H21
_    3  MESSAGES *         HELD      H   1 H   101 L  C4213H21
_    4  SASLOG   SAS       HELD      H   1 H    68 L  C4213H21
_    5  SASCLOG  SAS       DONE      H
_    6  SASLIST  SAS       HELD SEL  H   1 H    36 L  C4213H21
_    7  SYSUDUMP SAS       DONE      D
_    8  SASSNAP  SAS       DONE      D
```

2. You can view the output of your program by selecting **<u>SASLIST</u>**.

```
BROWSE - SASLIST              SAS        - Page  1     Line  1       Cols 41-120
COMMAND ===>                                          SCROLL ===> HALF
****************************** Top of Data ******************************
                    The SAS System                        14:29 Monday, Mar
                              First                                  °
        Obs    LastName       Name        JobTitle      Salary

         1     TORRES         JAN         Pilot          50000
         2     LANGKAMM       SARAH       Mechanic       80000
         3     SMITH          MICHAEL     Mechanic       40000
         4     LEISTNER       COLIN       Mechanic       36000
         5     WADE           KIRSTEN     Pilot          85000
         6     TOMAS          HARALD      Pilot         105000
         7     WAUGH          TIM         Pilot          70000
         8     LEHMANN        DAGMAR      Mechanic       64000
         9     TRETTHAHN      MICHAEL     Pilot         100000
        10     TIETZ          OTTO        Pilot          45000
        11     O'DONOGHUE     ART         Mechanic       52000
        12     WALKER         THOMAS      Pilot          95000
        13     NOROVIITA      JOACHIM     Mechanic       78000
        14     OESTERBERG     ANJA        Mechanic       80000
        15     LAUFFER        CRAIG       Mechanic       40000
        16     TORR           JUGDISH     Pilot          45000
        17     WAGSCHAL       NADJA       Pilot          77500
        18     TOERMOEN       JOCHEN      Pilot          65000
```

3. Because both the PRINT procedure and the MEANS procedure created output, SASLIST contains several reports. Use scrolling commands to see the other pages of output.

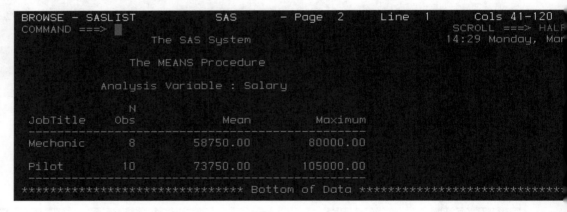

```
BROWSE - SASLIST              SAS        - Page  2     Line  1       Cols 41-120
COMMAND ===>                                          SCROLL ===> HALF
                    The SAS System                        14:29 Monday, Mar

                    The MEANS Procedure

                  Analysis Variable : Salary

                     N
        JobTitle    Obs           Mean            Maximum
        ------------------------------------------------------
        Mechanic     8         58750.00          80000.00

        Pilot       10         73750.00         105000.00
        ------------------------------------------------------
****************************** Bottom of Data ******************************
```

4. Return to the main job results screen and select <u>**SASLOG**</u> to see a record of your SAS session. Messages are written to the log in the order in which they are generated by the program.

```
BROWSE - SASLOG              SAS       - Page  1     Line  43     Cols 1-80
COMMAND ===> █                                       SCROLL ===> SCREEN
NOTE: 18 records were read from the infile '.prog1.rawdata(emplist)'.
NOTE: The data set WORK.STAFF has 18 observations and 4 variables.
NOTE: The DATA statement used 0.06 CPU seconds and 2706K.

6          proc print data=work.staff;
7          run;

NOTE: There were 18 observations read from the dataset WORK.STAFF.
NOTE: The PROCEDURE PRINT printed page 1.
NOTE: The PROCEDURE PRINT used 0.05 CPU seconds and 3541K.

8          proc means data=work.staff mean max;
9             class JobTitle;
10            var Salary;
11         run;

NOTE: There were 18 observations read from the dataset WORK.STAFF.
```

The SASLOG contains the programming statements that were submitted, as well as notes about

- any files that were read
- the records that were read
- the program execution and results.

In this example, the SASLOG contains no warning or error messages. If your program contains errors, relevant warning and error messages are also written to the SASLOG.

Exercises

1. **Submitting a Program**

   a. With the Program Editor window active, include a SAS program.

      Windows and UNIX: `include 'c2e1.sas'`

      OS/390:   `include '.prog1.sascode(c2e1)'`

   b. Submit the program for execution. Based on the report in the Output window, how many observations and variables are in the WORK.AIRPORTS data set?

   c. Examine the Log window. Based on the log notes, how many observations and variables are in the WORK.AIRPORTS data set?

   d. Clear the Log and Output windows.

2. **Using the KEYS Command (Optional)**

   The KEYS window is
   - a secondary window
   - used to browse or change function key definitions
   - closed by issuing the END command (Windows, UNIX, OS/390) or by clicking on ☒ (Windows, UNIX).

   a. Issue the KEYS command. Browse the contents of the window by scrolling vertically.

   b. Close the KEYS window.

2.3   Mastering Fundamental Concepts

Objectives

- Explain SAS syntax rules.
- Define a SAS data set and explain the descriptor portion and the data portion.
- Define a SAS variable.
- Identify a missing value and a SAS date value.
- State the naming conventions for SAS data sets and variables.
- Investigate a SAS data set using the CONTENTS and PRINT procedures.

18

SAS Syntax Rules

SAS statements
- usually begin with an identifying keyword
- always end with a semicolon.

```
data work.staff;
   infile 'emplist.dat';
   input LastName $ 1-20 FirstName $ 21-30
         JobTitle $ 36-43 Salary 54-59;
run;

proc print data=work.staff;
run;

proc means data=work.staff mean max;
   class JobTitle;
   var Salary;
run;
```

 In most situations, text in quotes is case-sensitive.

···

SAS Syntax Rules

SAS statements are free-format.

- They can begin and end in any column.
- One or more blanks or special characters can be used to separate words.
- A single statement can span multiple lines.
- Several statements can be on the same line.

Unconventional Spacing

```
data work.staff;
infile 'emplist.dat';
input LastName $ 1-20 FirstName $ 21-30
JobTitle $ 36-43 Salary 54-59;
run;
    proc means data=work.staff        mean max;
class JobTitle;     var Salary;run;
```

SAS Syntax Rules

Good spacing makes the program easier to read.

Conventional Spacing

```
data work.staff;
   infile 'emplist.dat';
   input LastName $ 1-20 FirstName $ 21-30
         JobTitle $ 36-43 Salary 54-59;
run;

proc print data=work.staff;
run;

proc means data=work.staff mean max;
   class JobTitle;
   var Salary;
run;
```

SAS programming statements are easier to read if you

- begin DATA, PROC, and RUN statements in column one and indent the other statements
- put blank lines between programming steps.

SAS Comments

- Type /* to begin a comment.
- Type your comment text.
- Type */ to end the comment.

```
 /* Create WORK.STAFF data set */
data work.staff;
   infile 'emplist.dat';
   input LastName $ 1-20 FirstName $ 21-30
         JobTitle $ 36-43 Salary 54-59;
run;

 /* Produce listing report of WORK.STAFF */
proc print data=work.staff;
run;
```

Avoid placing the /* comment symbols in columns 1 and 2. On some host systems, SAS may interpret these symbols as a request to end the SAS job or session.

SAS Data Sets

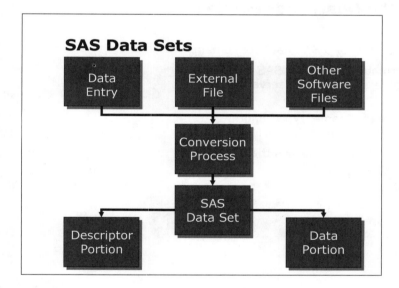

Data must be in the form of a SAS data set to be processed by many SAS procedures and some DATA step statements.

A *SAS data set* is a type of SAS file. A *SAS file* is a specially structured file that SAS software creates and organizes.

SAS Data Sets

SAS data sets have a descriptor and a data portion.

SAS Data Set

	General data set information
Descriptor Portion	* **data set name** * **data set label** * **date/time created** * **storage information** * **number of observations** **Information for each variable** * **Name** * **Informat** * **Length** * **Label** * **Type** * **Format** * **Position**
Data Portion	

The descriptor portion contains the metadata on the data set.

Browsing the Descriptor Portion

The *descriptor portion* of a SAS data set contains

- general information about the SAS data set (data set name, number of observations, and so on)

- variable attributes (name, type, length, position, informat, format, label).

The CONTENTS procedure displays the descriptor portion of a SAS data set.

28

Browsing the Descriptor Portion

General form of the CONTENTS procedure:

PROC CONTENTS DATA=*SAS-data-set*;
RUN;

Example:

```
proc contents data=work.staff;
run;
```

29

PROC CONTENTS Output

```
Data Set Name: WORK.STAFF          Observations:          18
Member Type:   DATA                Variables:             4
Engine:        V8                  Indexes:               0
Created:       21:52 Wednesday,    Observation Length:    48
               December 1, 1999
Last Modified: 21:52 Wednesday,    Deleted Observations:  0
               December 1, 1999
Protection:                        Compressed:            NO
Data Set Type:                     Sorted:                NO
Label:

        -----Alphabetic List of Variables and Attributes-----

            #      Variable    Type    Len    Pos
            -------------------------------------------
            2      FirstName   Char     10     28
            3      JobTitle    Char      8     38
            1      LastName    Char     20      8
            4      Salary      Num       8      0
```

This is a partial view of the default PROC CONTENTS output. The report also contains information about the physical location of the file and other data set information.

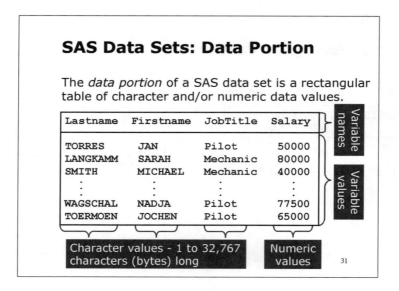

The *variables (columns)* in the table correspond to fields of data, and each data column is named.

The *observations (rows)* in the table correspond to records or data lines.

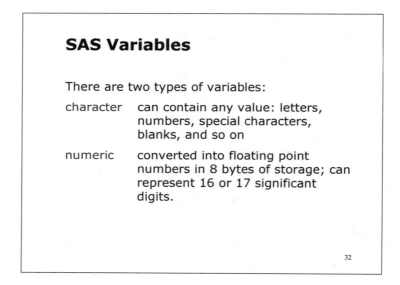

Character variables can be 1 to 32,767 bytes long. Each character is stored as one byte. If the character value does not use the entire length of the variable, blanks are added to the end of the value.

Numeric variables are stored as a double-precision floating point binary representation of the number. This storage method enables SAS to handle very large and very small numbers and provides very precise mathematical manipulations.

SAS Date Values

SAS stores date, time, and datetime values as numeric.

A *SAS date value* is interpreted as the number of days between January 1, 1960 and that date.

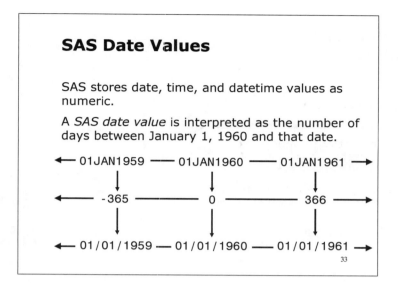

Dates, times, and datetimes are stored as numeric values so that they can easily be sorted and manipulated. SAS provides a wide variety of options for reading in and displaying these values.

Missing Data Values

A value must exist for every variable for each observation.

Missing values are valid values.

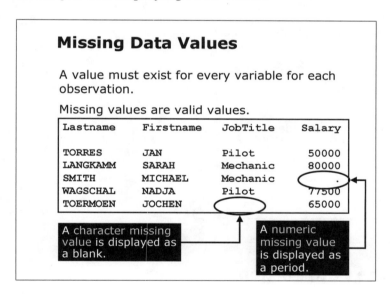

Lastname	Firstname	JobTitle	Salary
TORRES	JAN	Pilot	50000
LANGKAMM	SARAH	Mechanic	80000
SMITH	MICHAEL	Mechanic	.
WAGSCHAL	NADJA	Pilot	77500
TOERMOEN	JOCHEN		65000

A character missing value is displayed as a blank.

A numeric missing value is displayed as a period.

Naming SAS Data Sets and Variables

SAS names

- can be 32 characters long.
- can be uppercase, lowercase, or mixed case.
- must start with a letter or underscore. Subsequent characters can be letters, underscores, or numeric digits.

Special characters can be used if you put the name in quotes followed immediately by the letter N.

Example: `class 'Flight#'n;`

35

Browsing the Data Portion

The PRINT procedure displays the data portion of a SAS data set.

By default, PROC PRINT displays

- all observations
- all variables
- an OBS column on the left side.

36

Browsing the Data Portion

General form of the PRINT procedure:

PROC PRINT DATA=*SAS-data-set*;
RUN;

Example:

```
proc print data=work.staff;
run;
```

37

PROC PRINT Output

```
                  First
Obs   LastName    Name        JobTitle    Salary

1     TORRES      JAN         Pilot        50000
2     LANGKAMM    SARAH       Mechanic     80000
3     SMITH       MICHAEL     Mechanic     40000
4     LEISTNER    COLIN       Mechanic     36000
5     WADE        KIRSTEN     Pilot        85000
6     TOMAS       HARALD      Pilot       105000
7     WAUGH       TIM         Pilot        70000
8     LEHMANN     DAGMAR      Mechanic     64000
```

38

SAS Data Set Terminology

SAS documentation and text in the SAS windowing environment use the following terms interchangeably.

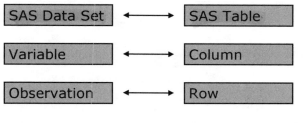

39

Investigating a SAS Data Set

File: c2s3d1.sas

- Use PROC CONTENTS to browse the descriptor portion of the SAS data set.

- Use PROC PRINT to browse the data portion of the SAS data set.

Browsing the Descriptor Portion

1. Use the CONTENTS procedure to browse the descriptor portion of the data set.

```
proc contents data=work.staff;
run;
```

2. Browse the output.

PROC CONTENTS lists general information about the SAS data set WORK.STAFF. The information varies slightly among operating environments.

SAS Output

```
                        The SAS System                         3
                                     14:21 Tuesday, June 27, 2000


                        The CONTENTS Procedure

Data Set Name: WORK.STAFF              Observations:          18
Member Type:   DATA                    Variables:             4
Engine:        V8                      Indexes:               0
Created:       16:12 Tuesday, June 27, 2000   Observation Length:    48
Last Modified: 16:12 Tuesday, June 27, 2000   Deleted Observations:  0
Protection:                            Compressed:            NO
Data Set Type:                         Sorted:                NO
Label:


                -----Engine/Host Dependent Information-----

Data Set Page Size:        4096
Number of Data Set Pages:  1
First Data Page:           1
Max Obs per Page:          84
Obs in First Data Page:    18
Number of Data Set Repairs: 0
File Name:                 C:\TEMP\SAS Temporary
                           Files\_TD323\staff.sas7bdat
Release Created:           8.0000M0
Host Created:              WIN_NT
```

It also lists the attributes of the variables.

SAS Output

```
-----Alphabetic List of Variables and Attributes-----

       #     Variable    Type    Len    Pos

       2     FirstName   Char     10     28
       3     JobTitle    Char      8     38
       1     LastName    Char     20      8
       4     Salary      Num       8      0
```

Browsing the Data Portion

1. Use PROC PRINT to browse the data portion of the SAS data set.

   ```
   proc print data=work.staff;
   run;
   ```

2. Browse the output.

SAS Output

```
                      The SAS System                       4
                          14:21 Tuesday, June 27, 2000

                   First
      Obs   LastName     Name       JobTitle    Salary

        1   TORRES       JAN        Pilot        50000
        2   LANGKAMM     SARAH      Mechanic     80000
        3   SMITH        MICHAEL    Mechanic     40000
        4   LEISTNER     COLIN      Mechanic     36000
        5   WADE         KIRSTEN    Pilot        85000
        6   TOMAS        HARALD     Pilot       105000
        7   WAUGH        TIM        Pilot        70000
        8   LEHMANN      DAGMAR     Mechanic     64000
        9   TRETTHAHN    MICHAEL    Pilot       100000
       10   TIETZ        OTTO       Pilot        45000
       11   O'DONOGHUE   ART        Mechanic     52000
       12   WALKER       THOMAS     Pilot        95000
       13   NOROVIITA    JOACHIM    Mechanic     78000
       14   OESTERBERG   ANJA       Mechanic     80000
       15   LAUFFER      CRAIG      Mechanic     40000
       16   TORR         JUGDISH    Pilot        45000
       17   WAGSCHAL     NADJA      Pilot        77500
       18   TOERMOEN     JOCHEN     Pilot        65000
```

2.4 SAS Data Libraries

Objectives

- Explain the concept of a SAS data library.
- State the difference between a permanent library and a temporary library.
- Use PROC CONTENTS and interactive windows to investigate a SAS data library.

42

SAS Data Libraries

A *SAS data library* is a collection of SAS files that are recognized as a unit by SAS.

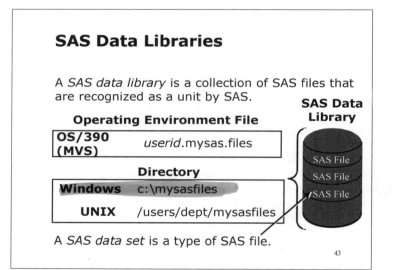

Operating Environment File		SAS Data Library
OS/390 (MVS)	*userid*.mysas.files	
Directory		
Windows	c:\mysasfiles	
UNIX	/users/dept/mysasfiles	

A *SAS data set* is a type of SAS file.

43

SAS Data Libraries

You can think of a SAS data library as a drawer in a filing cabinet and a SAS data set as one of the file folders in the drawer.

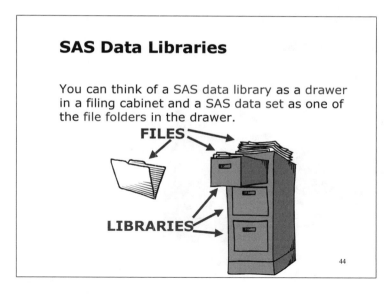

SAS Data Libraries

When you invoke SAS, you automatically have access to a temporary and a permanent SAS data library.

- WORK - temporary library
- SASUSER - permanent library

You can create and access your own permanent libraries.

- IA - permanent library

The *WORK library* and its SAS data files are deleted after your SAS session ends.

The *SASUSER library* and its SAS data files are saved after your SAS session ends.

Two-level SAS Filenames

Every SAS file has a two-level name.

libref.filename

- The first name (libref) refers to the library.

The data set WORK.STAFF is a SAS file in the WORK library.

- The second name (filename) refers to the file in the library.

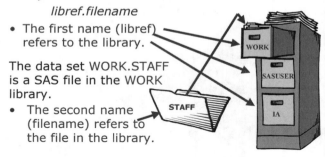

46

Browsing a SAS Data Library

You can use windows in your interactive SAS session to investigate the contents of a SAS data library.

In the LIBNAME window you can

- see a list of all the libraries available to your session

- drill down and see all members of a specific library.

47

Browsing a SAS Data Library

You can use the _ALL_ keyword to see the contents of an entire library:

PROC CONTENTS DATA=*libref._ALL_*;
RUN;

Example:

```
proc contents data=work._all_;
run;
```

48

Browsing a SAS Data Library

File: c2s4d1.sas

- Display a list of the SAS data libraries that are currently available in your SAS session.
- Display a list of the SAS data sets in the WORK library.

Investigating a Library Interactively

1. Issue the LIBNAME command to open the LIBNAME window.

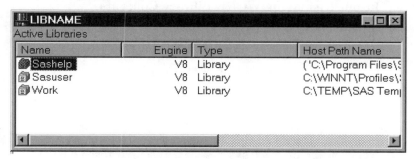

The LIBNAME window provides information for each library, including the name and the storage location.

2. Double click on the WORK library to display a list of files in the library. On OS/390, type **s** next to the WORK library.

3. Issue the END command (Windows, UNIX, OS/390) or click on ☒ (Windows, UNIX) to close the window.

Investigating a Library Programmatically

1. Use the CONTENTS procedure to browse the contents of the WORK
    library:

    ```
    proc contents data=work._all_;
    run;
    ```

2. Browse the output.

    PROC CONTENTS lists general information about the SAS library as
    well as information about each member of the library. The information
    varies slightly between operating environments.

    Partial SAS Output Displaying WORK Library Contents

    ```
                             The SAS System                         5
                                         14:10 Wednesday, June 28, 2000


                            The CONTENTS Procedure

                            -----Directory-----

            Libref:        WORK
            Engine:        V8
            Physical Name: C:\TEMP\SAS Temporary Files\_TD230
            File Name:     C:\TEMP\SAS Temporary Files\_TD230


                                   File
            #  Name    Memtype    Size  Last Modified

            1  ODSOUT  ITEMSTOR  13312   28JUN2000:14:10:33
            2  STAFF   DATA       5120   28JUN2000:14:11:35
    ```

When you use PROC CONTENTS to list the contents of the WORK
library, you may see information about system files that SAS creates
automatically. In this example, the ODSOUT file is a system file that
the SAS windowing environment uses to track items placed in the
Results window. The names and formats of these files vary among
releases of SAS.

Exercises

3. **Investigating a SAS Library Interactively**

   a. Issue the LIBNAME command to display the available SAS data libraries.

   b. Double-click on or select the SASUSER library. Browse the list of files in the SASUSER library.

   c. Close the LIBNAME window.

4. **Investigating a SAS Library with PROC CONTENTS**

   a. With the Program Editor window active, include a SAS program.

   Windows and UNIX: `include 'c2e4.sas'`

   OS/390:   `include '.prog1.sascode(c2e4)'`

   b. Submit the program for execution and browse the PROC CONTENTS output.

2.5 Diagnosing and Correcting Syntax Errors

Objectives

- Identify SAS syntax errors.
- Debug and edit a program with errors.
- Resubmit the corrected program.
- Save the corrected program.

52

Syntax Errors

Syntax errors include
- misspelled keywords
- missing or invalid punctuation
- invalid options.

```
daat work.staff;
    infile 'emplist.dat';
    input LastName $ 1-20 FirstName $ 21-30
        JobTitle $ 36-43 Salary 54-59;
run;

proc print data=work.staff
run;

proc means data=work.staff average max;
    class JobTitle;
    var Salary;
run;
```

53

When SAS encounters a syntax error, the following information is written to the SAS log:

- the word ERROR or WARNING
- the location of the error
- an explanation of the error.

Debugging a SAS Program

File: c2s5d1.sas

- Submit a SAS program that contains errors.
- Diagnose the errors.
- Correct the program.
- Save the corrected program.

Submit a SAS Program with Errors

```
daat work.staff;
   infile 'emplist.dat';
   input LastName $ 1-20 FirstName $ 21-30
         JobTitle $ 36-43 Salary 54-59;
run;

proc print data=work.staff
run;

proc means data=work.staff average max;
   class JobTitle;
   var Salary;
run;
```

Submit the program.

The SAS log contains error messages and warnings.

```
1     daat work.staff;
      ----
      14
WARNING 14-169: Assuming the symbol DATA was misspelled as daat.

2        infile 'emplist.dat';
3        input LastName $ 1-20 FirstName $ 21-30
4              JobTitle $ 36-43 Salary 54-59;
5     run;

NOTE: 18 records were read from the infile 'emplist.dat'.
      The minimum record length was 59.
      The maximum record length was 59.
NOTE: The data set WORK.STAFF has 18 observations and 4 variables.

6
7     proc print data=work.staff
8     run;
      ---
      22
         -
         200
ERROR 22-322: Syntax error, expecting one of the following: ;, (, DATA,
DOUBLE, HEADING, LABEL,
              N, NOOBS, OBS, ROUND, ROWS, SPLIT, UNIFORM, WIDTH.
ERROR 200-322: The symbol is not recognized and will be ignored.
9

NOTE: The SAS System stopped processing this step because of errors.

10    proc means data=work.staff average max;
                            ------- ---
                            22      202
ERROR 22-322: Syntax error, expecting one of the following: ;, (, ALPHA,
CHARTYPE, CLASSDATA, CLM, COMPLETETYPES, CSS, CV, DATA, DESCEND, DESCENDING,
DESCENDTYPES, EXCLNPWGT, EXCLNPWGTS, EXCLUSIVE, FW, IDMIN, KURTOSIS, LCLM,
MAX, MAXDEC, MEAN, MEDIAN, MIN, MISSING, N, NDEC, NMISS, NONOBS, NOPRINT,
NOTRAP, NWAY, ORDER, P1, P10, P25, P5, P50, P75, P90, P95, P99, PCTLDEF,
PRINT, PRINTALL, PRINTALLTYPES, PRINTIDS, PRINTIDVARS, PROBT, Q1, Q3,
QMARKERS, QMETHOD, QNTLDEF, QRANGE, RANGE, SKEWNESS, STDDEV, STDERR, SUM,
SUMSIZE, SUMWGT, T, UCLM, USS, VAR, VARDEF.
ERROR 202-322: The option or parameter is not recognized and will be ignored.
11       class JobTitle;
12       var Salary;
13    run;

NOTE: The SAS System stopped processing this step because of errors.
```

Debugging Your Program

The log indicates that

- SAS assumed the keyword DATA was misspelled and executed the DATA step
- SAS interpreted the word RUN as an option in the PROC PRINT statement (because there was a missing semicolon), so PROC PRINT was not executed
- SAS did not recognize the word AVERAGE as a valid option in the PROC MEANS statement, so the PROC MEANS step was not executed.

1. You can use the RECALL command or select **Run** ⇨ **Recall Last Submit** to recall the program you submitted back to the Program Editor.

    The original program is copied into the Program Editor.

2. Edit the program.

    a. Correct the spelling of DATA.

    b. Put a semicolon at the end of the PROC PRINT statement.

    c. Change the word AVERAGE to MEAN in the PROC MEANS statement.

```
data work.staff;
   infile 'emplist.dat';
   input LastName $ 1-20 FirstName $ 21-30
         JobTitle $ 36-43 Salary 54-59;
run;

proc print data=work.staff;
run;

proc means data=work.staff mean max;
   class JobTitle;
   var Salary;
run;
```

3. Submit the program. It runs successfully without errors and generates output.

Saving Your Program

You can use the FILE command to save your program to a file. The program must be in the Program Editor before you issue the FILE command.

OS/390:   `file '.prog1.sascode(myprog)'`

Windows or UNIX: `file 'myprog.sas'`

You can also select **File** ⇨ **Save As**.

A note appears that indicates the statements are saved to the file.

Submitting a SAS Program that Contains Unbalanced Quotes

The closing quote for the INFILE statement is missing.

```
data work.staff;
   infile 'emplist.dat;
   input LastName $ 1-20 FirstName $ 21-30
         JobTitle $ 36-43 Salary 54-59;
run;

proc print data=work.staff;
run;

proc means data=work.staff mean max;
   class JobTitle;
   var Salary;
run;
```

Submit the program and browse the SAS log.

```
Log - (Untitled)  DATA STEP running                                      _ □ x
151   data work.staff;
152      infile 'emplist.dat;
153      input LastName $ 1-20 FirstName $ 21-30
154            JobTitle $ 36-43 Salary 54-59;
155   run;
156
157   proc print data=work.staff;
158   run;
159
160   proc means data=work.staff mean max;
161      class JobTitle;
162      var Salary;
163   run;
```

There are no notes in the SAS log because all of the SAS statements after the INFILE statement have become part of the quoted string.

The banner on the window indicates the DATA step is still running because the RUN statement was not recognized.

Windows

1. To correct the problem in the Windows environment, press the Ctrl and Break keys.

2. Select **1. Cancel Submitted Statements** in the Tasking Manager window and select **OK**.

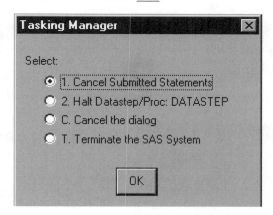

3. Select **Y to cancel submitted statements.** ⇨ **OK**.

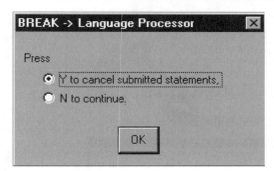

UNIX

1. To correct the problem in the UNIX operating environment, open the SAS: Session Management window and select **Interrupt**.

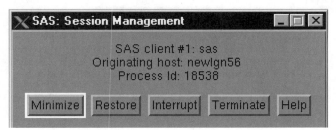

2. Select **1. Cancel Submitted Statements** in the SAS: Tasking Manager window.

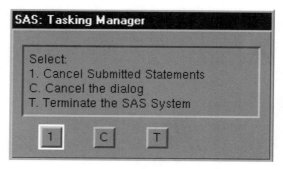

3. Select **Y**.

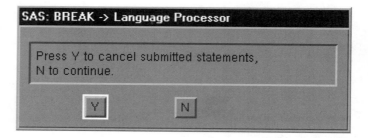

OS/390 (MVS)

1. To correct the problem in the OS/390 operating environment, press the Attention key or issue the ATTENTION command.

2. Select **1. Cancel Submitted Statements**.

3. Type **Y** and press Enter.

Resubmitting the Program

1. Recall the program into the Program Editor window.

2. Add a closing quote to the file reference on the INFILE statement.

3. Re-submit the program.

Partial SAS Log

```
27    data work.staff;
28       infile 'emplist.dat';
29       input LastName $ 1-20 FirstName $ 21-30
30             JobTitle $ 36-43 Salary 54-59;
31    run;

NOTE: 18 records were read from the infile 'emplist.dat'.
      The minimum record length was 59.
      The maximum record length was 59.
NOTE: The data set WORK.STAFF has 18 observations and 4 variables.
32
33    proc print data=work.staff;
34    run;

NOTE: There were 18 observations read from the dataset WORK.STAFF.
35
36    proc means data=work.staff mean max;
37       class JobTitle;
38       var Salary;
39    run;

NOTE: There were 18 observations read from the dataset WORK.STAFF.
```

Review: Recalling a Submitted Program

Program statements accumulate in a recall buffer each time you issue a SUBMIT command.

```
daat work.staff;
   infile 'emplist.dat';
   input LastName $ 1-20 FirstName $ 21-3
        JobTitle $ 36-43 Salary 54-59;
run;
proc print data=work.staff
run;
proc means data=work.staff average max;
   class JobTitle;
   var Salary;
run;
```
Submit Number 1

```
data work.staff;
   infile 'emplist.dat';
   input LastName $ 1-20 FirstName $ 21-3
        JobTitle $ 36-43 Salary 54-59;
run;
proc print data=work.staff;
run;
proc means data=work.staff mean max;
   class Jobtitle;
   var Salary;
run;
```
Submit Number 2

Review: Recalling a Submitted Program

Issue the RECALL command once to recall the most recently submitted program.

Submit Number 1

Issue RECALL once.

Submit Number 2

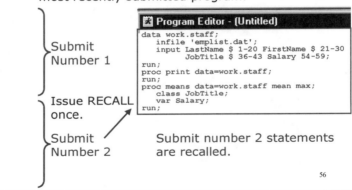

Program Editor - (Untitled)
```
data work.staff;
   infile 'emplist.dat';
   input LastName $ 1-20 FirstName $ 21-30
        JobTitle $ 36-43 Salary 54-59;
run;
proc print data=work.staff;
run;
proc means data=work.staff mean max;
   class JobTitle;
   var Salary;
run;
```

Submit number 2 statements are recalled.

56

Review: Recalling a Submitted Program

Issue the RECALL command again to recall submit number 1 statements.

Submit Number 1

Issue RECALL again.

Submit Number 2

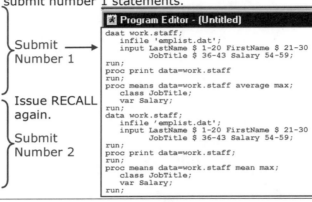

Program Editor - (Untitled)
```
daat work.staff;
   infile 'emplist.dat';
   input LastName $ 1-20 FirstName $ 21-30
        JobTitle $ 36-43 Salary 54-59;
run;
proc print data=work.staff
run;
proc means data=work.staff average max;
   class JobTitle;
   var Salary;
run;
data work.staff;
   infile 'emplist.dat';
   input LastName $ 1-20 FirstName $ 21-30
        JobTitle $ 36-43 Salary 54-59;
run;
proc print data=work.staff;
run;
proc means data=work.staff mean max;
   class JobTitle;
   var Salary;
run;
```

Review: Saving Your Program

Use the FILE command with the appropriate file naming convention for your operating environment.

OS/390 (MVS)

FILE `'userid.sas.programs(myprog)'`

UNIX

FILE `'/users/dept/programs/myprog.sas'`

Windows

FILE `'c:\coursedata\myprog.sas'`

58

OS/390:   The file reference '.SAS.PROGRAMS(MYPROG)' assumes *userid* is the first level of the filename.

Windows and UNIX: The file reference 'MYPROG.SAS' assumes the file will be stored in the current working folder.

Exercises

5. Correcting Errors

a. With the Program Editor window active, include and then submit the C2E5 program.

Windows and UNIX: `include 'c2e5.sas'`

OS/390: `include '.prog1.sascode(c2e5)'`

b. Use the SAS log notes to identify the error, correct the error, and resubmit the program.

2.6   Exploring Your SAS Environment (Self-Study)

Exploring Your SAS Environment under Windows

File: c2s6d1.sas

- Use the Enhanced Editor.
- Navigate around a SAS session.
- Explore SAS libraries and files.

Using the Enhanced Editor

1. If you are currently in an existing SAS session, exit SAS by issuing the BYE command or selecting **File** ⇨ **Exit**.

2. Invoke a new SAS session.

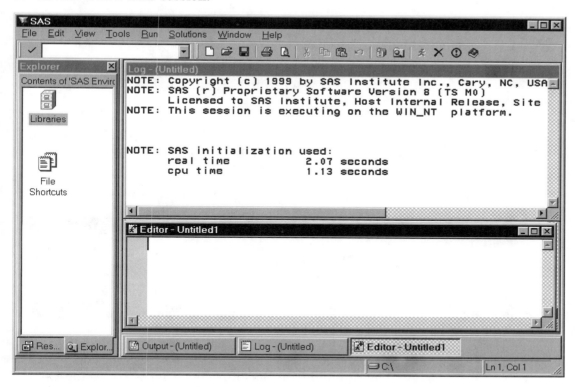

✎   If the Enhanced Editor is not the default editor, you can invoke it by selecting **View** ⇨ **Enhanced Editor**.

3. Include c2s6d1.sas by using the INCLUDE command or selecting **File** ⇨ **Open**. The window bar and the top border of the window reflect the name of the program.

```
c2s6d1.sas
data work.staff;
     infile 'emplist.dat';
     input LastName $ 1-20 FirstName $ 21-30
           JobTitle $ 36-43 Salary 54-59;
run;

proc print data=work.staff;
run;

proc means data=work.staff mean max;
     class JobTitle;
     var Salary;
run;
```

As you browse the program, notice the following:

- The syntax is color-coded to show
  - step boundaries
  - keywords
  - variable and data set names.
- A section boundary line separates each step.
- A minus sign ⊟ beside DATA or PROC indicates that the code has been expanded.

> 🖉 You can customize the appearance and functionality of the Enhanced Editor by selecting **Tools** ⇨ **Options** ⇨ **Enhanced Editor**.

4. Collapse the code by clicking on ⊟ to indicate the beginning of a step.

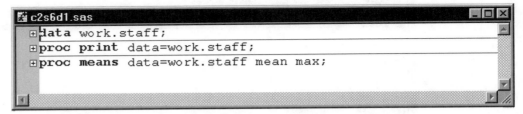

```
c2s6d1.sas
data work.staff;
proc print data=work.staff;
proc means data=work.staff mean max;
```

> 🖉 You can submit the code when it is collapsed. This is helpful if you want to highlight a portion of the program and submit only that portion. You can highlight the entire line that is visible for a step and submit it. To highlight the entire line, click to the left of the plus sign ⊞.

5. Expand the code by clicking on each ⊞. Delete the quotation mark from the end of the INFILE statement.

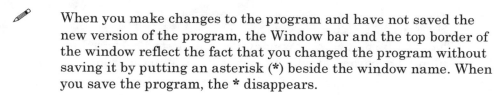

```
c2s6d1.sas *                                        _ □ ✕
⊟data work.staff;
    infile 'emplist.dat;
    input LastName $ 1-20 FirstName $ 21-30
          JobTitle $ 36-43 Salary 54-59;
run;

proc print data=work.staff;
run;

proc means data=work.staff mean max;
    class JobTitle;
    var Salary;
run;
```

Notice that

- the color of the rest of the program is the same as the file name, indicating that the code is considered part of the file name text

- there are no longer section boundary lines between the steps.

6. Correct the missing quotation mark on the INFILE statement and observe the colors and section boundary lines.

✎   When you make changes to the program and have not saved the new version of the program, the Window bar and the top border of the window reflect the fact that you changed the program without saving it by putting an asterisk (*****) beside the window name. When you save the program, the ***** disappears.

Navigating in Your SAS Session

1. Submit the program in the Enhanced Editor by issuing the SUBMIT command, selecting **Run** ⇨ **Submit**, or by clicking on [image of running person icon].

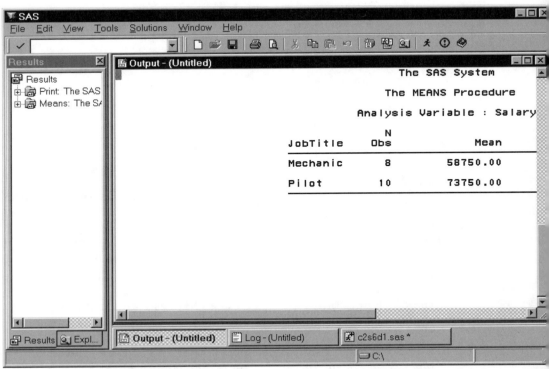

- The Results and Output windows remain in the background until you submit a program, at which point they come to the front.
- You can use the Ctrl and Tab keys to navigate between windows.
- You can use the SAS window bar at the bottom of the workspace to navigate between all of the windows in the SAS windowing environment or to restore minimized windows.
- Each window in the workspace has its own menu selections that reflect the actions you can perform when that window is active. This applies to pull-down, pop-up, and tool bar menus.

2. Return to the Enhanced Editor by selecting [c2s6d1.sas *] from the SAS window bar.

   Unlike the Program Editor, the code is not cleared from the Enhanced Editor after a submit so you do not need to use a RECALL command.

Exploring SAS Libraries and Files

1. Select Expl... on the SAS window bar or select **View** ⇨ **Explorer** to
    activate the Explorer window.

The functionality of the SAS Explorer is similar to explorers for
Windows-based systems. In addition to the single-pane view of folders
and files that opens by default, you can specify a tree view.

2. Select **View** ⇨ **Show Tree**.

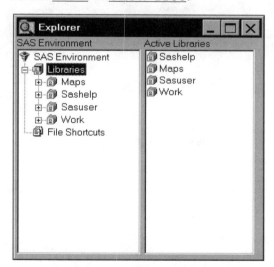

You can change the size of the windows by positioning the cursor on the
window divider so that the cursor becomes a double arrow. Drag the
window to the size you prefer.

3. Expand and collapse directories on the left. Drill-down and open specific
    files on the right.

4. Toggle this view off by selecting **View** ⇨ **Show Tree** again.

In addition to the tree view, you can view directories and files

- as large and small icons
- in a list format
- by their detail information.

You can investigate libraries and data sets using the SAS Explorer instead of issuing the LIBNAME command.

5. Double-click on the WORK library to show all members of that library.

6. Right-click on the STAFF data set and select **Properties**.

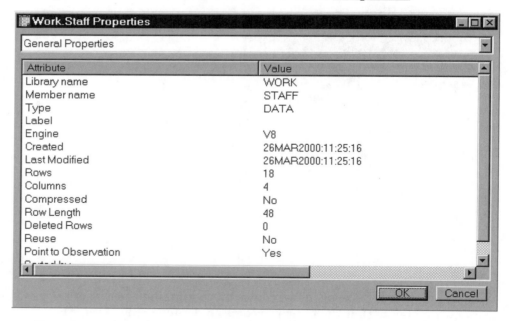

This default listing provides general information about the data set, such as the library in which it is stored, the type of information it contains, its creation date, the number of observations and variables, and so on. You can request specific information about the columns in the data table by using the list box pull-down menu at the top of the Properties window to select **Columns**.

7. Select ⊠ to close the Properties window.

8. You can view the contents of a data set by double-clicking on the file or right clicking on the file and selecting **Open**. This opens the data set in a VIEWTABLE window. A view of WORK.STAFF is shown below.

	LastName	FirstName	JobTitle	Salary
1	TORRES	JAN	Pilot	50000
2	LANGKAMM	SARAH	Mechanic	80000
3	SMITH	MICHAEL	Mechanic	40000
4	LEISTNER	COLIN	Mechanic	36000
5	WADE	KIRSTEN	Pilot	85000
6	TOMAS	HARALD	Pilot	105000
7	WAUGH	TIM	Pilot	70000
8	LEHMANN	DAGMAR	Mechanic	64000
9	TRETTHAHN	MICHAEL	Pilot	100000
10	TIETZ	OTTO	Pilot	45000
11	O'DONOGHUE	ART	Mechanic	52000
12	WALKER	THOMAS	Pilot	95000
13	NOROVIITA	JOACHIM	Mechanic	78000
14	OESTERBERG	ANJA	Mechanic	80000
15	LAUFFER	CRAIG	Mechanic	40000
16	TORR	JUGDISH	Pilot	45000

In addition to browsing SAS data sets, you can use the VIEWTABLE window to edit data sets, create data sets, and customize your view of a SAS data set. For example, you can

- sort your data
- change the color and fonts of variables
- display variable labels versus variable names
- remove and add variables.

9. Select ☒ to close the VIEWTABLE window.

Exploring Your SAS Environment under UNIX

- Explore SAS libraries and files.

Exploring SAS Libraries and Files

1. Select  on the SAS Toolbox or select **View** ⇨ **Explorer** to activate the Explorer window.

The functionality of the SAS Explorer is similar to explorers for GUI-based systems. You can choose to use a tree view or a single-pane view of folders and files. The screen above shows the tree view.

2. Select **View** ⇨ **Show Tree**. This selection toggles the tree view on or off.

The screen above shows the single-pane view.

3. Toggle the view so you are using the tree view.

   You can change the size of the windows by positioning the cursor on the window divider so that the cursor becomes a double arrow. Drag the window to the size you prefer.

4. Expand and collapse directories on the left. Drill-down and open specific files on the right.

5. Toggle the view so you are using the single pane view.

   In addition to the tree view, you can view directories and files
   - as large and small icons
   - in a list format
   - by their detail information.

   You can investigate libraries and data sets using the SAS Explorer instead of issuing the LIBNAME command.

6. Double-click on the WORK library to show all members of the library.

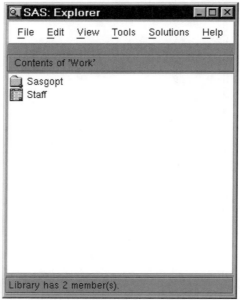

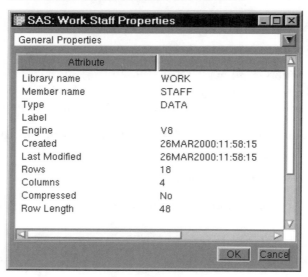

7. Right-click on the STAFF data set and select **Properties**.

This default listing provides general information about the data set, such as the library in which it is stored, the type of information it contains, its creation date, the number of observations and variables, and so on. You can request specific information about the columns in the data table by using the list box pull-down menu at the top of the Properties window to select **Columns**.

8. Select   OK   to close the Properties window.

9. You can view the contents of a data set by double-clicking on the file or right clicking on the file and selecting **Open**. This opens the data set in a VIEWTABLE window. A view of WORK.STAFF is shown below:

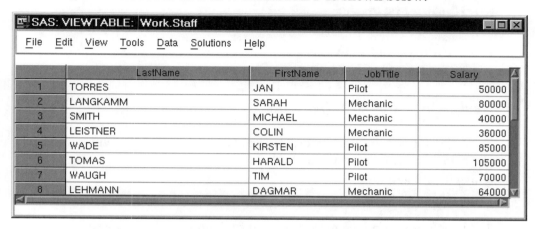

In addition to browsing SAS data sets, you can use the VIEWTABLE window to edit data sets, create data sets, and customize your view of a SAS data set. For example, you can

- sort your data
- change the color and fonts of variables
- display variable labels versus variable names
- remove and add variables.

10. Select **File** ⇨ **Close** to close the VIEWTABLE window.

Exploring Your SAS Environment under OS/390

- Navigate around a SAS session.
- Explore SAS libraries and files.

Navigating Your SAS Session

To perform tasks in your interactive SAS session, you can type commands on the command line or you can

- use pull-down menus
- use function keys.

1. Type **pmenu** on a command line to turn on pull-down menus.

If you have a mouse to control the cursor, you can click on a word to see the available actions for each pull-down menu item. Click on a word to select an item or click outside the pull-down area to **not** select an action.

You can also use your tab or arrow keys to move through the pull-down menu and action items. Press ENTER when the cursor is positioned on the item you want. Move your cursor away from the items and press ENTER to **not** select an action.

2. Select **Tools** ⇨ **Options** ⇨ **Turn All Menus Off** to turn off the pull-down menus and return to a command line.

Exploring SAS Libraries and Files

1. Issue the EXPLORER command to activate the Explorer window.

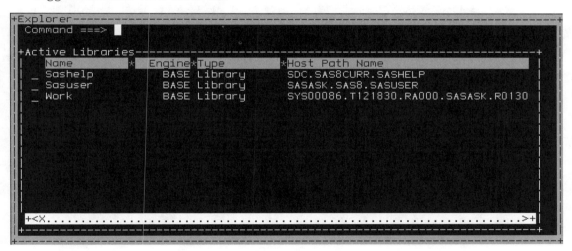

You can specify a tree view or a single-pane view of folders and files. The screen above shows the tree view.

2. Issue the TREE command or select **View** ⇨ **Show Tree**. This selection toggles the tree view on or off.

The screen above shows the single pane view.

3. If necessary, toggle the view to show the single pane view.

You can investigate libraries and data sets using the SAS Explorer instead of issuing the LIBNAME command.

4. Type **s** next to the WORK library to show all members of that library.

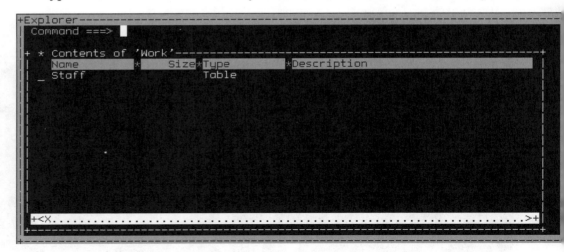

5. Type **?** next to the STAFF data set and select **Properties** or you can type **p** next to STAFF.

This default listing provides general information about the data set, such as the library in which it is stored, the type of information it contains, its creation date, the number of observations and variables, and so on.

6. Select ▮ OK ▮ to close the Properties window.

7. You can view the contents of a data set by typing **?** next to the file name and selecting **Open** or you can type **s** next to the file name. This opens the data set in an FSVIEW window. A view of WORK.STAFF is shown below:

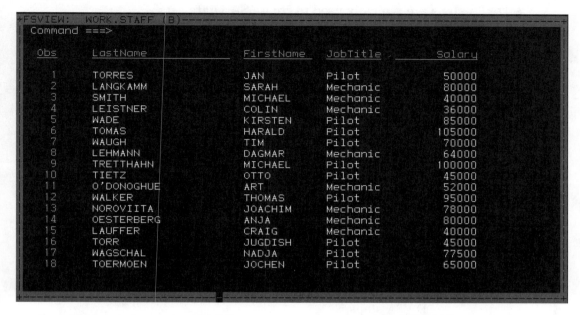

```
+FSVIEW:  WORK.STAFF (B)--------------------------------------------------+
| Command ===>                                                            |
|                                                                         |
|   Obs      LastName              FirstName   JobTitle        Salary      |
|                                                                         |
|     1      TORRES                JAN         Pilot            50000      |
|     2      LANGKAMM              SARAH       Mechanic         80000      |
|     3      SMITH                 MICHAEL     Mechanic         40000      |
|     4      LEISTNER              COLIN       Mechanic         36000      |
|     5      WADE                  KIRSTEN     Pilot            85000      |
|     6      TOMAS                 HARALD      Pilot           105000      |
|     7      WAUGH                 TIM         Pilot            70000      |
|     8      LEHMANN               DAGMAR      Mechanic         64000      |
|     9      TRETTHAHN             MICHAEL     Pilot           100000      |
|    10      TIETZ                 OTTO        Pilot            45000      |
|    11      O'DONOGHUE            ART         Mechanic         52000      |
|    12      WALKER                THOMAS      Pilot            95000      |
|    13      NOROVIITA             JOACHIM     Mechanic         78000      |
|    14      OESTERBERG            ANJA        Mechanic         80000      |
|    15      LAUFFER               CRAIG       Mechanic         40000      |
|    16      TORR                  JUGDISH     Pilot            45000      |
|    17      WAGSCHAL              NADJA       Pilot            77500      |
|    18      TOERMOEN              JOCHEN      Pilot            65000      |
|                                                                         |
+-------------------------------------------------------------------------+
```

In addition to browsing SAS data sets, you can use the FSVIEW window to edit data sets, create data sets, and customize your view of a SAS data set.

8. Issue the END command or select **File** ⇨ **Close** to close the FSVIEW window.

2.7 Chapter Summary

A SAS program is a sequence of steps to be submitted for execution.
- DATA steps are typically used to create SAS data sets.
- PROC steps are typically used to process SAS data sets (that is, generate reports and graphs, edit data, and sort data).

You can invoke SAS in
- interactive windowing mode (SAS windowing environment)
- interactive menu-driven mode (SAS/ASSIST, SAS/AF, or SAS/EIS software)
- interactive line mode
- batch mode
- noninteractive mode.

When you execute a SAS program, you generate two types of output:

SAS log   contains information about the processing of the SAS program, including warning and error messages

output   contains reports that are generated by SAS procedures and DATA steps.

The primary windows in the SAS windowing environment are the Program Editor window, the Output window, and the Log window.

Use the Program Editor window to
- access and edit SAS programs
- write new SAS programs
- submit SAS programs
- save programming statements to a file.

Issue the INCLUDE command in the Program Editor window to copy a program into your SAS session. Issue the FILE command to save the program to a file.

The output is displayed in the Output window. Use the BACKWARD and FORWARD commands to scroll vertically and the LEFT and RIGHT commands to scroll horizontally, or use the scrollbars. The Output window
- automatically accumulates output in the order in which it is generated. Issue the CLEAR command to clear the window contents.
- becomes the active window each time it receives output.

Issue the LOG command to activate the Log window. The Log window
- receives the programming statements that were submitted.
- acts as a record of your SAS session. Messages are written to the Log window in the order in which they are generated. Use the CLEAR command to clear the window contents.

SAS statements in a SAS program

- usually begin with an identifying keyword
- always end with a semicolon.

SAS statements are free-format.

- They can begin and end in any column.
- One or more blanks or special characters can be used to separate words.
- A single statement can span multiple lines.
- Several statements can be on the same line.

If you write and submit a program that contains misspelled SAS keywords, invalid options, or missing or invalid punctuation, a warning or error message is written to the SAS log that describes the error and identifies its location. These errors are syntax errors. Browse the log, use the RECALL command to recall the program to the Program Editor window, and edit the program as needed. Then resubmit the corrected program.

A SAS data set is a type of SAS file. A SAS file is a specially structured file that is created and organized by SAS software. The descriptor portion of a SAS data set contains general information about the data set and describes the variable attributes. The data portion of a SAS data set is a rectangular table of character data values, numeric data values, or both. The variables in the SAS data set correspond to fields of data and each variable is named. The observations in the data set correspond to records or data lines.

SAS data sets have two parts: the descriptor portion and the data portion. You can use the CONTENTS procedure to display the contents of the descriptor portion of a SAS data set. You can use the PRINT procedure to display the contents of the data portion of a SAS data set. The PRINT procedure produces a detailed list report.

A value must exist for every variable for every observation. Missing character variables are displayed as blanks, and missing numeric variables are displayed as periods.

SAS names (for SAS data sets and variables)

- can be 32 characters long.
- can be uppercase, lowercase, or mixed case.
- must start with a letter or underscore. Subsequent characters can be letters, underscores, or numeric digits.

A SAS data library is a collection of SAS files that SAS recognizes as a unit. When you invoke SAS, you automatically have access to the WORK library, which is temporary, and the SASUSER library, which is permanent. You can also create and access your own permanent libraries.

After your SAS session ends, temporary libraries are deleted and permanent libraries are saved.

Every SAS file has a two-level name in the form of *libref.filename*. The first name (*libref*) refers to the library. The second name (*filename*) refers to the file in the library.

You can use the LIBNAME window to browse information about a library, including its name and storage location.

2.8 Solutions to Exercises

1. **Submitting a Program**

   a. To activate the Program Editor window, issue the PGM command. Then issue the appropriate INCLUDE command or select **File** ⇨ **Open** to select the appropriate file.

   `Command ===> include 'operating-system-filename'`

   b. To submit your program for execution, issue the SUBMIT command or select **Submit**. Based on the report in the Output window, the WORK.AIRPORTS data set has 15 observations and 3 variables.

   c. To activate the Log window, issue the LOG command or select **Window** ⇨ **Log**. The log notes report that the WORK.AIRPORTS data set has 15 observations and 3 variables.

   d. To clear the Log window, issue the CLEAR command or select **Edit** ⇨ **Clear All**. To activate and clear the Output window, issue the OUTPUT command or select **Window** ⇨ **Output**. Then issue the CLEAR command or select **Edit** ⇨ **Clear All**.

5. **Correcting Errors**

   a. Activate the Program Editor window by issuing the PGM command or selecting **Window** ⇨ **Program Editor**. Then issue the appropriate INCLUDE command or select **File** ⇨ **Open** to select the appropriate file.

   `Command ===> include 'operating-system-filename'`

   To submit the program for execution, issue the SUBMIT command or select **Submit**.

   b. Activate the Log window by issuing the LOG command or selecting **Window** ⇨ **Log**. Scroll vertically to examine the SAS log notes. These notes confirm that the WORK.AIRPORTS data set was created. However, an error occurred in the PROC step. The name of the procedure is misspelled.

   To recall the program into the Program Editor window, activate the Program Editor window by issuing the PGM command or selecting **Window** ⇨ **Program Editor**. Then issue the RECALL command or select **Run** ⇨ **Recall Last Submit**.

   Edit the program to correct the spelling of the PRINT procedure.

   Resubmit your program by issuing the SUBMIT command or select **Submit**.

   If you do not see a report in the Output window, re-examine the SAS log notes, recall the program, correct the error, and resubmit the program.

Chapter 3   Importing Raw Data and Creating Basic Reports

3.1 Introduction

Business Scenario

International Airlines is preparing its yearly review of flight crew staff.

3

Business Scenario

The airline must

- write the flight crew data to a SAS data set so that it can be further processed

- create a report that lists all of the flight crew information

- categorize the flight crew by job code and salary

- determine the salary range that most pilots and flight attendants are paid.

4

Reading a Raw Data File

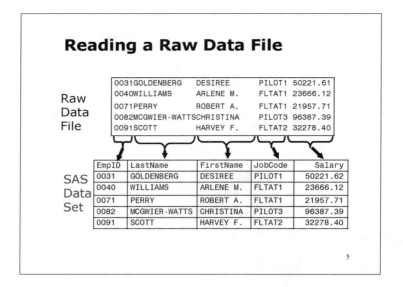

Browsing the Data Values

```
              Listing of Flight Crew Employees

       Emp                              Job
Obs    ID      LastName      FirstName  Code      Salary

1     0031     GOLDENBERG    DESIREE    PILOT1    50221.62
2     0040     WILLIAMS      ARLENE M.  FLTAT1    23666.12
3     0071     PERRY         ROBERT A.  FLTAT1    21957.71
4     0082     MCGWIER-WATTS CHRISTINA  PILOT3    96387.39
5     0091     SCOTT         HARVEY F.  FLTAT2    32278.40
6     0106     THACKER       DAVID S.   FLTAT1    24161.14
7     0275     GRAHAM        DEBORAH S. FLTAT2    32024.93
8     0286     DREWRY        SUSAN      PILOT1    55377.00
9     0309     HORTON        THOMAS L.  FLTAT1    23705.12
10    0334     DOWN          EDWARD     PILOT1    56584.87
11    0347     CHERVENY      BRENDA B.  FLTAT2    38563.45
12    0355     BELL          THOMAS B.  PILOT1    59803.16
13    0366     GLENN         MARTHA S.  PILOT3   120202.38
14    0730     BELL          CARLA      PILOT1    37397.93
15    0739     SAYRE         MARCO      PILOT1    59268.61
```

Categorizing the Flight Crew by Job Code

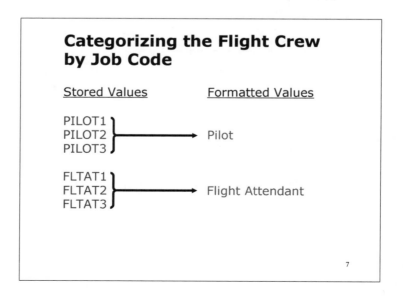

Categorizing the Flight Crew by Salary

Stored Values   Formatted Values

0-25000 $\longrightarrow$ < 25,000

25000-50000 $\longrightarrow$ 25,000 - 50,000

50000-200000 $\longrightarrow$ > 50,000

8

Generating a List Report with Formatted Values and Labels

```
              Flight Crew Employee Listing

First Name Last Name      Job Category      Salary Range

DESIREE    GOLDENBERG     Pilot             > 50,000
ARLENE M.  WILLIAMS       Flight Attendant  < 25,000
ROBERT A.  PERRY          Flight Attendant  < 25,000
CHRISTINA  MCGWIER-WATTS  Pilot             > 50,000
HARVEY F.  SCOTT          Flight Attendant  25,000 - 50,000
DAVID S.   THACKER        Flight Attendant  < 25,000
DEBORAH S. GRAHAM         Flight Attendant  25,000 - 50,000
SUSAN      DREWRY         Pilot             > 50,000
```

9

Calculating Job Code Frequencies

```
           Distribution of Job Categories

                                 Cumulative Cumulative
JobCode           Frequency Percent Frequency  Percent

Flight Attendant    128    68.82      128      68.82
Pilot                58    31.18      186     100.00
```

10

Calculating Job Code/Salary Frequencies

```
JobCode(Job Code)      Salary(Annual Salary)

    Frequency       |
    Percent         |
    Row Pct         |
    Col Pct         | < 25,000|25,000 -|> 50,000|  Total
                    |         |  50,000|        |
    ----------------+---------+--------+--------+--------
    Flight Attendant|     25  |   103  |     0  |   128
                    |  13.44  |  55.38 |  0.00  |  68.82
                    |  19.53  |  80.47 |  0.00  |
                    | 100.00  |  91.15 |  0.00  |
    ----------------+---------+--------+--------+--------
    Pilot           |      0  |    10  |    48  |    58
                    |   0.00  |   5.38 |  25.81 |  31.18
                    |   0.00  |  17.24 |  82.76 |
                    |   0.00  |   8.85 | 100.00 |
    ----------------+---------+--------+--------+--------
    Total                 25      113       48      186
                       13.44    60.75    25.81   100.00
```

11

3.2 Reading a Raw Data File Using Column Input

Objectives

- Create a SAS data set from a raw data file.
- Read a fixed-column raw data file using column input.
- Investigate the descriptor portion of a SAS data set using the CONTENTS procedure.
- Investigate the data portion of a SAS data set using the PRINT procedure.
- Examine data errors.

13

Accessing Data Sources

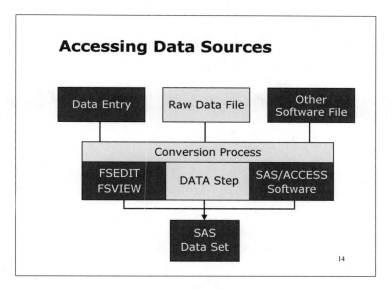

14

Data must be in the form of a SAS data set to be processed by many SAS procedures and some DATA step statements.

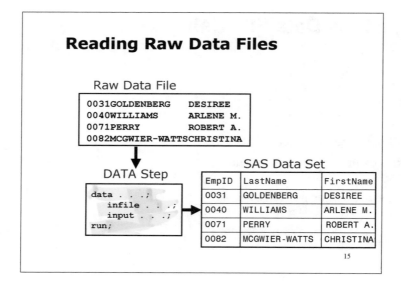

Reading Raw Data Files

In order to create a SAS data set from a raw data file, you must

- start a DATA step and name the SAS data set being created (DATA statement)

- identify the location of the raw data file to read (INFILE statement)

- describe how to read the data fields from the raw data file (INPUT statement).

16

Creating a SAS Data Set with the DATA Statement

General form of the DATA statement:

DATA *SAS-data-set(s);*

This DATA statement creates a SAS data set named WORK.EMPDATA:

```
data work.empdata;
```

17

The two major functions of the DATA statement are to
- signal the beginning of a DATA step
- name the SAS data set(s) being created.

The name of the SAS data set must follow the SAS naming conventions.

The SAS data set(s) being created can be either temporary or permanent.

Pointing to a Raw Data File with the INFILE Statement

General form of the INFILE statement:

INFILE *'filename'* *<options>;*

Examples:

OS/390	`infile 'edc.prog1.employee';`
UNIX	`infile '/prog1/employee.dat';`
WIN	`infile 'C:\prog1\employee.dat';`

18

The INFILE statement
- identifies an external file containing raw data
- must be after the DATA statement and before the INPUT statement.

Reading Raw Data Using Column Input

General form of column input:

> **INPUT** *variable <$> startcol-endcol ...;*

To read raw data values with column input

1. **name** the SAS variable you want to create
2. use a dollar sign ($) if the SAS variable is **character**
3. specify the **starting column**, a dash, and the **ending column** of the raw data field.

19

If the starting and ending columns of the raw data field are the same, specify the column number once without a dash.

What Is Column Input?

Column input is appropriate for reading

- data in fixed columns
- standard character and numeric data.

20

Some examples of standard numeric data are 15, -15, 15.4, +.05, 1.54E3, and −1.54E-3.

   Column input is one of several input methods available in the DATA step.

Reading Raw Data Using Column Input

```
              1    1    2    2    3    3    4    4
1---5----0----5----0----5----0----5----0----5

0031GOLDENBERG    DESIREE       PILOT1 50221.62


    input EmpID     $  1-4
          LastName  $  5-17
          FirstName $ 18-30
          JobCode   $ 31-36
          Salary      37-45;
```

                                                    26

This INPUT statement creates a character variable EMPID by reading data from columns 1 through 4, creates a character variable LASTNAME by reading data from columns 5 through 17, and so on.

Writing the DATA Step

```
data work.empdata;
   infile 'employee.dat';
   input EmpID     $  1-4
         LastName  $  5-17
         FirstName $ 18-30
         JobCode   $ 31-36
         Salary      37-45;
run;
```

                                                    27

Executing the DATA Step

The statements in a DATA step are executed sequentially.

```
data work.empdata;
   infile 'employee.dat';
   input EmpID      $  1-4
         LastName   $  5-17
         FirstName  $ 18-30
         JobCode    $ 31-36
         Salary       37-45;
run;
```

28

Executing the DATA Step

The INFILE statement executes and identifies the data source.

```
data work.empdata;
   infile 'employee.dat';
   input EmpID      $  1-4
         LastName   $  5-17
         FirstName  $ 18-30
         JobCode    $ 31-36
         Salary       37-45;
run;
```

29

Executing the DATA Step

The INPUT statement executes, reads a record from the file, and creates SAS variables.

```
data work.empdata;
   infile 'employee.dat';
   input EmpID      $  1-4
         LastName   $  5-17
         FirstName  $ 18-30
         JobCode    $ 31-36
         Salary       37-45;
run;
```

30

...

Executing the DATA Step

A new observation is written to
WORK.EMPDATA and processing returns to the
top of the DATA step.

```
data work.empdata;
   infile 'employee.dat';
   input EmpID     $  1-4
         LastName  $  5-17
         FirstName $ 18-30
         JobCode   $ 31-36
         Salary      37-45;
run;
```

OUTPUT

31

...

Executing the DATA Step

The INFILE statement executes and identifies
the data source.

```
data work.empdata;
   infile 'employee.dat';
   input EmpID     $  1-4
         LastName  $  5-17
         FirstName $ 18-30
         JobCode   $ 31-36
         Salary      37-45;
run;
```

32

...

Executing the DATA Step

The INPUT statement executes, reads the next
record from the file, and creates SAS variables.

```
data work.empdata;
   infile 'employee.dat';
   input EmpID     $  1-4
         LastName  $  5-17
         FirstName $ 18-30
         JobCode   $ 31-36
         Salary      37-45;
run;
```

33

···

Executing the DATA Step

A second observation is written to
WORK.EMPDATA and and processing returns to
the top of the DATA step.

```
data work.empdata;
    infile 'employee.dat';
    input EmpID      $  1-4
          LastName   $  5-17
          FirstName  $ 18-30
          JobCode    $ 31-36
          Salary        37-45;
run;
           OUTPUT
```

34

Executing the DATA Step

The DATA step stops when the end of the raw
data file is encountered.

```
data work.empdata;
    infile 'employee.dat';
    input EmpID      $  1-4
          LastName   $  5-17
          FirstName  $ 18-30
          JobCode    $ 31-36
          Salary        37-45;
run;
```

35

Reading a Raw Data File Using Column Input

File: c3s2d1.sas

- Use column input to read the flight crew raw data file.
- Use the CONTENTS procedure to browse the descriptor portion of the SAS data set.
- Use the PRINT procedure to browse the data portion of the SAS data set.

1. Write the DATA step, including the DATA statement, the INFILE statement, and the INPUT statement.

```
data work.empdata;
   infile 'employee.dat';
   input EmpID     $  1-4
         LastName  $  5-17
         FirstName $ 18-30
         JobCode   $ 31-36
         Salary      37-45;
run;
```

> ✎ The filename listed in the INFILE statement is different for OS/390 users:
>
> ```
> infile '.prog1.rawdata(employee)';
> ```

2.   Submit the program for execution and browse the SAS log.

Partial SAS Log

```
2     data work.empdata;
3        infile 'employee.dat';
4        input EmpID      $   1-4
5              LastName   $   5-17
6              FirstName  $  18-30
7              JobCode    $  31-36
8              Salary        37-45;
9     run;

NOTE: The infile 'employee.dat' is:
      File Name=c:\employee.dat,
      RECFM=V,LRECL=256

NOTE: 186 records were read from the infile 'employee.dat'.
      The minimum record length was 45.
      The maximum record length was 45.
NOTE: The data set WORK.EMPDATA has 186 observations and 5 variables.
```

The first note indicates that SAS found the raw data file that the INFILE statement points to. This note also includes some information about the raw data file.

The second note indicates how many records were read from the raw data file as well as the minimum and maximum length of the records in the raw data file.

The third note indicates that the SAS data set was created and lists the number of observations and variables in the new SAS data set.

3. Use PROC CONTENTS to browse the descriptor portion of
    WORK.EMPDATA.

    ```
    proc contents data=work.empdata;
    run;
    ```

SAS Output

```
                        The SAS System                    9
                                 10:29 Tuesday, May 16, 2000


                      The CONTENTS Procedure

Data Set Name: WORK.EMPDATA              Observations:        186
Member Type:   DATA                      Variables:           5
Engine:        V8                        Indexes:             0
Created:       10:38 Tuesday, May 16, 2000   Observation Length:  48
Last Modified: 10:38 Tuesday, May 16, 2000   Deleted Observations: 0
Protection:                              Compressed:          NO
Data Set Type:                           Sorted:              NO
Label:


              -----Engine/Host Dependent Information-----

Data Set Page Size:        4096
Number of Data Set Pages:  3
First Data Page:           1
Max Obs per Page:          84
Obs in First Data Page:    53
Number of Data Set Repairs: 0
File Name:                 C:\TEMP\SAS Temporary
                           Files\_TD258\empdata.sas7bdat
Release Created:           8.0000M0
Host Created:              WIN_NT

         -----Alphabetic List of Variables and Attributes-----

            #    Variable   Type    Len    Pos

            1    EmpID      Char     4      8
            3    FirstName  Char    13     25
            4    JobCode    Char     6     38
            2    LastName   Char    13     12
            5    Salary     Num      8      0
```

4. Use PROC PRINT to browse the data portion of WORK.EMPDATA.

```
proc print data=work.empdata;
run;
```

Partial SAS Output

```
                              The SAS System                              10
                                            10:29 Tuesday, May 16, 2000

          Emp                                    Job
Obs        ID    LastName        FirstName        Code      Salary

  1       0031   GOLDENBERG      DESIREE          PILOT1     50221.62
  2       0040   WILLIAMS        ARLENE M.        FLTAT1     23666.12
  3       0071   PERRY           ROBERT A.        FLTAT1     21957.71
  4       0082   MCGWIER-WATTS   CHRISTINA        PILOT3     96387.39
  5       0091   SCOTT           HARVEY F.        FLTAT2     32278.40
  6       0106   THACKER         DAVID S.         FLTAT1     24161.14
  7       0275   GRAHAM          DEBORAH S.       FLTAT2     32024.93
  8       0286   DREWRY          SUSAN            PILOT1     55377.00
  9       0309   HORTON          THOMAS L.        FLTAT1     23705.12
 10       0334   DOWN            EDWARD           PILOT1     56584.87
 11       0347   CHERVENY        BRENDA B.        FLTAT2     38563.45
 12       0355   BELL            THOMAS B.        PILOT1     59803.16
 13       0366   GLENN           MARTHA S.        PILOT3    120202.38
 14       0730   BELL            CARLA            PILOT1     37397.93
 15       0739   SAYRE           MARCO            PILOT1     59268.61
 16       0746   DIXON           MARTIN L.        PILOT3    110811.16
 17       0802   BETHEA          BARBARA ANN      FLTAT2     39844.72
 18       0803   DUNNING         SHELLEY S.       PILOT1     53713.81
```

What Are Data Errors?

The SAS System detects errors when SAS inputs raw data and

- invalid data is found in a field
- illegal arguments are used in functions
- impossible mathematical operations are requested.

37

Examining Data Errors

When SAS encounters a data error, SAS

1. prints a note that describes the error
2. displays the input record being read
3. displays the values in the SAS observation being created
4. assigns a missing value to the appropriate SAS variable
5. continues executing.

38

Examining Data Errors

File: c3s2d2.sas

- Use column input to read the raw data file.
- Examine the data error in the log.
- Use PROC PRINT to examine the data portion of the data set.

Partial Raw Data File

```
          1    1    2    2    3    3    4    4    5
1---5----0----5----0----5----0----5----0----5----0----
0031GOLDENBERG    DESIREE      PILOT1 50221.62
0040WILLIAMS      ARLENE M.    FLTAT1 23666.12
0071PERRY         ROBERT A.    FLTAT1 21957.71
0082MCGWIER-WATTSCHRISTINA     PILOT3 96387.39
0091SCOTT         HARVEY F.    FLTAT2 32278.40
0106THACKER       DAVID S.     FLTAT1 24161.14
0275GRAHAM        DEBORAH S.   FLTAT2 32024.93
0286DREWRY        SUSAN        PILOT1 55377.00
0309HORTON        THOMAS L.    FLTAT1 23705.12
0334DOWN          EDWARD       PILOT1 56%84.87
0347CHERVENY      BRENDA B.    FLTAT2 38563.45
0355BELL          THOMAS B.    PILOT1 59803.16
0366GLENN         MARTHA S.    PILOT3120202.38
0730BELL          CARLA        PILOT1 37397.93
0739SAYRE         MARCO        PILOT1 59268.61
```

1. Use a DATA step with column input to read the fields from the raw data file and create a SAS data set:

```
data work.empdata2;
   infile 'employe2.dat';
   input EmpID      $  1- 4
         LastName   $  5-17
         FirstName  $ 18-30
         JobCode    $ 31-36
         Salary        37-45;
run;
```

2. Examine the log.

SAS Log

```
16    data work.empdata2;
17       infile 'employe2.dat';
18       input EmpID      $  1- 4
19             LastName   $  5-17
20             FirstName  $ 18-30
21             JobCode    $ 31-36
22             Salary       37-45;
23    run;

NOTE: The infile 'employe2.dat' is:
      File Name=C:\employe2.dat,
      RECFM=V,LRECL=256

NOTE: Invalid data for Salary in line 10 37-45.
RULE:       ----+----1----+----2----+----3----+----4----+----5----+----6--
10          0334DOWN          EDWARD          PILOT1 56%84.87 45
EmpID=0334 LastName=DOWN FirstName=EDWARD JobCode=PILOT1 Salary=.
_ERROR_=1 _N_=10
NOTE: 15 records were read from the infile 'employe2.dat'.
      The minimum record length was 45.
      The maximum record length was 45.
NOTE: The data set WORK.EMPDATA2 has 15 observations and 5 variables.
```

The second note indicates that invalid data was found for the variable
SALARY in line 10 of the raw data file, in columns 37-45.

A ruler is drawn above the raw data record that contains the invalid data.
The ruler can help you locate the invalid data in the record.

SAS also displays the observation currently being created from the raw
data record. Notice the value of SALARY is set to missing.

During the processing of every DATA step, SAS automatically creates two
variables, _N_ and _ERROR_. However, they are **not** written to the SAS
data set.

3. Use PROC PRINT to examine the data portion of the SAS data set.

```
proc print data=work.empdata2;
run;
```

SAS Output

```
                            The SAS System                            14
                                           10:29 Tuesday, May 16, 2000

          Emp                                    Job
  Obs      ID    LastName       FirstName        Code      Salary

   1      0031   GOLDENBERG     DESIREE          PILOT1    50221.62
   2      0040   WILLIAMS       ARLENE M.        FLTAT1    23666.12
   3      0071   PERRY          ROBERT A.        FLTAT1    21957.71
   4      0082   MCGWIER-WATTS  CHRISTINA        PILOT3    96387.39
   5      0091   SCOTT          HARVEY F.        FLTAT2    32278.40
   6      0106   THACKER        DAVID S.         FLTAT1    24161.14
   7      0275   GRAHAM         DEBORAH S.       FLTAT2    32024.93
   8      0286   DREWRY         SUSAN            PILOT1    55377.00
   9      0309   HORTON         THOMAS L.        FLTAT1    23705.12
  10      0334   DOWN           EDWARD           PILOT1         .
  11      0347   CHERVENY       BRENDA B.        FLTAT2    38563.45
  12      0355   BELL           THOMAS B.        PILOT1    59803.16
  13      0366   GLENN          MARTHA S.        PILOT3   120202.38
  14      0730   BELL           CARLA            PILOT1    37397.93
  15      0739   SAYRE          MARCO            PILOT1    59268.61
```

A missing numeric value is displayed as a period and a missing character value is displayed as a blank.

Exercises

For these exercises, write DATA steps that read the raw data file that contains information on flights from San Francisco to various destinations.

Fill in the blank with the location of your raw data file. Use an INFILE statement in a DATA step to read the raw file.

```
data ...;
   infile '   SFOSCH.dat          ';
   .
   .
   .
```

Each exercise instructs you to read **some** of the fields shown in the following record layout. The complete record layout for the SFOSCH raw data file is shown below.

Variable Name	Field Description	Columns	Data Type
FLIGHTID	Flight ID Number	1-7	Character
ROUTEID	Route ID Number	8-14	Character
ORIGIN	Flight Origin	15-17	Character
DESTINATION	Flight Destination	18-20	Character
MODEL	Aircraft Model	21-40	Character
DEPARTDATE	Departure Date	41-49	Character 01JAN2000
DEPARTDAY	Departure Day of Week	51	Numeric 1=Sunday
FCLASSPASS	First Class Passengers	53-55	Numeric
BCLASSPASS	Business Class Passengers	57-59	Numeric
ECLASSPASS	Economy Class Passengers	61-63	Numeric
TOTPASSCAP	Aircraft Capacity – Total Passengers	65-67	Numeric
CARGOWT	Weight of Cargo in Pounds	69-73	Numeric
CARGOREV	Revenue from Cargo in Dollars	75-79	Numeric

1. **Reading Raw Data**

   a. Create a SAS data set named WORK.SANFRAN by writing a DATA step that uses column input to create only the variables FLIGHTID, ROUTEID, DESTINATION, MODEL, DEPARTDAY, and TOTPASSCAP.

   b. Read the log to answer the following questions:

      1) What is the name of the raw data file that was accessed?

      2) How many records were read from the raw data file?

      3) How many observations does the resulting SAS data set contain?

      4) How many variables does the resulting SAS data set contain?

   c. Use PROC PRINT to display the data portion of the data set.

   d. Use PROC CONTENTS to display the descriptor portion of the data set.

   e. Recall your DATA step program and save it in a file. If you are using Windows or UNIX, name your file ch3ex1.sas. If you are using OS/390, save your program to the appropriate partitioned data set with a member name of ch3ex1.

2. **Examining Data Errors**

   a. Create a SAS data set named WORK.SFPASS by writing a DATA step that uses column input to create only the variables FLIGHTID, DESTINATION, DEPARTDATE, FCLASSPASS, BCLASSPASS, and ECLASSPASS.

   b. Read the log and answer the following questions:

      1) What is the name of the raw data file that was accessed?

      2) How many records were read from the raw data file?

      3) How many observations are in the resulting SAS data set?

      4) How many variables are in the resulting SAS data set?

      5) What data errors are indicated in the SAS log?

   c. Use PROC PRINT to display the data portion of the data set.

   d. Use PROC CONTENTS to display the descriptor portion of the data set.

3.3 Reading Data Using the Import Wizard (Optional)

Objectives

- Create a SAS data set from data using the Import Wizard.

42

Business Scenario

International Airlines is preparing to review its flight crew. The immediate goal is to read an Excel spreadsheet and create a SAS data set.

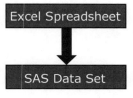

43

The flight crew employee data is stored in an Excel spreadsheet.

What Is the Import Wizard?

The *Import Wizard* is a point-and-click graphical interface that enables you to create a SAS data set from several types of external files including

- dBASE files (*.DBF)
- Excel spreadsheets (*.XLS)
- Microsoft Access tables
- delimited files (*.*)
- comma-separated values (*.CSV).

44

The data sources available to you depend on the SAS/ACCESS products that you have licensed. If you do not have any SAS/ACCESS products licensed, the only types of data source files available to you are

- .CSV
- .TXT
- delimited files.

Reading Raw Data with the Import Wizard

Use the Import Wizard to import the file EMPLOYEE.XLS into SAS. This is an Excel file that contains flight crew information. Name the resulting data set WORK.EMPDATA.

1. Select **File** ⇨ **Import Data...**. The Import Wizard – Select import type window opens.

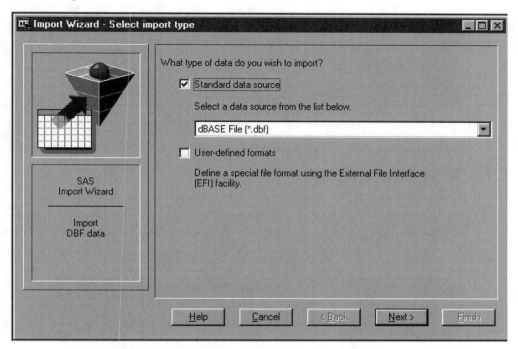

2. Select the drop-down button.

3. From the list box, select **Excel 97 or 2000 Spreadsheet (*.xls)**.

4. Select **Next >**. The Import Wizard – Select file window opens.

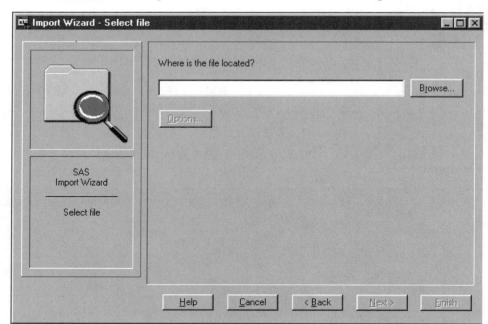

5. Type **employee.xls**, the name of the file to be imported.

    You can also select **Browse** to specify a file to import from the Open window. After you select the pathname, select **Open** to complete your selections and return to the Import Wizard – Select file window.

6. Select **Options** to browse the available import options.

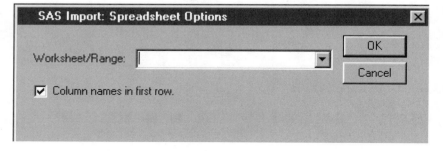

7. Select **OK** to accept the default values and close the window.

8. Select **Next >** to open the Import Wizard – Select library and member window, where you specify the storage location for the imported file.

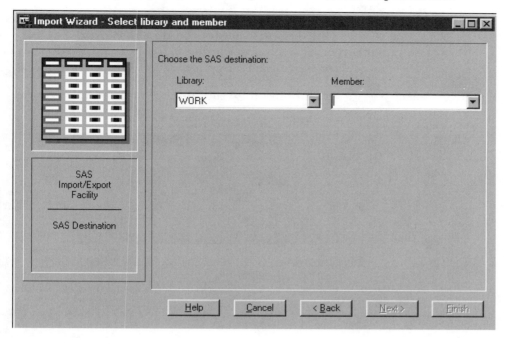

9. In the Library box on the left, leave the library as WORK. In the Member box on the right, type **empdata2**.

You can also select the down arrow in the Library box and select a different library. You can select the down arrow in the Member box and select an existing data set. If you select an existing data set, you will be asked later to verify that you want to replace it.

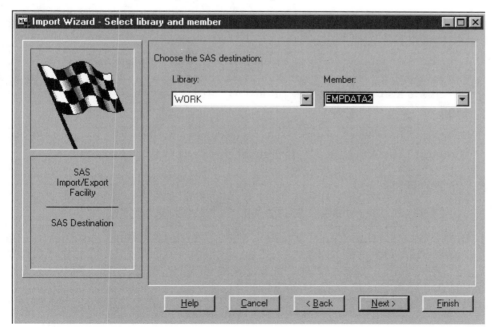

10. Select **Next >** to move to the next window or **Finish** to create the SAS data set from the Excel spreadsheet.

   If you select **Finish** and you select the name of an existing SAS data set for the name of your new SAS data set (in the Import Wizard – Select library and member window), you are prompted to determine whether or not you want to replace the existing data set. Select **OK** or **Cancel**.

   If you select **Next >**, you are taken to the Import Wizard – Create SAS Statements window.

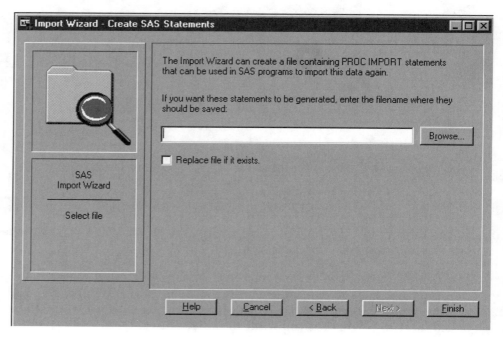

11. Type **import_code.sas**, which is the name of the location where you want to store the SAS code.

   You can also select **Browse** to specify a location from the Save As window. After you select the pathname, select **Save** to complete your selections and return to the Import Wizard – Create SAS Statements window.

   If the file already exists, you are prompted to replace the existing file, append to the existing file, or cancel the save.

12. Select **Finish**.

13. Check the log to see that the SAS data set is successfully created.

14. Go to the Program Editor window and open the SAS code created by the Import Wizard.

```
proc import out=work.empdata
            datafile="employee.xls"
            dbms=excel2000 replace;
    getnames=yes;
run;
```

The IMPORT Procedure

General form of the IMPORT procedure:

PROC IMPORT OUT=*SAS-data-set*
          DATAFILE='*external-file-name*`
          DBMS=*file-type*;
RUN;

46

The IMPORT procedure is a second method for reading data from an external data source and writing it to a SAS data set.

DATAFILE='*external-file-name*'

> specifies the complete path and filename of the input PC file, spreadsheet, or delimited external file.

OUT=*SAS-data-set*

> identifies the output SAS data set with either a one- or a two-level SAS name (library and member name).

DBMS=*file-type*

> specifies the type of data to import.

delimiter

Available DBMS Specifications

Identifier	Input Data Source	Extension
ACCESS	Microsoft Access database	.MDB
DBF	dBASE file	.DBF
WK1	Lotus 1 spreadsheet	.WK1
WK3	Lotus 3 spreadsheet	.WK3
WK4	Lotus 4 spreadsheet	.WK4
EXCEL	Excel Version 4 or 5 spreadsheet	.XLS
EXCEL4	Excel Version 4 spreadsheet	.XLS
EXCEL5	Excel Version 5 spreadsheet	.XLS
EXCEL97	Excel 97 spreadsheet	.XLS
EXCEL2000	Excel 2000 spreadsheet	.XLS
DLM	delimited file (default delimiter is a blank)	.*
CSV	delimited file (comma-separated values)	.CSV
TAB	delimited file (tab-delimited values)	.TXT

   The data sources available to you depend on the SAS/ACCESS products that you license. If you do not have SAS/ACCESS products licensed, the only types of data source files available to you are

- .CSV
- .TXT
- delimited files.

The OS/2 operating environment does not support Excel 5 and Excel 97 spreadsheets.

REPLACE	overwrites an existing SAS data set. If you do not specify REPLACE, PROC IMPORT does not overwrite an existing data set.
GETNAMES=YES | NO	for spreadsheets and delimited external files, determines whether to generate SAS variable names from the column names in the input file's first row of data. If you specify GETNAMES=NO or if the column names are not valid SAS names, PROC IMPORT uses the variable names VAR0, VAR1, VAR2, and so on.

Exercises (Applicable Only to Windows Users)

3. Reading an Excel Spreadsheet

a. The Excel 97 spreadsheet SFOSCH.XLS contains information about International Airlines flights originating in San Francisco. (It is the same data that is in the raw data file you used in the exercises in Section 3.2.)

Use the Import Wizard to create a SAS data set named WORK.SFOEXCEL from the Excel 97 spreadsheet.

Save the PROC IMPORT code that is generated to a file named IMPORTSFO.SAS.

b. Use PROC PRINT to display the data portion of the SAS data set WORK.SFOEXCEL.

c. Use PROC CONTENTS to display the descriptor portion of the WORK.SFOEXCEL data set.

4. Reading a Comma-delimited File

a. The file named SFOSCH.CSV (delimited file with comma-separated values) contains the same information about International Airlines flights as the Excel 97 spreadsheet named SFOSCH.XLS.

Include the program in the file named IMPORTSFO.SAS that you saved in the previous exercise. Alter the PROC IMPORT statement so it creates a SAS data set named WORK.SFOCSV from the comma-delimited file.

b. Use PROC PRINT to display the data portion of the WORK.SFOCSV data set.

c. Use PROC CONTENTS to display the descriptor portion of the WORK.SFOCSV data set.

3.4   Creating and Enhancing a List Report

Objectives

- Generate list reports using the PRINT procedure.
- Display selected variables in a list report using the VAR statement.
- Assign labels to variables using the LABEL statement.
- Define and modify titles and footnotes using the TITLE and FOOTNOTE statements.
- Apply SAS system options using the OPTIONS statement.

49

Business Scenario

International Airlines wants to create a custom report that lists all of the flight crew employees.

```
          Flight Crew Employee Listing

                              Job        Annual
     First Name  Last Name    Code       Salary

     DESIREE     GOLDENBERG    PILOT1    50221.62
     ARLENE M.   WILLIAMS      FLTAT1    23666.12
     ROBERT A.   PERRY         FLTAT1    21957.71
     CHRISTINA   MCGWIER-WATTS  PILOT3   96387.39
     HARVEY F.   SCOTT         FLTAT2    32278.40

                International Airlines
                Annual Employee Review
```

50

The final list report

- displays only selected variables
- uses labels instead of variable names as report column headers
- uses appropriate titles and footnotes
- eliminates the date and page number from the report.

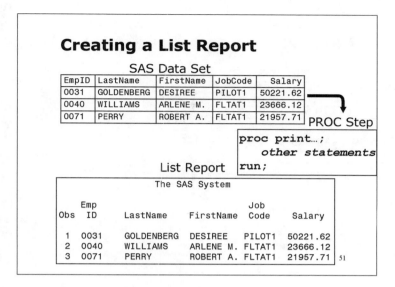

You can use PROC PRINT to create a quick listing of a SAS data set.

Creating a Default List Report

General form of the PRINT procedure:

PROC PRINT DATA=*SAS-data-set;*
RUN;

Example:

```
proc print data=work.empdata;
run;
```

52

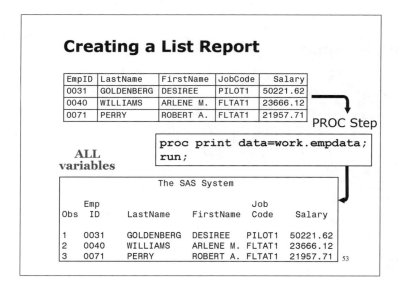

By default, PROC PRINT displays all the variables in the order they exist in the data set.

Printing Selected Variables

The VAR statement enables you to

- select variables to include in the list report
- select the order of the variables in the report.

General form of the VAR statement:

> **VAR** *variables(s);*

54

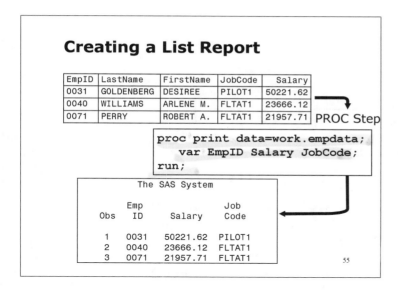

Creating a List Report

EmpID	LastName	FirstName	JobCode	Salary
0031	GOLDENBERG	DESIREE	PILOT1	50221.62
0040	WILLIAMS	ARLENE M.	FLTAT1	23666.12
0071	PERRY	ROBERT A.	FLTAT1	21957.71

PROC Step

```
proc print data=work.empdata;
   var EmpID Salary JobCode;
run;
```

```
                  The SAS System

           Emp                  Job
    Obs     ID      Salary      Code

     1     0031    50221.62    PILOT1
     2     0040    23666.12    FLTAT1
     3     0071    21957.71    FLTAT1
```

55

The VAR statement selects which variables are displayed and in what order left to right.

Assigning Report Column Labels

General form of the LABEL statement:

LABEL *variable*='*label*'
        variable='*label*';

'*label*'   specifies a label of up to 40 characters.

Labels are used

- automatically in many procedures
- by the PRINT procedure when the LABEL option is present in the PROC PRINT statement.

56

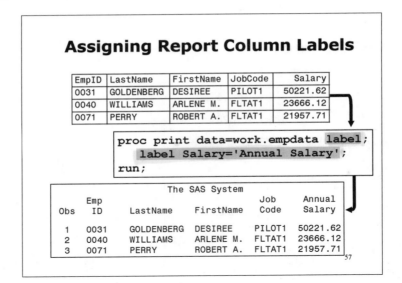

Assigning Report Column Labels

EmpID	LastName	FirstName	JobCode	Salary
0031	GOLDENBERG	DESIREE	PILOT1	50221.62
0040	WILLIAMS	ARLENE M.	FLTAT1	23666.12
0071	PERRY	ROBERT A.	FLTAT1	21957.71

```
proc print data=work.empdata label;
    label Salary='Annual Salary';
run;
```

```
                      The SAS System
        Emp                             Job    Annual
Obs     ID     LastName    FirstName     Code    Salary

  1    0031    GOLDENBERG  DESIREE      PILOT1  50221.62
  2    0040    WILLIAMS    ARLENE M.    FLTAT1  23666.12
  3    0071    PERRY       ROBERT A.    FLTAT1  21957.71
```

57

The LABEL **statement** specifies the column heading to use for SALARY. The LABEL **option** on the PROC PRINT statement tells the procedure to use any specified labels.

Assigning Report Column Labels

Labels associated with variables

- in a PROC step remain in effect only for that step
- in a DATA step are permanently assigned to that variable.

58

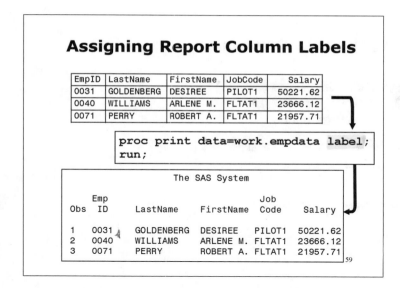

The LABEL option on the PROC PRINT statement has no affect because no label is defined for any of the variables displayed.

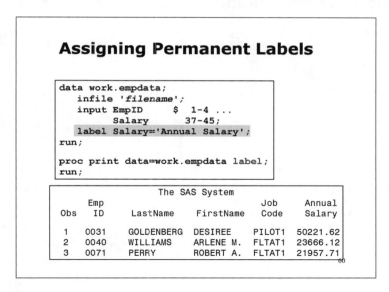

When the LABEL statement is part of the DATA step, the label becomes a permanent attribute of the variable. The variable label is then available for use by any procedure. You can tell PROC PRINT to use any existing variable labels as column headers by specifying the LABEL option on the PROC PRINT statement.

Suppressing the OBS Column

Use the NOOBS option to suppress the row numbers on the left side of the report.

General form of the NOOBS option:

PROC PRINT DATA=*SAS-data-set* **NOOBS**;
RUN;

Example:

```
proc print data=work.empdata noobs;
run;
```

61

Suppressing the OBS Column

EmpID	LastName	FirstName	JobCode	Salary
0031	GOLDENBERG	DESIREE	PILOT1	50221.62
0040	WILLIAMS	ARLENE M.	FLTAT1	23666.12
0071	PERRY	ROBERT A.	FLTAT1	21957.71

```
proc print data=work.empdata noobs;
run;
```

```
                        T e SAS System

     Emp                              Job
      ID      LastName    FirstName   Code     Salary

     0031     GOLDENBERG  DESIREE     PILOT1   50221.62
     0040     WILLIAMS    ARLENE M.   FLTAT1   23666.12
     0071     PERRY       ROBERT A.   FLTAT1   21957.71
```

62

Creating a List Report

File: c3s4d1.sas

- Use PROC PRINT to create a default list report.
- Specify variables to display on the list report and suppress the OBS column.
- Assign labels to replace the variable names as the column headers.
- Assign the labels permanently to the variables.
- Use the permanent labels in a list report.
- Replace a permanent label for a single list report.

1. Use PROC PRINT to create a default list report.

```
proc print data=work.empdata;
run;
```

Partial SAS Output

```
                            The SAS System                          27
                                      10:29 Tuesday, May 16, 2000

          Emp                                  Job
Obs        ID     LastName        FirstName    Code       Salary

 1        0031    GOLDENBERG      DESIREE       PILOT1     50221.62
 2        0040    WILLIAMS        ARLENE M.     FLTAT1     23666.12
 3        0071    PERRY           ROBERT A.     FLTAT1     21957.71
 4        0082    MCGWIER-WATTS    CHRISTINA    PILOT3     96387.39
 5        0091    SCOTT           HARVEY F.     FLTAT2     32278.40
 6        0106    THACKER         DAVID S.      FLTAT1     24161.14
 7        0275    GRAHAM          DEBORAH S.    FLTAT2     32024.93
 8        0286    DREWRY          SUSAN         PILOT1     55377.00
```

2. Use the VAR statement to select the variables and order them left to right on the page. Use the NOOBS option to suppress the row numbers.

```
proc print data=work.empdata noobs;
   var FirstName LastName JobCode Salary;
run;
```

Partial SAS Output

```
                            The SAS System                          31
                                      10:29 Tuesday, May 16, 2000

                                       Job
     FirstName      LastName           Code       Salary

     DESIREE        GOLDENBERG         PILOT1     50221.62
     ARLENE M.      WILLIAMS           FLTAT1     23666.12
     ROBERT A.      PERRY              FLTAT1     21957.71
     CHRISTINA      MCGWIER-WATTS      PILOT3     96387.39
```

3. Use PROC PRINT with the LABEL option and LABEL statement to
   assign labels to the report column headers.   *split='*'*

```
proc print data=work.empdata noobs label;
   var FirstName LastName JobCode Salary;
   label FirstName='First Name'
         LastName='Last Name'
         JobCode='Job Code'
         Salary='Annual Salary';
run;
```

Partial SAS Output

```
                              The SAS System                          35
                                          10:29 Tuesday, May 16, 2000

                                           Job        Annual
            First Name      Last Name      Code       Salary

            DESIREE         GOLDENBERG     PILOT1      50221.62
            ARLENE M.       WILLIAMS       FLTAT1      23666.12
            ROBERT A.       PERRY          FLTAT1      21957.71
            CHRISTINA       MCGWIER-WATTS  PILOT3      96387.39
            HARVEY F.       SCOTT          FLTAT2      32278.40
            DAVID S.        THACKER        FLTAT1      24161.14
            DEBORAH S.      GRAHAM         FLTAT2      32024.93
            SUSAN           DREWRY         PILOT1      55377.00
```

4. Assign the labels permanently by using the DATA step that created the
   data set. Create a listing report of the data and use the LABEL option to
   use the permanent labels in the data set.

```
data work.empdata;
   infile 'employee.dat';
   input EmpID     $  1-4
         LastName  $  5-17
         FirstName $ 18-30
         JobCode   $ 31-36
         Salary      37-45;
   label FirstName='First Name'
         LastName='Last Name'
         JobCode='Job Code'
         Salary='Annual Salary';
run;

proc print data=work.empdata noobs label;
   var FirstName LastName JobCode Salary;
run;
```

Partial SAS Output

```
                         The SAS System                      39
                                   10:29 Tuesday, May 16, 2000

                                      Job      Annual
         First Name      Last Name    Code     Salary

         DESIREE         GOLDENBERG    PILOT1   50221.62
         ARLENE M.       WILLIAMS      FLTAT1   23666.12
         ROBERT A.       PERRY         FLTAT1   21957.71
         CHRISTINA       MCGWIER-WATTS PILOT3   96387.39
         HARVEY F.       SCOTT         FLTAT2   32278.40
         DAVID S.        THACKER       FLTAT1   24161.14
         DEBORAH S.      GRAHAM        FLTAT2   32024.93
         SUSAN           DREWRY        PILOT1   55377.00
```

5. Use PROC PRINT to create a list report that uses the permanent labels and replaces two of the labels temporarily.

```
proc print data=work.empdata noobs label;
   var FirstName LastName JobCode Salary;
   label FirstName='Employee First Name'
         LastName='Employee Last Name';
run;
```

Partial SAS Output

```
                         The SAS System                      43
                                   10:29 Tuesday, May 16, 2000

         Employee        Employee      Job      Annual
         First Name      Last Name     Code     Salary

         DESIREE         GOLDENBERG    PILOT1   50221.62
         ARLENE M.       WILLIAMS      FLTAT1   23666.12
         ROBERT A.       PERRY         FLTAT1   21957.71
         CHRISTINA       MCGWIER-WATTS PILOT3   96387.39
         HARVEY F.       SCOTT         FLTAT2   32278.40
         DAVID S.        THACKER       FLTAT1   24161.14
         DEBORAH S.      GRAHAM        FLTAT2   32024.93
         SUSAN           DREWRY        PILOT1   55377.00
```

Defining Titles

You can enhance reports by adding titles.

General form of the TITLE statement:

TITLE*n* *'text'*;

Example:

```
title1 'Flight Crew Employee Listing';
```

64

Defining Titles

Features of titles are
- titles appear at the top of the page
- the default title is The SAS System
- the value of *n* can be from 1 to 10
- an unnumbered TITLE is equivalent to TITLE1
- titles remain in effect until they are changed, cancelled, or you end your SAS session
- the null TITLE statement `title;` cancels all titles.

65

You can use the TITLES window to define titles.

Be certain to match quotes.

Defining Footnotes

General form of the FOOTNOTE statement:

FOOTNOTE*n* *'text'*;

Example:

```
footnote2 'Employee Review';
```

66

TITLE and FOOTNOTE are global statements. They do not have to be part of a step. They can be submitted outside of a DATA or PROC step. Titles and footnotes are assigned as soon as the TITLE or FOOTNOTE statement is encountered by SAS.

Defining Footnotes

Features of footnotes are

- footnotes appear at the bottom of the page
- no footnote is printed unless one is specified
- the value of *n* can be from 1 to 10
- an unnumbered FOOTNOTE is equivalent to FOOTNOTE1
- footnotes remain in effect until they are changed, cancelled, or you end your SAS session
- the null FOOTNOTE statement **footnote;** cancels all footnotes.

67

You can use the FOOTNOTES window to define footnotes.

Be certain to match quotes.

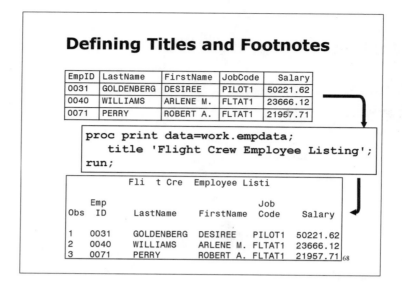

Defining Titles and Footnotes

EmpID	LastName	FirstName	JobCode	Salary
0031	GOLDENBERG	DESIREE	PILOT1	50221.62
0040	WILLIAMS	ARLENE M.	FLTAT1	23666.12
0071	PERRY	ROBERT A.	FLTAT1	21957.71

```
proc print data=work.empdata;
   title 'Flight Crew Employee Listing';
run;
```

```
                Fli   t Cre   Employee Listi

         Emp                              Job
 Obs     ID        LastName    FirstName  Code    Salary

  1     0031      GOLDENBERG   DESIREE    PILOT1  50221.62
  2     0040      WILLIAMS     ARLENE M.  FLTAT1  23666.12
  3     0071      PERRY        ROBERT A.  FLTAT1  21957.71
```

68

Changing Titles and Footnotes

TITLE*n* or FOOTNOTE*n*

- replaces a previous title or footnote with the same number

- cancels all titles or footnotes with higher numbers.

69

You can use the TITLES and FOOTNOTES windows to change or delete existing titles and footnotes without affecting higher numbered ones.

Defining Titles and Footnotes

PROC PRINT Code	Resultant Title(s)

`proc print data=work.march;`
`    title1 'The First Line';`
`    title2 'The Second Line';`
`run;`	

`proc print data=work.march;`
`    title2 'The Next Line';`
`run;`	

`proc print data=work.march;`
`    title 'The Top Line';`
`run;`	

`proc print data=work.march;`
`    title3 'The Third Line';`
`run;`	

`proc print data=work.march;`
`    title;`
`run;`	

If each of these programs were submitted in order in a single SAS session, what would be the resultant titles?

Defining Titles and Footnotes

PROC PRINT Code	Resultant Title(s)

`proc print data=work.march;`
`    title1 'The First Line';`
`    title2 'The Second Line';`
`run;`
	The First Line
	The Second Line

`proc print data=work.march;`
`    title2 'The Next Line';`
`run;`
	The First Line
	The Next Line

`proc print data=work.march;`
`    title 'The Top Line';`
`run;`
	The Top Line

`proc print data=work.march;`
`    title3 'The Third Line';`
`run;`
	The Top Line
	
	The Third Line

`proc print data=work.march;`
`    title;`
`run;`	

75

Altering Titles

EmpID	LastName	FirstName	JobCode	Salary
0031	GOLDENBERG	DESIREE	PILOT1	50221.62
0040	WILLIAMS	ARLENE M.	FLTAT1	23666.12
0071	PERRY	ROBERT A.	FLTAT1	21957.71

```
proc print data=work.empdata;
   title2 'New Salary Figures';
run;
```

```
                 Flight Crew Employee Listing
                      New Salary Figures

        Emp                             Job
  Obs   ID        LastName    FirstName  Code     Salary

  1     0031      GOLDENBERG  DESIREE    PILOT1   50221.62
  2     0040      WILLIAMS    ARLENE M.  FLTAT1   23666.12
  3     0071      PERRY       ROBERT A.  FLTAT1   21957.71
```

76

The first title line of Flight Crew Employee Listing was already in effect for this SAS session. Submitting a TITLE2 statement added another title line to the existing title.

Using SAS System Options

You can use SAS system options to change the appearance of a report.

General form of the OPTIONS statement:

> **OPTIONS** *option ...;*

The OPTIONS statement is **not** usually included in a PROC or DATA step.

77

Using SAS System Options

Selected SAS system options are

DATE   specifies to print the date and time the SAS session began at the top of each page of the SAS output.

NODATE   specifies not to print the date and time the SAS session began.

continued...

78

Using SAS System Options

Selected SAS system options are

NUMBER   specifies that page numbers be printed on the first title line of each page of SAS output.

NONUMBER   specifies that page numbers not be printed.

79

Additional SAS system options:

PAGENO=*n*   specifies a beginning page number for the next page of output produced by SAS. *n* specifies the page number.

LINESIZE=*width*   specifies the line size for the SAS log and the SAS procedure output. The alias for this option is LS=. *width* specifies the line width. The programs shown in this course were run with a linesize of 72.

PAGESIZE=*n*   specifies the number of lines that can be printed per page of SAS output. The alias for this option is PS=. *n* specifies the number of lines.

CENTER   specifies that SAS procedure output is centered instead of left justified, which is the default.

NOCENTER   specifies that SAS procedure output is left justified.

Defining Titles, Footnotes, and SAS System Options

File: c3s4d2.sas

- Use the OPTIONS statement to remove the date and time, as well as the page number, from the list report.
- Define appropriate titles and footnotes for the list report using the TITLE and FOOTNOTE statements.
- Override existing titles and footnotes in a second list report.

1. Use the OPTIONS statement to suppress the date and page number. Use the PRINT procedure to create a list report with labels. Use TITLE and FOOTNOTE statements to create titles and footnotes.

```
options nodate nonumber;

proc print data=work.empdata noobs label;
   var FirstName LastName JobCode Salary;
   label FirstName='First Name'
         LastName='Last Name'
         JobCode='Job Code'
         Salary='Annual Salary';
   title 'Flight Crew Employee Listing';
   footnote 'International Airlines';
   footnote2 'Annual Employee Review';
run;
```

Partial SAS Output

```
                       Flight Crew Employee Listing

                                        Job        Annual
         First Name        Last Name    Code       Salary

         DESIREE           GOLDENBERG     PILOT1      50221.62
         ARLENE M.         WILLIAMS       FLTAT1      23666.12
         ROBERT A.         PERRY          FLTAT1      21957.71
         CHRISTINA         MCGWIER-WATTS  PILOT3      96387.39
         HARVEY F.         SCOTT          FLTAT2      32278.40
         DAVID S.          THACKER        FLTAT1      24161.14
         DEBORAH S.        GRAHAM         FLTAT2      32024.93
         SUSAN             DREWRY         PILOT1      55377.00
         THOMAS L.         HORTON         FLTAT1      23705.12
         EDWARD            DOWN           PILOT1      56584.87
         BRENDA B.         CHERVENY       FLTAT2      38563.45
         THOMAS B.         BELL           PILOT1      59803.16
         MARTHA S.         GLENN          PILOT3     120202.38
         CARLA             BELL           PILOT1      37397.93
         MARCO             SAYRE          PILOT1      59268.61
         MARTIN L.         DIXON          PILOT3     110811.16
         BARBARA ANN       BETHEA         FLTAT2      39844.72
         SHELLEY S.        DUNNING        PILOT1      53713.81
         WILLIAM R.        GOOLSBY        FLTAT1      24759.34
         LAURA             DUNLAP         FLTAT2      34873.28
         MICHAEL           KRYNICKI       PILOT1      58480.79
         ROBERT            SANDY          PILOT2      64915.31
         SUE A.            MCGRATH        PILOT3     118578.17
         JEFFREY J.        WIERSMA        PILOT1      54140.94
         MARY P.           EAKES          FLTAT2      40264.00
         DOROTHY E         CHU            FLTAT2      40177.86
         CARL F.           GAMBINI        FLTAT3      42821.35
         DARWIN            BOND           FLTAT3      43467.37
         GREGORY O.        FERNANDEZ      FLTAT2      26065.74
         STEPHANIE         WILSON         FLTAT3      43357.39
         SANDRA H.         WONG           FLTAT2      34522.33
         COLLEEN T.        WEISS          PILOT1      41715.27
         SUSAN             WICKLIN        PILOT1      63810.15
         ROBERT L.         GOLDTHWAITE    FLTAT3      40564.86
         CINDY             LATOUR         FLTAT2      32166.86
         MARK J.           LEONARD        FLTAT3      42705.23
         GOLDIE A.         WILSON         FLTAT3      43067.31
         JOHN MCDONALD     BONNEY         FLTAT3      41393.37
         MARTHA            EDDS           FLTAT3      40289.63
         DOUGLAS B.        WILLIAMS       FLTAT2      39418.71
         MICHAEL J.        MERTENS        PILOT1      52614.06
         JANINE M.         GOULD          FLTAT2      32429.60
         DIANE L.          SECOSKY        FLTAT3      40500.55
         PATRICIA A        LABARR         FLTAT1      24919.23
         JOANNE            TELENKO        FLTAT1      22598.17
         CAROL G.          MORGAN         FLTAT1      18452.53

                       International Airlines
                       Annual Employee Review
```

2. Create another list report and use TITLE and FOOTNOTE statements to override existing titles and footnotes.

```
proc print data=work.empdata noobs;
   title2 'New Salary Figures';
   footnote;
run;
```

Partial SAS Output

```
                        Flight Crew Employee Listing
                           New Salary Figures

    Emp                                    Job
    ID      LastName        FirstName      Code       Salary

    0031    GOLDENBERG      DESIREE        PILOT1      50221.62
    0040    WILLIAMS        ARLENE M.      FLTAT1      23666.12
    0071    PERRY           ROBERT A.      FLTAT1      21957.71
    0082    MCGWIER-WATTS   CHRISTINA      PILOT3      96387.39
    0091    SCOTT           HARVEY F.      FLTAT2      32278.40
    0106    THACKER         DAVID S.       FLTAT1      24161.14
    0275    GRAHAM          DEBORAH S.     FLTAT2      32024.93
    0286    DREWRY          SUSAN          PILOT1      55377.00
    0309    HORTON          THOMAS L.      FLTAT1      23705.12
    0334    DOWN            EDWARD         PILOT1      56584.87
    0347    CHERVENY        BRENDA B.      FLTAT2      38563.45
    0355    BELL            THOMAS B.      PILOT1      59803.16
    0366    GLENN           MARTHA S.      PILOT3     120202.38
    0730    BELL            CARLA          PILOT1      37397.93
    0739    SAYRE           MARCO          PILOT1      59268.61
    0746    DIXON           MARTIN L.      PILOT3     110811.16
    0802    BETHEA          BARBARA ANN    FLTAT2      39844.72
    0803    DUNNING         SHELLEY S.     PILOT1      53713.81
    0898    GOOLSBY         WILLIAM R.     FLTAT1      24759.34
    0903    DUNLAP          LAURA          FLTAT2      34873.28
    0937    KRYNICKI        MICHAEL        PILOT1      58480.79
    0942    SANDY           ROBERT         PILOT2      64915.31
    0977    MCGRATH         SUE A.         PILOT3     118578.17
    0980    WIERSMA         JEFFREY J.     PILOT1      54140.94
    1003    EAKES           MARY P.        FLTAT2      40264.00
    1018    CHU             DOROTHY E      FLTAT2      40177.86
    1030    GAMBINI         CARL F.        FLTAT3      42821.35
    1170    BOND            DARWIN         FLTAT3      43467.37
    1191    FERNANDEZ       GREGORY O.     FLTAT2      26065.74
    1215    WILSON          STEPHANIE      FLTAT3      43357.39
    1245    WONG            SANDRA H.      FLTAT2      34522.33
    1253    WEISS           COLLEEN T.     PILOT1      41715.27
    1254    WICKLIN         SUSAN          PILOT1      63810.15
    1288    GOLDTHWAITE     ROBERT L.      FLTAT3      40564.86
    1293    LATOUR          CINDY          FLTAT2      32166.86
    1295    LEONARD         MARK J.        FLTAT3      42705.23
    1340    WILSON          GOLDIE A.      FLTAT3      43067.31
    1341    BONNEY          JOHN MCDONALD  FLTAT3      41393.37
    1345    EDDS            MARTHA         FLTAT3      40289.63
    1535    WILLIAMS        DOUGLAS B.     FLTAT2      39418.71
```

Exercises

For these exercises, write a DATA step that reads the raw data file containing information on flights from San Francisco to various destinations.

> Fill in the blank with the location of your raw data file. Use an INFILE statement in a DATA step to read the raw file.
>
> ```
> data ...;
>    infile '_____';
>    .
>    .
>    .
> ```

Here is the complete record layout for the SFOSCH raw data file:

Variable Name	Field Description	Columns	Data Type
FLIGHTID	Flight ID Number	1-7	Character
ROUTEID	Route ID Number	8-14	Character
ORIGIN	Flight Origin	15-17	Character
DESTINATION	Flight Destination	18-20	Character
MODEL	Aircraft Model	21-40	Character
DEPARTDATE	Departure Date	41-49	Character 01JAN2000
DEPARTDAY	Departure Day of Week	51	Numeric 1=Sunday
FCLASSPASS	First Class Passengers	53-55	Numeric
BCLASSPASS	Business Class Passengers	57-59	Numeric
ECLASSPASS	Economy Class Passengers	61-63	Numeric
TOTPASSCAP	Aircraft Capacity – Total Passengers	65-67	Numeric
CARGOWT	Weight of Cargo in Pounds	69-73	Numeric
CARGOREV	Revenue from Cargo in Dollars	75-79	Numeric

5. **Reading Raw Data**

Create a SAS data set named WORK.SANFRAN by writing a DATA step that uses column input to read **all** the columns. You can save time by including and modifying the program you stored in Exercise 1 in Section 3.2 (ch3ex1.sas for Windows and UNIX, *userid*.PROG1.SASCODE(CH3EX1) for OS/390). You can also find the completed program in BKUP31 (bkup31.sas for Windows and UNIX, *userid*.PROG1.SASCODE(BKUP31) for OS/390.

6. **Creating List Reports**

    a. Use PROC PRINT to produce a list report that displays only the variables FLIGHTID, DESTINATION, DEPARTDAY, CARGOWT, and CARGOREV.

    Place a title `Cargo Information` and a footnote `Flights from San Francisco` on the report.

Partial SAS Output

```
                          Cargo Information                           29
                                   16:24 Wednesday, July 12, 2000

            Flight                Depart   Cargo    Cargo
   Obs        ID     Destination    Day      Wt      Rev

     1      IA11200      HND          4     61300    79077
     2      IA01804      SEA          4     10300    13287
     3      IA02901      HNL          5     47400    61146
     4      IA03100      ANC          5     24800    31992
     5      IA02901      HNL          6     48200    62178
     6      IA03100      ANC          6     25600    33024
     7      IA00800      RDU          7     25600    33024
     8      IA01805      SEA          7     10100    13029
     9      IA01804      SEA          2     12500    16125
    10      IA03101      ANC          2     28000    36120
    11      IA01802      SEA          3      8500    10965
    12      IA11200      HND          4     56700    73143
    13      IA03101      ANC          4     26400    34056
    14      IA01804      SEA          4     10700    13803
    15      IA11201      HND          5     61100    78819
    16      IA03100      ANC          5     27200    35088
    17      IA01805      SEA          6      9300    11997
    18      IA01803      SEA          7      7300     9417
    19      IA11201      HND          1     60100    77529
    20      IA11200      HND          2     60500    78045
    21      IA03100      ANC          2     25800    33282
    22      IA01802      SEA          2     11500    14835
    23      IA01804      SEA          2     11700    15093
    24      IA01805      SEA          2     10300    13287
    25      IA11201      HND          3     62700    80883
    26      IA00801      RDU          3     30200    38958
    27      IA01803      SEA          4     13700    17673
    28      IA00801      RDU          5     29000    37410
    29      IA01800      SEA          5      9300    11997
    30      IA01803      SEA          6     13900    17931
    31      IA01803      SEA          7      8500    10965
    32      IA00801      RDU          1     33600    43344
    33      IA03100      ANC          2     34600    44643
    34      IA00801      RDU          2     33000    42570
    35      IA01803      SEA          2     12700    16383
    36      IA01801      SEA          3     13300    17157
    37      IA11200      HND          4     59700    77013
    38      IA01800      SEA          6     12300    15867
    39      IA02901      HNL          6     43200    55728
    40      IA03101      ANC          6     27000    34830
    41      IA01801      SEA          6     11700    15093
    42      IA01802      SEA          7      8300    10707
    43      IA01805      SEA          7     12100    15609
    44      IA00800      RDU          1     24600    31734
    45      IA01800      SEA          1      9300    11997
    46      IA01801      SEA          1     10900    14061

                      Flights from San Francisco
```

b.   Recall the program.

Modify it so that the list report displays labels instead of variable names. Use the field descriptions in the table on the earlier page for the labels.

Specify SAS system options to suppress the display of page numbers and the current date.

Only specify labels for the variables you are printing.

Partial SAS Output

```
                              Cargo Information

          Flight            Departure   Weight of    Revenue from
           ID      Flight    Day of     Cargo in      Cargo in
   Obs    Number  Destination  Week      Pounds        Dollars

    1    IA11200     HND        4        61300         79077
    2    IA01804     SEA        4        10300         13287
    3    IA02901     HNL        5        47400         61146
    4    IA03100     ANC        5        24800         31992
    5    IA02901     HNL        6        48200         62178
    6    IA03100     ANC        6        25600         33024
    7    IA00800     RDU        7        25600         33024
    8    IA01805     SEA        7        10100         13029
    9    IA01804     SEA        2        12500         16125
   10    IA03101     ANC        2        28000         36120
   11    IA01802     SEA        3         8500         10965
   12    IA11200     HND        4        56700         73143
   13    IA03101     ANC        4        26400         34056
   14    IA01804     SEA        4        10700         13803
   15    IA11201     HND        5        61100         78819
   16    IA03100     ANC        5        27200         35088
   17    IA01805     SEA        6         9300         11997
   18    IA01803     SEA        7         7300          9417
   19    IA11201     HND        1        60100         77529
   20    IA11200     HND        2        60500         78045
   21    IA03100     ANC        2        25800         33282
   22    IA01802     SEA        2        11500         14835
   23    IA01804     SEA        2        11700         15093
   24    IA01805     SEA        2        10300         13287
   25    IA11201     HND        3        62700         80883
   26    IA00801     RDU        3        30200         38958
   27    IA01803     SEA        4        13700         17673
   28    IA00801     RDU        5        29000         37410
   29    IA01800     SEA        5         9300         11997
   30    IA01803     SEA        6        13900         17931
   31    IA01803     SEA        7         8500         10965
   32    IA00801     RDU        1        33600         43344
   33    IA03100     ANC        2        34600         44643
   34    IA00801     RDU        2        33000         42570
   35    IA01803     SEA        2        12700         16383
   36    IA01801     SEA        3        13300         17157
   37    IA11200     HND        4        59700         77013
   38    IA01800     SEA        6        12300         15867
   39    IA02901     HNL        6        43200         55728
   40    IA03101     ANC        6        27000         34830
   41    IA01801     SEA        6        11700         15093
   42    IA01802     SEA        7         8300         10707
   43    IA01805     SEA        7        12100         15609
   44    IA00800     RDU        1        24600         31734
   45    IA01800     SEA        1         9300         11997
   46    IA01801     SEA        1        10900         14061

                        Flights from San Fransisco
```

c. Recall the program.

Add a second title `Weight and Revenue` to the report and cancel the footnote.

Partial SAS Output

```
                          Cargo Information
                         Weight and Revenue

        Flight                   Departure   Weight of   Revenue from
          ID          Flight     Day of      Cargo in      Cargo in
 Obs    Number     Destination    Week        Pounds       Dollars

   1    IA11200        HND          4          61300         79077
   2    IA01804        SEA          4          10300         13287
   3    IA02901        HNL          5          47400         61146
   4    IA03100        ANC          5          24800         31992
   5    IA02901        HNL          6          48200         62178
   6    IA03100        ANC          6          25600         33024
   7    IA00800        RDU          7          25600         33024
   8    IA01805        SEA          7          10100         13029
   9    IA01804        SEA          2          12500         16125
  10    IA03101        ANC          2          28000         36120
  11    IA01802        SEA          3           8500         10965
  12    IA11200        HND          4          56700         73143
  13    IA03101        ANC          4          26400         34056
  14    IA01804        SEA          4          10700         13803
  15    IA11201        HND          5          61100         78819
  16    IA03100        ANC          5          27200         35088
  17    IA01805        SEA          6           9300         11997
  18    IA01803        SEA          7           7300          9417
  19    IA11201        HND          1          60100         77529
  20    IA11200        HND          2          60500         78045
  21    IA03100        ANC          2          25800         33282
  22    IA01802        SEA          2          11500         14835
  23    IA01804        SEA          2          11700         15093
  24    IA01805        SEA          2          10300         13287
  25    IA11201        HND          3          62700         80883
  26    IA00801        RDU          3          30200         38958
  27    IA01803        SEA          4          13700         17673
  28    IA00801        RDU          5          29000         37410
  29    IA01800        SEA          5           9300         11997
  30    IA01803        SEA          6          13900         17931
  31    IA01803        SEA          7           8500         10965
  32    IA00801        RDU          1          33600         43344
  33    IA03100        ANC          2          34600         44643
  34    IA00801        RDU          2          33000         42570
  35    IA01803        SEA          2          12700         16383
  36    IA01801        SEA          3          13300         17157
  37    IA11200        HND          4          59700         77013
  38    IA01800        SEA          6          12300         15867
  39    IA02901        HNL          6          43200         55728
  40    IA03101        ANC          6          27000         34830
  41    IA01801        SEA          6          11700         15093
  42    IA01802        SEA          7           8300         10707
  43    IA01805        SEA          7          12100         15609
  44    IA00800        RDU          1          24600         31734
  45    IA01800        SEA          1           9300         11997
  46    IA01801        SEA          1          10900         14061
  47    IA01802        SEA          1           9300         11997
```

3.5 Recoding Data Values

Objectives

- Display formatted values using SAS formats in a list report.
- Permanently associate a format with a variable.
- Create user-defined formats using the FORMAT procedure.
- Apply user-defined formats to variables in a list report.

83

Business Scenario

Enhance the readability of reports
by formatting the data values.

```
              Flight Crew Employee Listing

                                   Job          Annual
First Name         Last Name       Code         Salary

DESIREE            GOLDENBERG       PILOT1     50,221.62
ARLENE M.          WILLIAMS         FLTAT1     23,666.12
ROBERT A.          PERRY            FLTAT1     21,957.71
CHRISTINA          MCGWIER-WATTS    PILOT3     96,387.39
HARVEY F.          SCOTT            FLTAT2     32,278.40
DAVID S.           THACKER          FLTAT1     24,161.14
```

84

Business Scenario

Create custom formats to categorize data values.

```
              Flight Crew Employee Listing

First Name Last Name       Job Category      Salary Range

DESIREE     GOLDENBERG     Pilot                 > 50,000
ARLENE M.   WILLIAMS       Flight Attendant      < 25,000
ROBERT A.   PERRY          Flight Attendant      < 25,000
CHRISTINA   MCGWIER-WATTS  Pilot                 > 50,000
HARVEY F.   SCOTT          Flight Attendant  25,000 - 50,000
DAVID S.    THACKER        Flight Attendant      < 25,000
DEBORAH S.  GRAHAM         Flight Attendant  25,000 - 50,000
SUSAN       DREWRY         Pilot                 > 50,000
```

85

Formatting Data Values

You can enhance reports by using SAS formats to format data values.

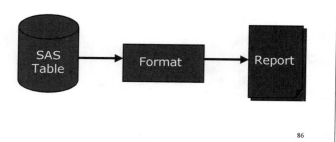

86

Formatting Data Values

To apply a format to a specific SAS variable, use the FORMAT statement.

General form of the FORMAT statement:

FORMAT *variable(s) format;*

Example:

```
proc print data=work.empdata;
   format Salary comma14.2;
run;
```

87

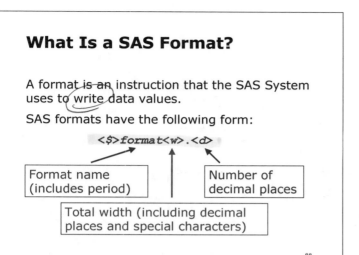

What Is a SAS Format?

A format is an instruction that the SAS System uses to write data values.

SAS formats have the following form:

<$>format<w>.<d>

Format name (includes period)

Number of decimal places

Total width (including decimal places and special characters)

88

$ indicates a character format; its absence indicates a numeric format.

format   is the name of the format.

w   is the maximum number of columns used to display the data values.

d   is an optional number of decimal places for numeric values; the default number of decimal places is 0.

.   is a required part of a name for a format. All formats **must** contain a period as part of the name.

SAS Formats

Selected SAS formats:

w.d	standard numeric format
$w.	standard character format
COMMA*w.d*	commas in a number: 12,234.21
DOLLAR*w.d*	dollar signs and commas in a number: $12,234.41

89

Refer to the online SAS System Help for a complete list of available formats.

SAS Formats

Stored Value	Format	Displayed Value
27134.2864	COMMA12.2	27,134.29
27134.2864	12.2	27134.29
27134.2864	DOLLAR12.2	$27,134.29
27134.2864	DOLLAR9.2	$27134.29
27134.2864	DOLLAR8.2	27134.29

90

SAS Formats

Selected SAS date formats:

MMDDYY*w.*   101692 (MMDDYY6.)

10/16/92 (MMDDYY8.)

10/16/1992 (MMDDYY10.)

DATE*w.*   16OCT92 (DATE7.)

16OCT1992 (DATE9.)

91

SAS Formats

Stored Value	Format	Displayed Value
0	MMDDYY8.	01/01/60
0	MMDDYY10.	01/01/1960
0	DATE9.	01JAN1960
0	DDMMYY10.	01/01/1960
0	WORDDATE.	January 1, 1960
0	WEEKDATE.	Friday, January 1, 1960

92

Formatting Data Values

Formats associated with variables

- in a PROC step, remain in effect only for that step

- in a DATA step, are permanently assigned to that variable.

Temporary

93

Formatting Data Values

EmpID	LastName	FirstName	JobCode	Salary
0031	GOLDENBERG	DESIREE	PILOT1	50221.62
0040	WILLIAMS	ARLENE M.	FLTAT1	23666.12
0071	PERRY	ROBERT A.	FLTAT1	21957.71

```
proc print data=work.empdata;
   format Salary comma10.2;
run;
```

```
            Flight Crew Employee Listing

      Emp                           Job
Obs   ID      LastName    FirstName  Code     Salary

  1   0031    GOLDENBERG  DESIREE    PILOT1   50,221.62
  2   0040    WILLIAMS    ARLENE M.  FLTAT1   23,666.12
  3   0071    PERRY       ROBERT A.  FLTAT1   21,957.71
```

94

You can specify a format for any variable in your report. The format alters the appearance of the data in the report without altering the data stored in the data set. When you specify the FORMAT statement in a PROC step, the format is only in effect for that PROC step.

Assigning Permanent Formats

```
data work.empdata;
   infile 'filename';
   input EmpID     $  1-4 ...
         Salary       37-45;
   format Salary comma10.2;
run;
proc print data=work.empdata;
run;
```

```
              Flight Crew Employee Listing

      Emp                           Job
Obs   ID      LastName    FirstName  Code      Salary

 1   0031    GOLDENBERG  DESIREE    PILOT1   50,221.62
 2   0040    WILLIAMS    ARLENE M.  FLTAT1   23,666.12
 3   0071    PERRY       ROBERT A.  FLTAT1   21,957.71    95
```

When the FORMAT statement is part of the DATA step, the format becomes a permanent attribute of the variable. When any procedure displays the SALARY data, it automatically uses the COMMA10.2 format.

Using SAS Formats

File: c3s5d1.sas

- Format the data in a column of a list report.
- Assign a format permanently to a variable.
- Use the permanent format in a list report.
- Replace a permanent format for a single list report.

1. Display the SALARY data with commas and two decimal places.

```
proc print data=work.empdata noobs label;
   var FirstName LastName JobCode Salary;
   format Salary comma10.2;
   title 'Flight Crew Employee Listing';
run;
```

Partial SAS Output

```
                  Flight Crew Employee Listing

                                    Job        Annual
      First Name      Last Name     Code       Salary

      DESIREE         GOLDENBERG     PILOT1     50,221.62
      ARLENE M.       WILLIAMS       FLTAT1     23,666.12
      ROBERT A.       PERRY          FLTAT1     21,957.71
      CHRISTINA       MCGWIER-WATTS  PILOT3     96,387.39
      HARVEY F.       SCOTT          FLTAT2     32,278.40
      DAVID S.        THACKER        FLTAT1     24,161.14
      DEBORAH S.      GRAHAM         FLTAT2     32,024.93
```

2. Use a DATA step to permanently associate the COMMA10.2 format with the SALARY variable. Create a list report.

```
data work.empdata;
   infile 'employee.dat';
   input EmpID     $  1-4
         LastName  $  5-17
         FirstName $ 18-30
         JobCode   $ 31-36
         Salary      37-45;
   label FirstName='First Name'
         LastName='Last Name'
         JobCode='Job Code'
         Salary='Annual Salary';
   format Salary comma10.2;
run;

proc print data=work.empdata noobs label;
   var FirstName LastName JobCode Salary;
run;
```

Partial SAS Output

```
                     Flight Crew Employee Listing

                                          Job        Annual
           First Name        Last Name    Code       Salary

           DESIREE           GOLDENBERG    PILOT1     50,221.62
           ARLENE M.         WILLIAMS      FLTAT1     23,666.12
           ROBERT A.         PERRY         FLTAT1     21,957.71
           CHRISTINA         MCGWIER-WATTS PILOT3     96,387.39
           HARVEY F.         SCOTT         FLTAT2     32,278.40
           DAVID S.          THACKER       FLTAT1     24,161.14
           DEBORAH S.        GRAHAM        FLTAT2     32,024.93
```

3. Use a FORMAT statement in PROC PRINT to temporarily override the permanent format. Display the SALARY values with a dollar sign, commas, and no decimal places.

```
proc print data=work.empdata noobs label;
   var FirstName LastName JobCode Salary;
   format Salary dollar7.;
run;
```

Partial SAS Output

```
                     Flight Crew Employee Listing

                                          Job        Annual
           First Name        Last Name    Code       Salary

           DESIREE           GOLDENBERG    PILOT1     $50,222
           ARLENE M.         WILLIAMS      FLTAT1     $23,666
           ROBERT A.         PERRY         FLTAT1     $21,958
           CHRISTINA         MCGWIER-WATTS PILOT3     $96,387
           HARVEY F.         SCOTT         FLTAT2     $32,278
           DAVID S.          THACKER       FLTAT1     $24,161
           DEBORAH S.        GRAHAM        FLTAT2     $32,025
```

Creating User-defined Formats

The SAS System provides standard formats as well as the FORMAT procedure to define custom formats.

To create formats,

1. use the FORMAT procedure to create the format

2. apply the format to specific variable(s) by using a FORMAT statement.

97

Creating User-defined Formats

General form of a PROC FORMAT step:

```
PROC FORMAT;
     VALUE format-name range1='label'
                       range2='label'
                       ...;
RUN;
```

98

Creating User-defined Formats

Format-name

- names the format you are creating

- for character values, must have a dollar sign ($) as the first character and no more than seven additional characters, numbers, and underscores

- for numeric values, can be up to eight characters, numbers, and underscores

- cannot end in a number

continued...

99

Creating User-defined Formats

Format-name

- cannot be the name of a SAS System format
- does not end with a period in the VALUE statement.

Labels must be

- 200 characters or fewer in length
- enclosed in quotes.

100

Creating User-defined Formats

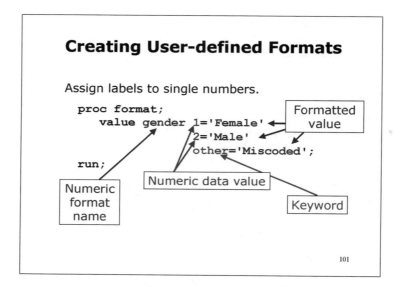

Assign labels to single numbers.

```
proc format;
    value gender 1='Female'
                 2='Male'
                 other='Miscoded';
run;
```

Formatted value

Numeric data value

Keyword

Numeric format name

101

Once created, the GENDER. format can be used with any numeric variable. If the variable has a value of 1, then `Female` is displayed. If the variable has a value of 2, then `Male` is displayed. If the variable has any other value, then `Miscoded` is displayed.

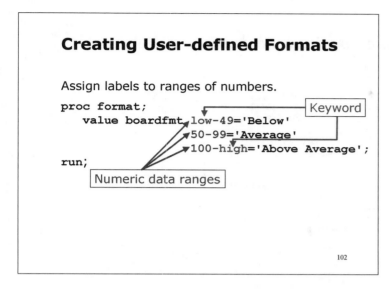

For numeric formats, OTHER includes missing values. If OTHER is not used, a default format is applied to values not specified in the format.

For numeric formats, LOW does not include missing values.

For character formats, LOW includes missing values.

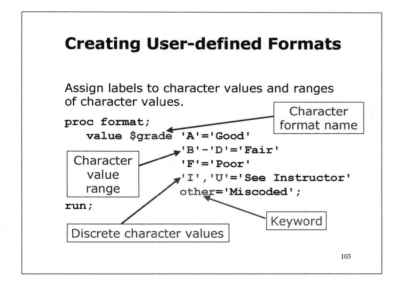

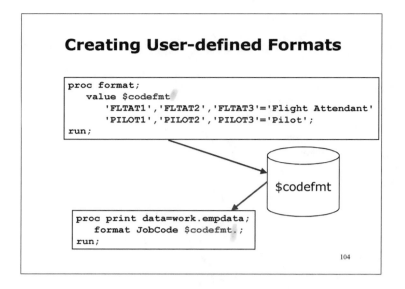

Creating User-defined Formats

```
proc format;
    value $codefmt
        'FLTAT1','FLTAT2','FLTAT3'='Flight Attendant'
        'PILOT1','PILOT2','PILOT3'='Pilot';
run;
```

$codefmt

```
proc print data=work.empdata;
    format JobCode $codefmt.;
run;
```

104

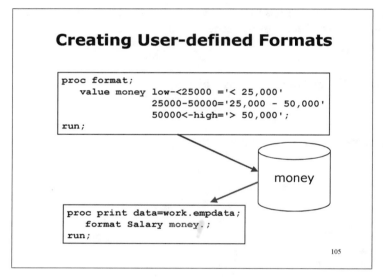

Creating User-defined Formats

```
proc format;
    value money low-<25000 ='< 25,000'
                25000-50000='25,000 - 50,000'
                50000<-high='> 50,000';
run;
```

money

```
proc print data=work.empdata;
    format Salary money.;
run;
```

105

Creating and Applying User-Defined Formats to Recode SAS Data Values

File: c3s5d2.sas

- Use the FORMAT procedure to define a format that displays all of the pilot job codes with the value `Pilot` and all of the flight attendant job codes with the value `Flight Attendant`.
- Use the FORMAT procedure to define a format that displays numeric values up to 25,000 as `< 25,000`, the values from 25,000 to 50,000 as `25,000 - 50,000`, and the values higher than 50,000 as `> 50,000`.
- Apply the user-defined formats to the JOBCODE and SALARY variables in a list report.

1. Use the FORMAT procedure to categorize the values of JOBCODE.

```
proc format;
   value $codefmt
         'FLTAT1','FLTAT2','FLTAT3'='Flight Attendant'
         'PILOT1','PILOT2','PILOT3'='Pilot';
run;
```

Submit the program and browse the log. There should no errors or messages in the log.

2. Use the FORMAT procedure to categorize the values of salary.

```
proc format;
   value money low-<25000 ='< 25,000'
               25000-50000='25,000 - 50,000'
               50000<-high='> 50,000';
run;
```

Submit the program and browse the log. There should no errors or messages in the log.

3. Apply the user-defined formats to JOBCODE and SALARY in a list report.

```
proc print data=work.empdata noobs label;
   var FirstName LastName JobCode Salary;
   format JobCode $codefmt. Salary money.;
   label JobCode='Job Category'
         Salary='Salary Range';
   title 'Flight Crew Employee Listing';
run;
```

Partial SAS Output

```
                       Flight Crew Employee Listing

       First Name        Last Name        Job Category        Salary Range

       DESIREE           GOLDENBERG       Pilot               > 50,000
       ARLENE M.         WILLIAMS         Flight Attendant    < 25,000
       ROBERT A.         PERRY            Flight Attendant    < 25,000
       CHRISTINA         MCGWIER-WATTS    Pilot               > 50,000
       HARVEY F.         SCOTT            Flight Attendant    25,000 - 50,000
       DAVID S.          THACKER          Flight Attendant    < 25,000
       DEBORAH S.        GRAHAM           Flight Attendant    25,000 - 50,000
       SUSAN             DREWRY           Pilot               > 50,000
       THOMAS L.         HORTON           Flight Attendant    < 25,000
```

Exercises

7. Using SAS Formats and Creating User-defined Formats

For this exercise, use the WORK.SANFRAN data set. If necessary, recall and run the program you created in Exercise 5 in Section 3.4 or you can include the BKUP35 file (bkup35.sas on Windows and UNIX, *userid*.PROG1.SASCODE(BKUP35) on OS/390).

   a. Using the WORK.SANFRAN data set, create a numeric format named DAYWORD that enables you to display the values of DEPARTDAY as Sunday, Monday, and so on, where 1=Sunday, 2=Monday, ..., 7=Saturday.

   b. The values of DESTINATION are airport codes. Create a character format named $CITY that enables you to display the values of DESTINATION as city names.
   * ANC=Anchorage, AK
   * HND=Hatteras, NC
   * HNL=Honolulu, HI
   * RDU=Raleigh-Durham, NC
   * SEA=Seattle, WA.

   c. Produce a list report of the WORK.SANFRAN data set that displays the variables FLIGHTID, DESTINATION, DEPARTDAY, FCLASSPASS, BCLASSPASS, ECLASSPASS, and CARGOWT.

   Display the values of CARGOWT with commas, use the DAYWORD format you created to recode the DEPARTDAY values, and use the $CITY format you created to recode the values of DESTINATION.

   Add an appropriate title to the report.

Partial SAS Output

```
                     Flight Information

     Flight                            FClass BClass EClass  Cargo
Obs    ID    Destination     DepartDay  Pass   Pass   Pass    Wt

  1 IA11200 Hatteras, NC     Wednesday   19     31    171   61,300
  2 IA01804 Seattle, WA      Wednesday   10      .    123   10,300
  3 IA02901 Honolulu, HI     Thursday    13     24    138   47,400
  4 IA03100 Anchorage, AK    Thursday    13     22    250   24,800
  5 IA02901 Honolulu, HI     Friday      14     25    132   48,200
  6 IA03100 Anchorage, AK    Friday      16      .    243   25,600
  7 IA00800 Raleigh-Durham, NC Saturday  16      .    243   25,600
  8 IA01805 Seattle, WA      Saturday    11      .    123   10,100
  9 IA01804 Seattle, WA      Monday      11     12    111   12,500
 10 IA03101 Anchorage, AK    Monday      14     26    233   28,000
```

3.6 Creating a Frequency Report

Objectives

- Create a one-way frequency table using the FREQ procedure.
- Restrict the variables processed by the FREQ procedure using the TABLES statement.
- Use formats to create frequency reports on groups of data.
- Create a two-way frequency table using the FREQ procedure.

109

Business Scenario

International Airlines wants to calculate how frequently each value of JOBCODE occurs.

Job Code	Frequency	Percent	Cumulative Frequency	Cumulative Percent
FLTAT1	25	13.44	25	13.44
FLTAT2	44	23.66	69	37.10
FLTAT3	59	31.72	128	68.82
PILOT1	36	19.35	164	88.17
PILOT2	11	5.91	175	94.09
PILOT3	11	5.91	186	100.00

110

Business Scenario

International Airlines wants to use formats to categorize the flight crew by job code and salary.

<u>Stored values</u>   <u>Formatted values</u>

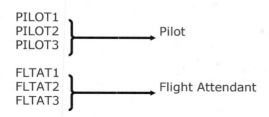

PILOT1
PILOT2   Pilot
PILOT3

FLTAT1
FLTAT2   Flight Attendant
FLTAT3

111

Business Scenario

International Airlines wants to use the categorized job code and salary values to calculate frequencies of job code and salary combinations.

```
JobCode(Job Code)      Salary(Annual Salary)

Frequency
Percent
Row Pct
Col Pct          < 25,000|25,000 -|> 50,000|  Total
                         | 50,000 |        |

Flight Attendant      25 |    103 |      0 |    128
                   13.44 |  55.38 |   0.00 |  68.82
                   19.53 |  80.47 |   0.00 |
                  100.00 |  91.15 |   0.00 |

Pilot                  0 |     10 |     48 |     58
                    0.00 |   5.38 |  25.81 |  31.18
                    0.00 |  17.24 |  82.76 |
                    0.00 |   8.85 | 100.00 |

Total                 25 |    113 |     48 |    186
                   13.44 |  60.75 |  25.81 | 100.00
```
112

Creating a Frequency Report

The FREQ procedure displays frequency counts of the data values in a SAS data set.

General form of a simple PROC FREQ step:

> **PROC FREQ** DATA=*SAS-data-set*;
> **RUN;**

Example:

```
proc freq data=work.empdata;
run;
```

113

Creating a Frequency Report

By default, PROC FREQ

- analyzes every variable in the SAS data set
- displays each distinct data value
- calculates the number of observations in which each data value appears (and the corresponding percentage)
- indicates for each variable how many observations have missing values.

114

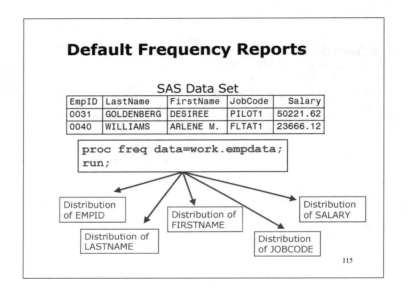

Default Frequency Reports

SAS Data Set

EmpID	LastName	FirstName	JobCode	Salary
0031	GOLDENBERG	DESIREE	PILOT1	50221.62
0040	WILLIAMS	ARLENE M.	FLTAT1	23666.12

```
proc freq data=work.empdata;
run;
```

Distribution of EMPID

Distribution of LASTNAME

Distribution of FIRSTNAME

Distribution of JOBCODE

Distribution of SALARY

115

By default, PROC FREQ creates a report on every variable in the data set. For example, the EMPID report displays every unique value of EMPID, counts how many observations have each value, and provides percentages and cumulative statistics.

You do not typically create frequency reports for variables with a large number of distinct values, like EMPID, or for analysis variables, like SALARY. You usually create frequency reports for categorical variables, like JOBCODE. You can group variables into categories by creating and applying formats.

Creating a One-Way Frequency Report

Use the TABLES statement to limit the variables included in the frequency counts. These are typically variables that have a limited number of distinct values.

General form of a PROC FREQ step:

```
PROC FREQ DATA=SAS-data-set;
    TABLES SAS-variables;
RUN;
```

116

A separate table is created for each variable listed on the TABLES statement.

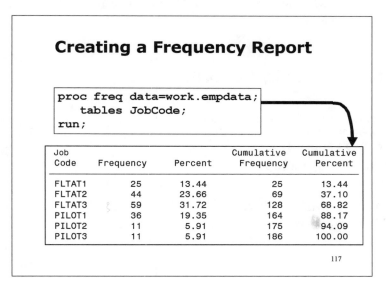

Creating a Frequency Report

```
proc freq data=work.empdata;
    tables JobCode;
run;
```

Job Code	Frequency	Percent	Cumulative Frequency	Cumulative Percent
FLTAT1	25	13.44	25	13.44
FLTAT2	44	23.66	69	37.10
FLTAT3	59	31.72	128	68.82
PILOT1	36	19.35	164	88.17
PILOT2	11	5.91	175	94.09
PILOT3	11	5.91	186	100.00

117

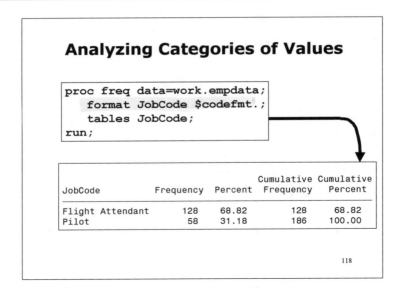

The $CODEFMT. format groups individual job codes into job categories. PROC FREQ automatically uses the formatted value of a variable for calculations if a format is present.

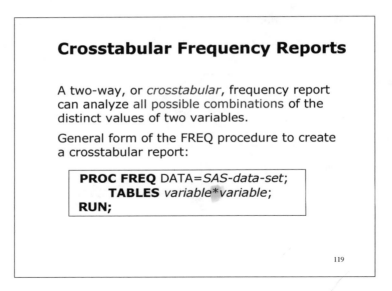

The asterisk operator indicates a crosstabulation.

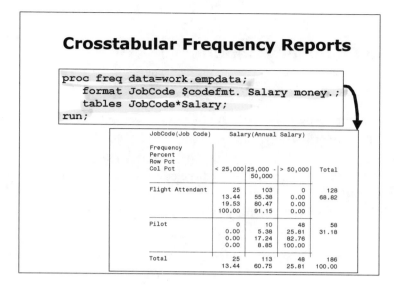

Crosstabular Frequency Reports

```
proc freq data=work.empdata;
   format JobCode $codefmt. Salary money.;
   tables JobCode*Salary;
run;
```

```
JobCode(Job Code)      Salary(Annual Salary)

  Frequency
  Percent
  Row Pct
  Col Pct     < 25,000|25,000 -|> 50,000|  Total
                      | 50,000 |        |

Flight Attendant   25 |   103 |      0 |    128
                13.44 | 55.38 |   0.00 |  68.82
                19.53 | 80.47 |   0.00 |
               100.00 | 91.15 |   0.00 |

Pilot               0 |    10 |     48 |     58
                 0.00 |  5.38 |  25.81 |  31.18
                 0.00 | 17.24 |  82.76 |
                 0.00 |  8.85 | 100.00 |

Total              25 |   113 |     48 |    186
                13.44 | 60.75 |  25.81 | 100.00
```

The values of the first SAS variable on the TABLES statement form the rows of the frequency table and the values of the second SAS variable form the columns of the frequency table.

Creating Frequency Reports

File: c3s6d1.sas

- Create a report that displays the distribution of the values of JOBCODE.
- Create a report that displays the distribution of the job categories.
- Create two reports, one that displays the distribution of the job categories and one that displays the distribution of the salary categories using a single TABLES statement.
- Create a crosstabulation report that displays the frequencies of each salary range for each job category.

1. Use PROC FREQ with a TABLES statement to generate a frequency report for the values of JOBCODE.

    ```
    proc freq data=work.empdata;
       tables JobCode;
       title 'Distribution of Job Code Values';
    run;
    ```

    SAS Output

Distribution of Job Code Values				
The FREQ Procedure				
Job Code				
Job Code	Frequency	Percent	Cumulative Frequency	Cumulative Percent
FLTAT1	25	13.44	25	13.44
FLTAT2	44	23.66	69	37.10
FLTAT3	59	31.72	128	68.82
PILOT1	36	19.35	164	88.17
PILOT2	11	5.91	175	94.09
PILOT3	11	5.91	186	100.00

2. Add a FORMAT statement to generate a frequency report for the formatted values of JOBCODE (job categories).

    ```
    proc freq data=work.empdata;
       format JobCode $codefmt.;
       tables JobCode;
       title 'Distribution of Job Categories';
    run;
    ```

SAS Output

```
                    Distribution of Job Categories

                         The FREQ Procedure

                            Job Code

                                          Cumulative    Cumulative
  JobCode            Frequency    Percent   Frequency      Percent
  ─────────────────────────────────────────────────────────────────
  Flight Attendant      128       68.82        128         68.82
  Pilot                  58       31.18        186        100.00
```

3. Add SALARY to the TABLES statement to display a second report and format SALARY with the MONEY. format.

```
proc freq data=work.empdata;
   format JobCode $codefmt. Salary money.;
   tables JobCode Salary;
   title 'Distribution of Job and Salary Categories';
run;
```

SAS Output

```
                Distribution of Job and Salary Categories

                         The FREQ Procedure

                            Job Code

                                          Cumulative    Cumulative
  JobCode            Frequency    Percent   Frequency      Percent
  ─────────────────────────────────────────────────────────────────
  Flight Attendant      128       68.82        128         68.82
  Pilot                  58       31.18        186        100.00

                           Annual Salary

                                          Cumulative    Cumulative
        Salary       Frequency    Percent   Frequency      Percent
  ─────────────────────────────────────────────────────────────────
  < 25,000                25       13.44         25         13.44
  25,000 - 50,000        113       60.75        138         74.19
  > 50,000                48       25.81        186        100.00
```

4. Request a crosstabulation by placing an asterisk between JOBCODE and SALARY on the TABLES statement.

```
proc freq data=work.empdata;
   format JobCode $codefmt. Salary money.;
   tables JobCode*Salary;
   title 'Cross-tabulation of';
   title2 'Job and Salary Categories';
run;
```

SAS Output

```
                      Cross-tabulation of
                    Job and Salary Categories

                        The FREQ Procedure

                    Table of JobCode by Salary


    JobCode(Job Code)        Salary(Annual Salary)


    Frequency
    Percent
    Row Pct
    Col Pct          < 25,000 25,000 - > 50,000   Total
                              50,000

    Flight Attendant       25       103        0     128
                        13.44     55.38     0.00   68.82
                        19.53     80.47     0.00
                       100.00     91.15     0.00

    Pilot                   0        10       48      58
                         0.00      5.38    25.81   31.18
                         0.00     17.24    82.76
                         0.00      8.85   100.00

    Total                  25       113       48     186
                        13.44     60.75    25.81  100.00
```

Exercises

8. Creating Frequency Reports

For this exercise, use the WORK.SANFRAN data set. If necessary, recall and run the program you stored in Exercise 5 in Section 3.4 or you can include the BKUP35 file (bkup35.sas on Windows and UNIX, *userid*.PROG1.SASCODE(BKUP35) on OS/390).

a. Using the WORK.SANFRAN data set, use PROC FREQ to produce a frequency table that displays the number of flights that departed from San Francisco on each day of the week.

Place the title `Flights from San Francisco by Day of Week` on the report. Eliminate any active footnotes.

SAS Output

```
              Flights from San Fransisco by Day of Week

                       The FREQ Procedure

                                        Cumulative     Cumulative
    DepartDay    Frequency    Percent    Frequency       Percent

        1            6        11.54          6           11.54
        2           13        25.00         19           36.54
        3            5         9.62         24           46.15
        4            7        13.46         31           59.62
        5            7        13.46         38           73.08
        6            8        15.38         46           88.46
        7            6        11.54         52          100.00
```

b. Use one TABLES statement in a PROC FREQ step to produce two frequency tables: one that displays the number of flights to each destination and one that displays the number of flights flown on each model of aircraft.

Add the title `Flights from San Francisco` to the reports.

SAS Output

```
                        Flights from San Fransisco

                           The FREQ Procedure

                                           Cumulative    Cumulative
     Destination    Frequency    Percent    Frequency      Percent

     ANC               10         19.23         10          19.23
     HND                8         15.38         18          34.62
     HNL                3          5.77         21          40.38
     RDU                6         11.54         27          51.92
     SEA               25         48.08         52         100.00

                                           Cumulative    Cumulative
     Model          Frequency    Percent    Frequency      Percent

     JetCruise LF5100    3         5.77          3           5.77
     JetCruise LF5200    3         5.77          6          11.54
     JetCruise LF8000    2         3.85          8          15.38
     JetCruise LF8100    9        17.31         17          32.69
     JetCruise MF2100    2         3.85         19          36.54
     JetCruise MF4000   11        21.15         30          57.69
     JetCruise SF1000   22        42.31         52         100.00
```

c. Produce a two-way frequency table that shows the number of flights made on each day of the week to each destination city. Display the DEPARTDAY variable with the DAYWORD format you created earlier (if you did not previously create the format, you can include the BKUP37 file (bkup37.sas on Windows and UNIX, *userid*.PROG1.SASCODE(BKUP37) on OS/390).

SAS Output

```
                        Flights from San Francisco

                          The FREQ Procedure

                    Table of DepartDay by Destination

DepartDay
          Destination

Frequency |
Percent   |
Row Pct   |
Col Pct   | ANC    | HND    | HNL    | RDU    | SEA    | Total
----------+--------+--------+--------+--------+--------+
Sunday    |      0 |      1 |      0 |      2 |      3 |      6
          |   0.00 |   1.92 |   0.00 |   3.85 |   5.77 |  11.54
          |   0.00 |  16.67 |   0.00 |  33.33 |  50.00 |
          |   0.00 |  12.50 |   0.00 |  33.33 |  12.00 |
----------+--------+--------+--------+--------+--------+
Monday    |      3 |      2 |      0 |      1 |      7 |     13
          |   5.77 |   3.85 |   0.00 |   1.92 |  13.46 |  25.00
          |  23.08 |  15.38 |   0.00 |   7.69 |  53.85 |
          |  30.00 |  25.00 |   0.00 |  16.67 |  28.00 |
----------+--------+--------+--------+--------+--------+
Tuesday   |      1 |      1 |      0 |      1 |      2 |      5
          |   1.92 |   1.92 |   0.00 |   1.92 |   3.85 |   9.62
          |  20.00 |  20.00 |   0.00 |  20.00 |  40.00 |
          |  10.00 |  12.50 |   0.00 |  16.67 |   8.00 |
----------+--------+--------+--------+--------+--------+
Wednesday |      1 |      3 |      0 |      0 |      3 |      7
          |   1.92 |   5.77 |   0.00 |   0.00 |   5.77 |  13.46
          |  14.29 |  42.86 |   0.00 |   0.00 |  42.86 |
          |  10.00 |  37.50 |   0.00 |   0.00 |  12.00 |
----------+--------+--------+--------+--------+--------+
Thursday  |      3 |      1 |      1 |      1 |      1 |      7
          |   5.77 |   1.92 |   1.92 |   1.92 |   1.92 |  13.46
          |  42.86 |  14.29 |  14.29 |  14.29 |  14.29 |
          |  30.00 |  12.50 |  33.33 |  16.67 |   4.00 |
----------+--------+--------+--------+--------+--------+
Friday    |      2 |      0 |      2 |      0 |      4 |      8
          |   3.85 |   0.00 |   3.85 |   0.00 |   7.69 |  15.38
          |  25.00 |   0.00 |  25.00 |   0.00 |  50.00 |
          |  20.00 |   0.00 |  66.67 |   0.00 |  16.00 |
----------+--------+--------+--------+--------+--------+
Saturday  |      0 |      0 |      0 |      1 |      5 |      6
          |   0.00 |   0.00 |   0.00 |   1.92 |   9.62 |  11.54
          |   0.00 |   0.00 |   0.00 |  16.67 |  83.33 |
          |   0.00 |   0.00 |   0.00 |  16.67 |  20.00 |
----------+--------+--------+--------+--------+--------+
Total           10        8        3        6       25       52
             19.23    15.38     5.77    11.54    48.08   100.00
```

    d. **(Optional)** You can specify many options on the TABLES statement to control the calculations and appearance of a frequency table. The option NOCUM suppresses the printing of the cumulative frequencies and cumulative percentages. You can specify options on a TABLES statement in the following way:

```
tables variable / options;
```

Recall your program from part B and add the NOCUM option to the TABLES statement.

SAS Output

```
                    Flights from San Francisco

                        The FREQ Procedure

            Destination   Frequency      Percent

            ANC                  10        19.23
            HND                   8        15.38
            HNL                   3         5.77
            RDU                   6        11.54
            SEA                  25        48.08


            Model              Frequency     Percent

            JetCruise LF5100          3        5.77
            JetCruise LF5200          3        5.77
            JetCruise LF8000          2        3.85
            JetCruise LF8100          9       17.31
            JetCruise MF2100          2        3.85
            JetCruise MF4000         11       21.15
            JetCruise SF1000         22       42.31
```

3.7 Chapter Summary

Data must be in the form of a SAS data set to be processed by many SAS procedures and some DATA step statements. You can use a DATA step to read raw data and create a SAS data set. You must

- start a DATA step and name the SAS data set being created (DATA statement)
- identify the location of the raw data file to be read (INFILE statement)
- describe how to read the data fields from the raw data file (INPUT statement).

You can use column input to read data that is stored in a fixed-field raw data file. The raw data values must be standard character and numeric values to be read with column input. You can use an INPUT statement to read the data values by

- naming the SAS variable that you want to create
- use a dollar sign ($) if the SAS variable is character
- specify the starting column, a dash, and the ending column of the raw data field.

The SAS System detects data errors when

- invalid data is found in a field
- illegal arguments are used in functions
- impossible mathematical operations are requested.

When a data error is encountered, SAS

- prints a note that describes the error
- displays the input record being read
- displays the values in the SAS observation being created
- assigns a missing value to the appropriate SAS variable
- continues executing.

The Import Wizard is a point-and-click graphical interface that enables you to create a SAS data set from several types of external files. The data sources available to you depend on the SAS/ACCESS products that you license. The Import Wizard can also generate the appropriate IMPORT procedure code. You can write the IMPORT procedure statements to access the external files.

You can use the PRINT procedure to create a detailed list report. You can control the appearance of the report by selecting the variables to include and their order in the report (VAR statement).

You can further enhance a list report by

- defining report titles and footnotes (TITLE and FOOTNOTE statements)
- using SAS system options (OPTIONS statement, not part of a PROC or DATA step)
- using the NOOBS option to suppress the row numbers on the left side of the report
- assigning report column labels to variables (LABEL statement and, for PROC PRINT, the LABEL option)
- displaying the stored SAS values differently by assigning formats to variables (FORMAT statement).

The SAS System provides a number of formats but you can also create user-defined formats when you use the FORMAT procedure.

Labels and formats can be temporarily assigned to a variable in a PROC step or permanently assigned in a DATA step. If a label or format is permanently associated with a variable, it is stored in the descriptor portion of the data set.

You can use the FREQ procedure to generate one-way and two-way tabular reports.

By default, the FREQ procedure

- analyzes every variable in the SAS data set
- displays each distinct data value
- calculates the number of observations in which each data value appears (frequency), and the corresponding percentage, cumulative frequency, and cumulative percentage
- indicates the number of missing values for each variable.

Use the TABLES statement to select the variables to analyze and create either a one-way or two-way tabular report. A two-way report analyzes all possible combinations of the distinct values of two variables.

General form of the DATA statement:

DATA *SAS-data-set(s)*;

General form of the INFILE statement:

INFILE *'filename' <options>*;

General form of the INPUT statement (column input):

INPUT *variable <$> startcol-endcol* . . . ;

General form of the DATA step with column input:

DATA *SAS-data-set*(s);
    INFILE '*filename*' <*options*>;
    INPUT *variable $ startcol-endcol* ...;
RUN;

General form of a PROC CONTENTS step:

PROC CONTENTS DATA=*SAS-data-set;*
RUN;

General form of a PROC PRINT step:

PROC PRINT DATA=*SAS-data-set*;
RUN;

General form of a VAR statement:

VAR *variable(s)*;

General form of a TITLE statement:

TITLE*n* '*text*';

General form of a FOOTNOTE statement:

FOOTNOTE*n* '*text*';

General form of an OPTIONS statement:

OPTIONS *option* ...;

General form of a LABEL statement:

LABEL *variable* = '*label*'
     variable = '*label*';

General form of a FORMAT statement:

FORMAT *variable(s) format*;

General form of a PROC FORMAT step

PROC FORMAT;
    VALUE *format-name range1* = '*label*'
                   range2 = '*label*'
                   ...;
RUN;

General form of a PROC FREQ step:

```
PROC FREQ DATA=SAS-data-set;
    TABLES SAS-variables;
RUN;
```

3.8 Solutions

1. Reading Raw Data

a.

```
data work.sanfran;
   infile 'raw-data-file-name';
   input FlightID    $  1-7
         RouteID     $  8-14
         Destination $ 18-20
         Model       $ 21-40
         DepartDay      51
         TotPassCap     65-67;
run;
```

b.

1) The name of the raw data file is sfosch.dat (Windows and UNIX) or .prog1.workshop(sfosch) (OS/390).

2) Fifty-two records were read from the raw data file.

3) The data set has 52 observations.

4) The data set has 6 variables.

c.

```
proc print data=work.sanfran;
run;
```

Partial SAS Output

```
                      The SAS System                            14
                            16:24 Wednesday, July 12, 2000

                                                         Tot
       Flight                                  Depart    Pass
Obs      ID     RouteID   Destination   Model    Day     Cap

  1   IA11200  0000112       HND    JetCruise LF8100    4     255
  2   IA01804  0000018       SEA    JetCruise SF1000    4     150
  3   IA02901  0000029       HNL    JetCruise LF5200    5     207
  4   IA03100  0000031       ANC    JetCruise LF8100    5     255
  5   IA02901  0000029       HNL    JetCruise LF5200    6     207
  6   IA03100  0000031       ANC    JetCruise MF4000    6     267
  7   IA00800  0000008       RDU    JetCruise MF4000    7     267
  8   IA01805  0000018       SEA    JetCruise SF1000    7     150
  9   IA01804  0000018       SEA    JetCruise LF5100    2     165
 10   IA03101  0000031       ANC    JetCruise LF8100    2     255
 11   IA01802  0000018       SEA    JetCruise SF1000    3     150
 12   IA11200  0000112       HND    JetCruise LF8100    4     255
```

d.

```
proc contents data=work.sanfran;
run;
```

Partial SAS Output

```
    -----Alphabetic List of Variables and Attributes-----

    #     Variable        Type     Len     Pos

    5     DepartDay       Num       8       0
    3     Destination     Char      3      30
    1     FlightID        Char      7      16
    4     Model           Char     20      33
    2     RouteID         Char      7      23
    6     TotPassCap      Num       8       8
```

2. Examining Data Errors

a.

```
data work.sfpass;
   infile 'raw-data-file-name';
   input FlightID     $  1-7
         Destination $ 18-20
         DepartDate  $ 41-49
         FClassPass    53-55
         BClassPass    57-59
         EClassPass    61-63;
run;
```

b.

1) The name of the raw data file is sfosch.dat (Windows and UNIX) or .prog1.workshop(sfosch) (OS/390).

2) Fifty-two records were read from the raw data file.

3) The data set has 52 observations.

4) The data set has 6 variables.

5) The log indicates two data errors: invalid data for BCLASSPASS in records 11 and 26 of the raw data file.

c.

```
proc print data=work.sfpass;
run;
```

Partial SAS Output

```
                         The SAS System                          17
                                16:24 Wednesday, July 12, 2000

         Flight                   Depart    FClass   BClass   EClass
Obs        ID     Destination      Date      Pass     Pass     Pass

 1      IA11200      HND        01DEC1999     19       31      171
 2      IA01804      SEA        01DEC1999     10        .      123
 3      IA02901      HNL        02DEC1999     13       24      138
 4      IA03100      ANC        02DEC1999     13       22      250
 5      IA02901      HNL        03DEC1999     14       25      132
 6      IA03100      ANC        03DEC1999     16        .      243
 7      IA00800      RDU        04DEC1999     16        .      243
 8      IA01805      SEA        04DEC1999     11        .      123
 9      IA01804      SEA        06DEC1999     11       12      111
10      IA03101      ANC        06DEC1999     14       26      233
11      IA01802      SEA        07DEC1999     10        .      132
12      IA11200      HND        08DEC1999     17       33      194
```

d.

```
proc contents data=work.sfpass;
run;
```

Partial SAS Output

```
        -----Alphabetic List of Variables and Attributes-----

           #    Variable      Type    Len    Pos

           5    BClassPass    Num      8      8
           3    DepartDate    Char     9     34
           2    Destination   Char     3     31
           6    EclassPass    Num      8     16
           4    FClassPass    Num      8      0
           1    FlightID      Char     7     24
```

3. Reading an Excel Spreadsheet

a.
```
proc import out= work.sfoexcel
              datafile= "sfosch.xls"
              dbms=excel2000 replace;
     getnames=yes;
run;
```
b.
```
proc print data=work.sfoexcel;
run;
```

Partial SAS Output

```
                           The SAS System                         20
                                    16:24 Wednesday, July 12, 2000

      Flight                                                Depart
Obs   ID        RouteID  Origin  Destination  Model         Date

   1  IA11200   0000112  SFO      HND          JetCruise LF8100  01DEC1999
   2  IA01804   0000018  SFO      SEA          JetCruise SF1000  01DEC1999
   3  IA02901   0000029  SFO      HNL          JetCruise LF5200  02DEC1999
   4  IA03100   0000031  SFO      ANC          JetCruise LF8100  02DEC1999
   5  IA02901   0000029  SFO      HNL          JetCruise LF5200  03DEC1999
   6  IA03100   0000031  SFO      ANC          JetCruise MF4000  03DEC1999
   7  IA00800   0000008  SFO      RDU          JetCruise MF4000  04DEC1999
   8  IA01805   0000018  SFO      SEA          JetCruise SF1000  04DEC1999
   9  IA01804   0000018  SFO      SEA          JetCruise LF5100  06DEC1999
  10  IA03101   0000031  SFO      ANC          JetCruise LF8100  06DEC1999


      Depart  FClass  BClass  EClass  TotPass
Obs   Day     Pass    Pass    Pass    Cap    CargoWt  CargoRev

   1    4      19      31      171     255    61300    79077
   2    4      10       .      123     150    10300    13287
   3    5      13      24      138     207    47400    61146
   4    5      13      22      250     255    24800    31992
   5    6      14      25      132     207    48200    62178
   6    6      16       .      243     267    25600    33024
   7    7      16       .      243     267    25600    33024
   8    7      11       .      123     150    10100    13029
   9    2      11      12      111     165    12500    16125
  10    2      14      26      233     255    28000    36120
```

c.

```
proc contents data=work.sfoexcel;
run;
```

Partial SAS Output

```
-----Alphabetic List of Variables and Attributes-----

 #    Variable       Type   Len   Pos   Format    Informat   Label

 9    BClassPass     Num     8    16    BEST8.    BEST8.     BClassPass
13    CargoRev       Num     8    48    BEST8.    BEST8.     CargoRev
12    CargoWt        Num     8    40    BEST8.    BEST8.     CargoWt
 6    DepartDate     Char    9    92    $9.       $255.      DepartDate
 7    DepartDay      Num     8     0    BEST8.    BEST8.     DepartDay
 4    Destination    Char    3    73    $3.       $255.      Destination
10    EClassPass     Num     8    24    BEST8.    BEST8.     EClassPass
 8    FClassPass     Num     8     8    BEST8.    BEST8.     FClassPass
 1    FlightID       Char    7    56    $7.       $255.      FlightID
 5    Model          Char   16    76    $16.      $255.      Model
 3    Origin         Char    3    70    $3.       $255.      Origin
 2    RouteID        Char    7    63    $7.       $255.      RouteID
11    TotPassCap     Num     8    32    BEST8.    BEST8.     TotPassCap
```

4.   Reading a Comma-delimited File

a.

```
proc import out=work.sfocsv
            datafile="sfosch.csv"
            dbms=csv replace;
    getnames=yes;
run;
```

b.

```
proc print data=work.sfocsv;
run;
```

Partial SAS Output

```
                         The SAS System                          24
                              16:24 Wednesday, July 12, 2000

     Flight
Obs  ID            RouteID   Origin    Destination    Model

  1  IA11200          112     SFO          HND       JetCruise LF8100
  2  IA01804           18     SFO          SEA       JetCruise SF1000
  3  IA02901           29     SFO          HNL       JetCruise LF5200
  4  IA03100           31     SFO          ANC       JetCruise LF8100
  5  IA02901           29     SFO          HNL       JetCruise LF5200
  6  IA03100           31     SFO          ANC       JetCruise MF4000
  7  IA00800            8     SFO          RDU       JetCruise MF4000
  8  IA01805           18     SFO          SEA       JetCruise SF1000
  9  IA01804           18     SFO          SEA       JetCruise LF5100
 10  IA03101           31     SFO          ANC       JetCruise LF8100


Obs  DepartDate   DepartDay   FClassPass    BClassPass    EClassPass

  1  1-Dec-99         4           19            31           171
  2  1-Dec-99         4           10             .           123
  3  2-Dec-99         5           13            24           138
  4  2-Dec-99         5           13            22           250
  5  3-Dec-99         6           14            25           132
  6  3-Dec-99         6           16             .           243
  7  4-Dec-99         7           16             .           243
  8  4-Dec-99         7           11             .           123
  9  6-Dec-99         2           11            12           111
 10  6-Dec-99         2           14            26           233


Obs    TotPassCap      CargoWt      CargoRev

  1        255          61300        79077
  2        150          10300        13287
  3        207          47400        61146
  4        255          24800        31992
  5        207          48200        62178
  6        267          25600        33024
  7        267          25600        33024
  8        150          10100        13029
  9        165          12500        16125
 10        255          28000        36120
```

c.

```
proc contents data=work.sfocsv;
run;
```

Partial SAS Output

```
 -----Alphabetic List of Variables and Attributes-----

    #    Variable      Type    Len    Pos    Format     Informat

    9    BClassPass    Num      8     24     BEST12.    BEST32.
   13    CargoRev      Num      8     56     BEST12.    BEST32.
   12    CargoWt       Num      8     48     BEST12.    BEST32.
    6    DepartDate    Char     9     93     $9.        $9.
    7    DepartDay     Num      8      8     BEST12.    BEST32.
    4    Destination   Char     3     74     $3.        $3.
   10    EClassPass    Num      8     32     BEST12.    BEST32.
    8    FClassPass    Num      8     16     BEST12.    BEST32.
    1    FlightID      Char     7     64     $7.        $7.
    5    Model         Char    16     77     $16.       $16.
    3    Origin        Char     3     71     $3.        $3.
    2    RouteID       Num      8      0     BEST12.    BEST32.
   11    TotPassCap    Num      8     40     BEST12.    BEST32.
```

5. Reading Raw Data

```
data work.sanfran;
   infile 'raw-data-file-name';
   input FlightID      $  1-7
         RouteID       $  8-14
         Origin        $ 15-17
         Destination   $ 18-20
         Model         $ 21-40
         DepartDate    $ 41-49
         DepartDay        51
         FClassPass       53-55
         BClassPass       57-59
         EClassPass       61-63
         TotPassCap       65-67
         CargoWt          69-73
         CargoRev         75-79;
run;
```

6. Creating List Reports

a.

```
proc print data=work.sanfran;
   var FlightID Destination DepartDay
       CargoWt CargoRev;
   title 'Cargo Information';
   footnote 'Flights from San Fransisco';
run;
```

b.

Issue the RECALL command and modify the program:

```
options nonumber nodate;
proc print data=work.sanfran label;
   var FlightID Destination DepartDay
      CargoWt CargoRev;
   label FlightID='Flight ID Number'
         Destination='Flight Destination'
         DepartDay='Departure Day of Week'
         CargoWt='Weight of Cargo in Pounds'
         CargoRev='Revenue from Cargo in Dollars';
   title 'Cargo Information';
   footnote 'Flights from San Fransisco';
run;
```

c.

```
options nonumber nodate;
proc print data=work.sanfran label;
   var FlightID Destination DepartDay
      CargoWt CargoRev;
   label FlightID='Flight ID Number'
         Destination='Flight Destination'
         DepartDay='Departure Day of Week'
         CargoWt='Weight of Cargo in Pounds'
         CargoRev='Revenue from Cargo in Dollars';
   title 'Cargo Information';
   title2 'Weight and Revenue';
   footnote;
run;
```

7. **Using SAS Formats and Creating User-defined Formats**

a.

```
proc format;
   value dayword 1='Sunday'
                 2='Monday'
                 3='Tuesday'
                 4='Wednesday'
                 5='Thursday'
                 6='Friday'
                 7='Saturday';
run;
```

b.

```
proc format;
   value $city 'ANC'='Anchorage, AK'
               'HND'='Hatteras, NC'
               'HNL'='Honolulu, HI'
               'RDU'='Raleigh-Durham, NC'
               'SEA'='Seattle, WA';
run;
```

c.

```
proc print data=work.sanfran;
    var FlightID Destination DepartDay FClassPass
        BClassPass EClassPass CargoWt;
    format CargoWt comma6.
           DepartDay dayword.
           Destination $city.;
    title 'Flight Information';
run;
```

8. **Creating Frequency Reports**

a.

```
proc freq data=work.sanfran;
    tables DepartDay;
    title 'Flights from San Fransisco by Day of Week';
    footnote;
run;
```

b.

```
proc freq data=work.sanfran;
    tables Destination Model;
    title 'Flights from San Fransisco';
run;
```

c.

```
proc freq data=work.sanfran;
    tables Destination*DepartDay;
    format DepartDay dayword.;
run;
```

d. (Optional)

```
proc freq data=work.sanfran;
    tables Destination Model / nocum;
    title 'Flights from San Fransisco';
run;
```

Chapter 4   Importing and Transforming Raw Data and Creating Graphical Reports

4.1 Introduction

Business Scenario

International Airlines is considering the replacement of its older aircraft.

3

Business Scenario

The airline wants to

- store the aircraft service records in a SAS data set

- report beginning service dates for the aircraft

- calculate the age of aircraft in service

- create a report that includes only aircraft that are 15 years or older

- depict results graphically.

4

The Raw Data

The aircraft data is stored in a fixed-column raw data file.

Partial data:

	aircraft ID	last maintenance date

```
              1    1    2    2    3    3    4    4
1---5----0----5----0----5----0----5----0----5
JetCruise LF5200 030003 04/05/1994 03/11/2001
JetCruise LF5200 030005 02/15/1999 07/05/2001
JetCruise LF5200 030008 03/06/1996 04/02/2002
JetCruise LF5200 030009 10/14/1998 09/15/2001
JetCruise LF5200 030011 09/04/1998 08/31/2001
```

aircraft model	date in service

5

Reading a Raw Data File

Use formatted input to read date values and convert them to SAS date values.

07/25/1994		InService
06/06/1999	→	12624
02/06/1999		14401
		14281

6

Browsing the Data Attributes

Browse the descriptor portion of the data.

```
-----Alphabetic List of Variables and Attributes-----

     #     Variable      Type    Len    Pos

     2     AircraftID    Char     6      32
     3     InService     Num      8       0
     4     LastMaint     Num      8       8
     1     Model         Char    16      16
```

7

Browsing the Data Values

Print the SAS data set to display the data values.

```
                Aircraft Service Records

                      Aircraft
   Model                 ID        InService   LastMaint

JetCruise LF5200        030003      05APR1994   11MAR2001
JetCruise LF5200        030005      15FEB1999   05JUL2001
JetCruise LF5200        030008      06MAR1996   02APR2002
JetCruise LF5200        030009      14OCT1998   15SEP2001
JetCruise LF5200        030011      04SEP1998   31AUG2001
```

8

Reporting with a Vertical Bar Chart

Use a vertical bar chart to depict the values for beginning year of service, in intervals.

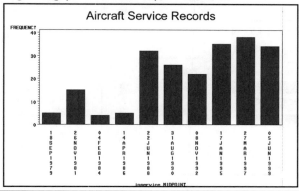

Adding a New Variable

Subtract the beginning year of service from the current year to determine aircraft age.

2000-1994=6

2000-1991=9

2000-1996=4

11

Reporting with a Horizontal Bar Chart

Use a horizontal bar chart to depict the mean age for the aircraft.

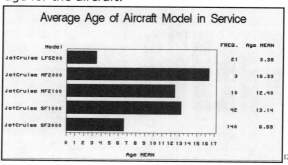

12

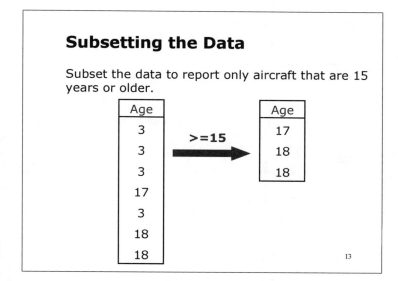

You can use SAS to report your results in a variety of ways, including

- list reports
- summary reports
- charts and graphs.

A graphical report is a good choice for presentation purposes.

4.2   Reading a Raw Data File

Objectives

- Define formatted input.
- Define a SAS informat.
- Define SAS date values.
- Use formatted input to read a raw data file.
- Use the CONTENTS procedure to browse the descriptor portion of the data set.
- Print the data set and apply formats in the PROC PRINT step.

15

Business Scenario

International Airlines is preparing to review its aircraft service records. The immediate goal is to read the raw data and create a SAS data set.

```
            Aircraft Service Records

                  Aircraft
       Model         ID       InService   LastMaint
JetCruise LF5200   030003    05APR1994   11MAR2001
JetCruise LF5200   030005    15FEB1999   05JUL2001
JetCruise LF5200   030008    06MAR1996   02APR2002
JetCruise LF5200   030009    14OCT1998   15SEP2001
JetCruise LF5200   030011    04SEP1998   31AUG2001
```

16

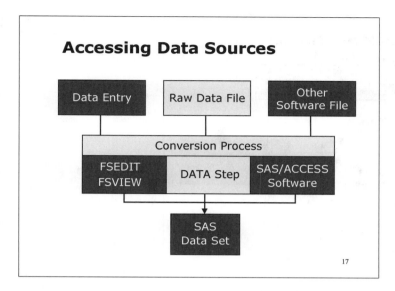

Remember that data must be in the form of a SAS data set to be processed by many SAS procedures and some DATA step statements.

✎   SAS can access and read data from a variety of storage places, including

- raw data files
- Excel spreadsheets
- SAS data sets.

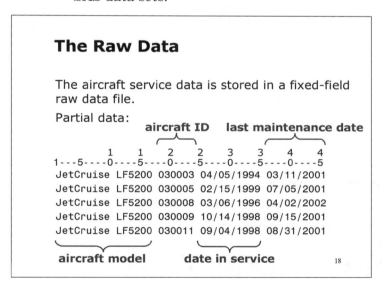

Using Formatted Input

Raw Data File

```
JetCruise LF5200 030003 04/05/1994 03/11/2001
JetCruise LF5200 030005 02/15/1999 07/05/2001
JetCruise LF5200 030008 03/06/1996 04/02/2002
```

DATA Step

```
data sas-data-set-name;
    infile raw-filename;
    input pointer-control
          variable
          informat-name;
run;
```

The raw data file will be read with formatted input.

SAS Data Set

Model	AircraftID	InService	LastMaint
JetCruise	030003	05APR1994	11MAR2001
JetCruise	030005	15FEB1999	05JUL2001
JetCruise	030008	06MAR1996	02APR2002

19

Using Formatted Input

Formatted input is appropriate for reading

- data in fixed columns
- standard and nonstandard character and numeric data
- calendar values to be converted to SAS date values.

20

Using Formatted Input

General form of the INPUT statement with formatted input:

INPUT *pointer-control variable informat* ...;

Pointer control:

@*n*   moves the pointer to column *n*.

+*n*   moves the pointer *n* positions.

21

Using Formatted Input

Formatted input can be used to read non-standard data values by

- moving the input pointer to the starting position of the field
- specifying a variable name
- specifying an informat.

An *informat* specifies the width of the input field and how to read the data values that are stored in the field.

22

Using Formatted Input

General form of an informat:

$informat-namew.d

$	indicates a character informat.
informat-name	names the informat.
w	is an optional field width.
.	is the required delimiter.
d	optionally, specifies a decimal for numeric informats.

23

An informat must contain a period as part of its name.

Selected Informats

7. or 7.0	reads seven columns of numeric data.
7.2	reads seven columns of numeric data and may insert a decimal point in the data value.
$5.	reads five columns of character data and removes leading blanks.
$CHAR5.	reads five columns of character data and preserves leading blanks.

24

Selected Informats

COMMA7.	reads seven columns of numeric data and removes selected nonnumeric characters, such as dollar signs and commas.
PD4.	reads four columns of packed decimal numeric data.
MMDDYY10.	reads dates of the form 01/20/2000.

25

Working with Date Values

The raw data file contains date values. These date values will be read with the MMDDYY10. informat.

```
            1    1    2    2    3    3    4    4
1---5----0----5----0----5----0----5----0----5
Jetcruise LF5200 030003 04/05/1990 3/11/2001
Jetcruise LF5200 030005 02/15/1990 7/05/2001
Jetcruise LF5200 030008 03/06/1990 4/02/2002
```

26

Working with Date Values

Date values that are stored as SAS dates are special numeric values.

A *SAS date value* is interpreted as the number of days between January 1, 1960, and a specific date.

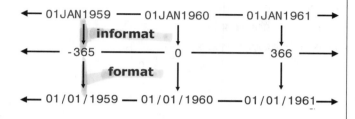

Converting Dates to SAS Date Values

SAS uses date **informats** to **read** and **convert** dates to SAS date values, for example,

Stored Value	Informat	Converted Value
10/29/1999	MMDDYY10.	14546
29OCT1999	DATE9.	14546
29/10/1999	DDMMYY10.	14546

28

Writing SAS Date Values

SAS uses date **formats** to **write** values from columns that represent dates, for example,

Stored Value	Format	Displayed Value
0	MMDDYY10.	01/01/1960
0	DATE9.	01JAN1960
0	DDMMYY10.	01/01/1960
0	WEEKDATE.	Friday, January 1, 1960

29

For a complete list of SAS formats and informats, see the online SAS documentation.

Self-Study

Reading and Writing SAS Time and SAS Datetime Values

SAS Time Values

SAS date informats and formats can be used to read and write SAS time values.

```
  ←——  12:00 AM  ————  9:30 AM   ——→
        05JUN1989        05JUN1989
          │                │
          ↓                ↓
          0              34200
```

30

 # OF seconds since Jan 1, 1960

A *SAS time value* is interpreted as the number of seconds since midnight of the current day.

Cannot have a negative time value.

SAS Datetime Values

SAS date informats and formats can also be used to read and write SAS datetime values.

```
  ←——  12:00 AM  ————  9:30 AM   ——→
        01JUN1960        05JUN1989
          │                │
          ↓                ↓
          0            928661400
```

31

A *SAS datetime value* is interpreted as the number of seconds between midnight, January 1, 1960, and a specified date and time.

Reading a Raw Data File with Formatted Input

Locating and Browsing the Raw Data File

Browse the raw data file and determine the column layout and type.
Partial raw data file:

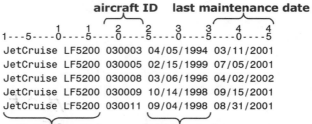

```
                            aircraft ID    last maintenance date
            1    1    2    2    3    3    4    4
1---5----0----5----0----5----0----5----0----5
JetCruise LF5200 030003 04/05/1994 03/11/2001
JetCruise LF5200 030005 02/15/1999 07/05/2001
JetCruise LF5200 030008 03/06/1996 04/02/2002
JetCruise LF5200 030009 10/14/1998 09/15/2001
JetCruise LF5200 030011 09/04/1998 08/31/2001
```

  aircraft model   **date in service**   32

Starting the DATA Step

Use the DATA statement to begin the DATA step and name the SAS data set.

```
data work.aircraft;
   other SAS statements
run;
```

Use the INFILE statement to identify the input raw data file.

```
data work.aircraft;
   infile 'aircraft.dat';
   other SAS statements
run;
```

33

Writing the INPUT Statement

Use the INPUT statement and pointer control to
read the record starting with the first column.
Read the value with the $16. informat and assign
it to the variable MODEL.

```
          1    1    2    2    3    3    4    4
1---5----0----5----0----5----0----5----0----5

JetCruise LF5200 030003 04/05/1994 03/11/2001

data work.aircraft;
   infile 'aircraft.dat';
   input @1 Model $16.;
run;
```

⤷ I am naming the variable

Writing the INPUT Statement

Use the INPUT statement and pointer control to
read the record starting with column 18. Read
the value with the $6. informat and assign the
value to AIRCRAFTID.

```
          1    1    2    2    3    3    4    4
1---5----0----5----0----5----0----5----0----5

JetCruise LF5200 030003 04/05/1994 03/11/2001

data work.aircraft;
   infile 'aircraft.dat';
   input @1 Model $16. @18 AircraftID $6.;
run;
```

35

Writing the INPUT Statement

Use the INPUT statement and pointer control to
read the record starting with column 25. Read
the value with the MMDDYY10. informat and
assign the value to INSERVICE.

```
          1    1    2    2    3    3    4    4
1---5----0----5----0----5----0----5----0----5

JetCruise LF5200 030003 04/05/1994 03/11/2001

data work.aircraft
   infile 'aircraft.dat';
   input @1 Model $16. @18 AircraftID $6.
      @25 InService mmddyy10.;
run;
```

36

Writing the INPUT Statement

Use the INPUT statement and pointer control to read the record starting with column 36. Read the value with the MMDDYY10. informat and assign the value to LASTMAINT.

```
           1    1    2    2    3    3    4    4
1---5----0----5----0----5----0----5----0----5
JetCruise LF5200 030003 04/05/1994 03/11/2001

data work.aircraft;
   infile 'aircraft.dat';
   input @1 Model $16. @18 AircraftID $6.
         @25 InService mmddyy10.
         @36 LastMaint mmddyy10.;
run;
                                          37
```

without period = sixth col.
with " = six col.

Reading a Raw Data File and Creating a Report with Formatted Values

File: c4s2d1.sas

Read the aircraft raw data file and create the SAS data set WORK.AIRCRAFT.

- Use formatted input to read the raw data file.
- Use the CONTENTS procedure to browse the descriptor portion of the data.
- Use the PRINT procedure with a FORMAT statement to print and browse the resulting list report.

Reading a Raw Data File with Formatted Input

1. Locate the raw data file and open it. Determine its column layout and type.

2. Write the DATA step.

   ```
   data work.aircraft;
      infile 'aircraft.dat';
      input @1  Model $16. @18 AircraftID $6.
            @25 InService mmddyy10.
            @36 LastMaint mmddyy10.;
   run;
   ```

3. Submit the program for execution and browse the SAS log. The SAS log
   - contains no warnings or error messages
   - points to the raw data file
   - indicates that 216 records were read
   - indicates that the SAS data set contains 216 observations and 4 variables.

Browsing the Descriptor Portion of the Data

1. Use the CONTENTS procedure to browse the descriptor portion of the SAS data set.

   ```
   proc contents data=work.aircraft;
      title;
   run;
   ```

2. Submit the program and browse the output. PROC CONTENTS lists general information about the table WORK.AIRCRAFT.

Partial SAS Output

```
                        The CONTENTS Procedure

Data Set Name: WORK.AIRCRAFT                  Observations:          216
Member Type:   DATA                           Variables:             4
Engine:        V8                             Indexes:               0
Created:       11:28 Thursday, December 16, 1999 Observation Length: 40
Last Modified: 11:28 Thursday, December 16, 1999 Deleted Observations: 0
Protection:                                   Compressed:            NO
Data Set Type:                                Sorted:                NO
Label:
```

It also lists the attributes for the four variables.

Partial SAS Output

```
            -----Alphabetic List of Variables and Attributes-----

            #    Variable     Type    Len    Pos

            2    AircraftID   Char     6      32
            3    InService    Num      8      0
            4    LastMaint    Num      8      8
            1    Model        Char     16     16
```

✎ If you run SAS interactively, you can also issue the VAR command to browse the descriptor portion of the data.

Browsing the Data Portion

1. Use the PRINT procedure to browse a list report of the data. Include a FORMAT statement to format the printed data values and a TITLE statement.

```
proc print data=work.aircraft noobs;
   format InService LastMaint date9.;
   title 'Aircraft Service Records';
run;
```

2. Submit the program.

✎ The FORMAT statement associates the DATE9. format with both variables listed in the statement.

Partial SAS Output

```
                      Aircraft Service Records

                         Aircraft
           Model            ID       InService    LastMaint

      JetCruise LF5200     030003    05APR1994    11MAR2001
      JetCruise LF5200     030005    15FEB1999    05JUL2001
      JetCruise LF5200     030008    06MAR1996    02APR2002
      JetCruise LF5200     030009    14OCT1998    15SEP2001
      JetCruise LF5200     030011    04SEP1998    31AUG2001
      JetCruise LF5200     030012    02JAN1994    29MAR2001
      JetCruise LF5200     030013    01FEB1996    23NOV2002
      JetCruise LF5200     030015    24JUN1998    06FEB2001
      JetCruise LF5200     030016    23NOV1999    10MAR2002
      JetCruise LF5200     030018    25APR1999    14JUN2001
      JetCruise LF5200     030019    12MAY1998    15JUL2001
      JetCruise LF5200     030022    12MAY1994    18FEB2001
      JetCruise LF5200     030025    19OCT1994    13DEC2002
      JetCruise LF5200     030026    09MAR1996    03NOV2002
      JetCruise LF5200     030027    31JAN1996    28NOV2002
      JetCruise LF5200     030030    25JUL1994    19DEC2001
      JetCruise LF5200     030031    06JUN1999    26FEB2002
      JetCruise LF5200     030033    06FEB1999    15MAY2002
```

✎ Remember that by default PROC PRINT displays all observations and variables.

Testing a DATA Step

Typically, a DATA step reads raw data from an external file.

```
data work.aircraft;
   infile 'aircraft.dat';
   input @1 Model $16. @18 AircraftID $6.
         @25 InService mmddyy10.
         @36 LastMaint mmddyy10.;
run;
```

39

Testing a DATA Step

When you test code, it is not always convenient to create an external file to read. However, this DATA step requires a data source.

```
data work.aircraft;
   infile ?;
   input @1 Model $16. @18 AircraftID $6.
         @25 InService mmddyy10.
         @36 LastMaint mmddyy10.;
run;
```

40

Using Imbedded Data

You can imbed lines of data in a DATA step by

1. placing the DATALINES statement after the last statement in the DATA step

2. following the statement with rows of data

3. ending with a RUN statement on a line alone.

General form of the DATALINES statement:

DATALINES;

41

Using Imbedded Data

Test a DATA step with two imbedded rows
of data.

```
data work.aircraft;
    input @1 Model $16. @18 AircraftID $6.
          @25 InService mmddyy10.
          @36 LastMaint mmddyy10.;
datalines;
JetCruise LF5200 030003 04/05/1994 03/11/2001
JetCruise LF5200 030005 02/15/1999 07/05/2001;
run;
```

42

To include the data
into your Program
add "datalines"

The CARDS statement has the same functionality as the DATALINES
statement.

 No INFILE statement is required if a DATALINES or CARDS
statement is used in the DATA step.

Testing a DATA Step with Imbedded Data

File: c4s2d2.sas

Read the imbedded aircraft data and create the SAS data set WORK.TEST.

- Use formatted input to read imbedded data rows.
- Use the PRINT procedure with a FORMAT statement to print and browse the resulting list report.

Reading a Raw Data File with Formatted Input

Write the DATA step.

```
data work.test;
   input @1  Model $16. @18 AircraftID $6.
         @25 InService mmddyy10.
         @36 LastMaint mmddyy10.;
datalines;
JetCruise LF5200 030003 04/05/1994 03/11/2001
JetCruise LF5200 030005 02/15/1999 07/05/2001
JetCruise LF5200 030008 03/06/1996 04/02/2002
JetCruise LF5200 030009 10/14/1998 09/15/2001
run;
```

Submit the program for execution and browse the SAS log.

Browsing the Data Portion

1. Use the PRINT procedure to browse a list report of the data. Include a FORMAT statement to format the printed data values and a TITLE statement.

```
proc print data=work.test noobs;
   format InService LastMaint date9.;
   title 'Aircraft Service Records';
run;
```

Submit the program.

SAS Output

```
                        Aircraft Service Records

                        Aircraft
            Model          ID      InService     LastMaint

      JetCruise LF5200    030003   05APR1994     11MAR2001
      JetCruise LF5200    030005   15FEB1999     05JUL2001
      JetCruise LF5200    030008   06MAR1996     02APR2002
      JetCruise LF5200    030009   14OCT1998     15SEP2001
```

Exercises

1. Reading a Raw Data File with Formatted Input

This exercise requires that you read from a raw data file called EMPLOYE1. Fill in the blank with the location of your raw data file. Use an INFILE statement in a DATA step to read the raw file.

```
data ...;
    infile '_____';
    .
    .
    .
```

International Airlines must read employee information from a raw data file and write it to a SAS data set.

a. A ruler and the first three records of the raw data file are shown below. Use these records to create a record layout, and use the table below to record the results. You use the information in the table to compose your INPUT statement.

```
----+----1----+----2----+----3----+----4----+----5----+----6----+----7----

16OCT1989JUDD         CAROL A.      CARY      2061 E00004 FACMNT$42,000

15FEB1992BADINE       DAVID         TORONTO   1000 E00008 OFFMGR$85,000

20NOV1991TENGESDAL    ANDERS        OSLO      1029 E00070 RESCLK$24,000
```

Field Description	Character or numeric?	Starting Column	Informat
Date of hire			DATE9.
Last name			
First name			
Employee location			
Telephone number			
Employee number			
Job code			
Annual salary			

b. Use formatted input in a DATA step to read the raw data file into a SAS data set WORK.EMPLOYEE. Create the following variables in the order specified:

- HIREDATE
- LASTNAME
- FIRSTNAME
- LOCATION
- PHONE
- EMPID
- JOBCODE
- SALARY.

Submit the DATA step. Browse the Log window to

- verify that 72 records were read from the raw data file
- verify that 72 observations were written to the SAS data set WORK.EMPLOYEE
- determine whether there were any invalid values in the raw data file.

c. Examine the descriptor portion of the data set WORK.EMPLOYEE.

Partial SAS Output

```
-----Alphabetic List of Variables and Attributes-----

  #     Variable      Type     Len     Pos
  _____

  6     EmpID         Char      6      60
  3     FirstName     Char     14      32
  1     HireDate      Num       8       0
  7     JobCode       Char      6      66
  2     LastName      Char     16      16
  4     Location      Char     10      46
  5     Phone         Char      4      56
  8     Salary        Num       8       8
```

d. Print the data portion of the table and assign a descriptive title. Examine the values that you read in from the date of hire field. What do these values represent?

Partial SAS Output

```
                            Employee Database

                        F
     H   L              i            L
     i   a              r            o                   J
     r   s              s            c                   o    S
     e   t              t            a       P    E      b    a
     D   N              N            t       h    m      C    l
O    a   a              a            i       o    p      o    a
b    t   m              m            o       n    I      d    r
s    e   e              e            n       e    D      e    y

1 10881 JUDD            CAROL A.     CARY    2061 E00004 FACMNT 42000
2 11733 BADINE          DAVID        TORONTO 1000 E00008 OFFMGR 85000
3 11646 TENGESDAL       ANDERS       OSLO    1029 E00070 RESCLK 24000
4 11117 DUNLAP          PEGGY H.     CARY    1565 E00120 FLTAT2 30000
5  9121 SAWYER          STEPHANIE    AUSTIN  1079 E00216 MECHO3 22000
```

e. Recall your PROC PRINT step and alter the code to display each employee's date of hire as shown in the output below. Assign a format in the PROC step. Re-assign a descriptive title.

Partial SAS Output

```
                          Employee Database


        Obs      HireDate      LastName          FirstName

         1      10/16/1989     JUDD              CAROL A.
         2      02/15/1992     BADINE            DAVID
         3      11/20/1991     TENGESDAL         ANDERS
         4      06/09/1990     DUNLAP            PEGGY H.
         5      12/21/1984     SAWYER            STEPHANIE
         6      12/24/1988     BRASWELL          JANINE
         7      10/11/1985     WEISS             MARY E.
         8      08/10/1989     RIPPERTON         DAVID D.
         9      10/30/1988     HARTZ             GRAY
        10      05/01/1991     SCHWEDE           REINHARD
        11      02/20/1992     RODRIGUEZ         MELISSA A.
        12      03/01/1980     ZIMMERMAN         ROSEMARY C
        13      12/25/1991     BENSON            JESSE R.
        14      03/24/1993     HOESCHEL          JUERGEN
        15      01/26/1983     MOORE             MICHAEL


                                                   Job
        Obs      Location      Phone    EmpID      Code      Salary

         1      CARY           2061     E00004     FACMNT     42000
         2      TORONTO        1000     E00008     OFFMGR     85000
         3      OSLO           1029     E00070     RESCLK     24000
         4      CARY           1565     E00120     FLTAT2     30000
         5      AUSTIN         1079     E00216     MECHO3     22000
         6      ROCKVILLE      1007     E00227     MKTCLK     36000
         7      CARY           1547     E00262     PILOT3     36000
         8      CARY           2670     E00308     MECHO1     22000
         9      PITTSBURGH     1003     E00373     SALCLK     31000
        10      FRANKFURT      1175     E00568     FLTAT3     27000
        11      CARY           2687     E00701     GRCREW     21000
        12      CARY           3249     E00781     BAGCLK     19000
        13      CARY           1148     E00788     PILOT3     20000
        14      FRANKFURT      1067     E00886     GRCREW     34000
        15      CARY           1357     E01076     FLTAT1     38000
```

Scroll to the 59th observation. How is the invalid data value represented?

f.   (Optional) Create a data set named WORK.TEST by using the first three records of the EMPLOYE1 raw data file as imbedded data.

HINT: Use the same input statement you used in the DATA step you wrote in part **b**. You can include the BKUP41 file into your SAS program instead of typing the first three lines of the raw data file (bkup41.sas for Windows and UNIX, *userid*.PROG1.SASCODE(BKUP41) for OS/390).

Use PROC PRINT to view your data set to verify that your DATA step executed properly.

SAS Output

Obs	Hire Date	LastName	First Name	Location	Phone	EmpID	Job Code	Salary
				Employee Database				
1	12302	HOLLEMAN	JOHN W	CARY	1937	E03009	PILOT2	43000
2	7746	CAVILL	RODNEY	SYDNEY	1012	E03018	FINCLK	17000
3	8163	SEMMLER	BARBARA	FRANKFURT	1132	E03102	PILOT1	64000

4.3   Creating a Graph Report

Objectives

- Explain the GCHART procedure.
- Explain chart variables.
- Explain the VBAR and HBAR statements.
- Explain RUN-group processing.
- Use the GCHART procedure to create a vertical bar chart with a numeric chart variable.

46

Business Scenario

International Airlines is considering the replacement of some older aircraft. One step will be to determine the year each aircraft was placed into service.

47

Business Scenario

The airline chose to present its findings graphically at an upcoming meeting.

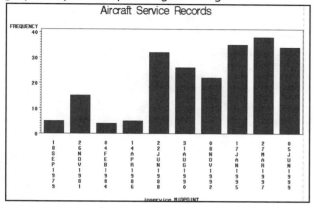

Using the GCHART Procedure

You can use the GCHART procedure to create presentation-quality graphs and charts.

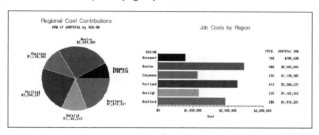

49

Using the GCHART Procedure

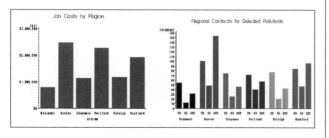

50

Using the GCHART Procedure

The GCHART procedure summarizes data and depicts the summarized information as

- bars within a vertical or horizontal bar chart (also called a histogram)

- blocks within a three-dimensional block chart

- slices within a pie chart

- spines or slices within a star chart.

51

Charts that are created with the GCHART procedure

- depict a variable value or the relationship between two or more variables

- represent the value of a statistic calculated for one or more variables in a SAS data set.

 If you do not have access to SAS/GRAPH software, you can use the CHART procedure, which is part of base SAS software.

Creating a Chart with the GCHART Procedure

General form of the PROC GCHART statement:

> **PROC GCHART** DATA=*SAS-data-set*;

DATA=*SAS-data-set* specifies the SAS data set that contains the variable(s) to chart. By default, the procedure uses the most recently created SAS data set.

52

Creating a Chart with the GCHART Procedure

General syntax of the VBAR|HBAR|PIE statement

HBAR|VBAR|PIE *chart-variable(s) </option(s)>;*

The *chart-variable(s)*

- identifies the chart variable and determines the number of bars or slices that are produced

- can be character or numeric.

53

In charts that are created with the HBAR, VBAR, or PIE statement, the length or height of the bars or the size of the slice of the pie represents the value of the chart statistic for each category of data. Three dimensional bars and pies are also available.

 All variables must be in the input SAS data set. Multiple variables must be separated with blanks.

Using the GCHART Procedure to Create a Vertical Bar Chart

Creating a Vertical Bar Chart with the GCHART Procedure

Write the PROC GCHART step.

Use the PROC GCHART statement to start the procedure and identify WORK.AIRCRAFT as the input SAS data set.

```
proc gchart data=work.aircraft;
   other statements
run;
```

54

Creating a Vertical Bar Chart with the GCHART Procedure

In the VBAR statement, specify the chart variable as INSERVICE.

```
proc gchart data=work.aircraft;
   vbar InService;
run;
```

55

The numeric variable INSERVICE will be used to create a default bar graph.

Creating a Vertical Bar Chart with the GCHART Procedure

Write a FORMAT statement to apply the DATE9. format to INSERVICE.

```
proc gchart data=work.aircraft;
   format InService date9.;
   vbar InService;
run;
```

56

Creating a Vertical Bar Chart with the GCHART Procedure

Add a TITLE statement and the RUN and QUIT statements.

```
proc gchart data=work.aircraft;
   format InService date9.;
   vbar InService;
   title 'Aircraft Service Records';
run;
quit;
```

57

Using RUN-Group Processing

RUN-group processing is in effect for the GCHART procedure. RUN-group processing enables you to

- keep the procedure in memory
- submit new statements without resubmitting the PROC statement.

Use the QUIT statement to end RUN-group processing.

5

General form of the QUIT statement:

> **QUIT**;

 You can also end RUN-group processing by

- submitting another PROC statement or DATA step
- ending the current SAS session.

Using a Numeric Chart Variable

The variable INSERVICE is numeric. When the chart variable is numeric,

- the values of the variable are treated as continuous numeric data
- the range of values of the variable are divided into intervals
- each interval is represented as a bar (or the appropriate counterpart for other graphs)
- the bar is labeled with the interval midpoint value.

5

Using the GCHART Procedure to Create a Vertical Bar Chart

File: c4s3d1.sas

Create a vertical bar chart that illustrates the beginning year of service for International Airlines' aircraft.

- Use the VBAR statement to request a vertical bar chart.
- Use a FORMAT statement to apply the DATE9. format to the values of INSERVICE.

1. Write the PROC GCHART step, including a VBAR statement, FORMAT and TITLE statements, and a RUN statement. Add a QUIT statement.

```
proc gchart data=work.aircraft;
   format InService date9.;
   vbar InService;
   title 'Aircraft Service Records';
run;
quit;
```

2. Submit the program for execution.

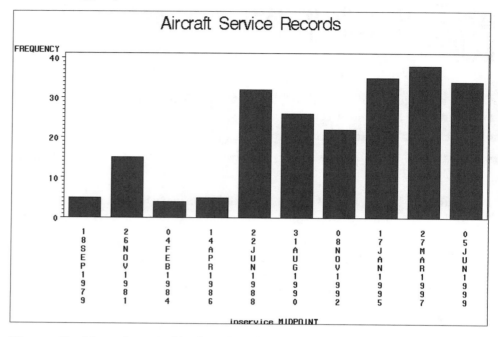

The vertical bar chart is displayed with the name of the chart variable at the bottom of the chart. Each bar is displayed with a midpoint value based on the data in WORK.AIRCRAFT.

✎ If you run a program interactively, the output is displayed in the GRAPH window.

The chart shows that most of the airplanes were put into service after 1983.

3. Check the SAS log. The program contains no errors.

Exercises

2. Creating Vertical and Horizontal Bar Charts

This exercise requires that you include a DATA step that is contained in a program file called SCHEDULE. Use an INCLUDE command to read the file.

> **INCLUDE '_____'**

a. Include the DATA step contained in the program file. The DATA step reads in a raw data file and creates a SAS table.

Examine the DATA step and complete the following table.

Name of the SAS data set created:	
Name of the raw data file read:	
Number of variables in the SAS data set:	
Names of the character variables in the SAS data set:	
Names of the numeric variables in the SAS data set:	
Name of the informat used to read in the DATE variable:	
Name of the informat used to read in the CARGOCAP variable:	

b. When you complete the table, submit the DATA step. Examine the SAS log for any data errors. Are there any?

c. Examine the descriptor portion of the resulting SAS data set.

d. Print the data portion of the resulting SAS data set.

e. Create a vertical bar chart of the SAS data set that displays the frequency of values for DATE. Format the values of DATE as shown in the output below. Display the values of scheduled flight date by using the DATE9. format. Add an appropriate TITLE statement. What does each vertical bar represent?

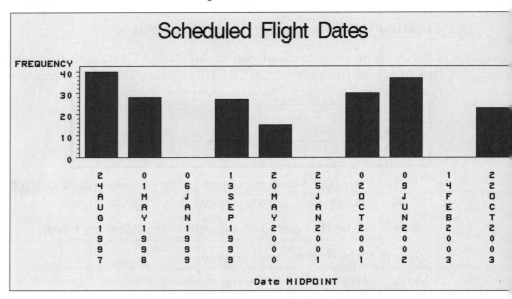

f. Create a horizontal bar chart that displays the frequency of values for DATE. Note the differences in the output between the horizontal and the vertical bar charts.

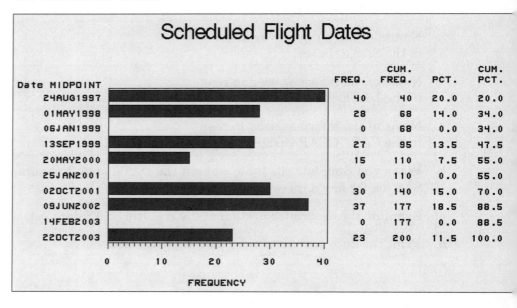

4.4 Creating a New Variable and Reporting the Results Graphically

Objectives

- Explain the assignment statement.
- Explain SAS functions.
- Use SAS functions to manipulate SAS date values.
- Use the GCHART procedure to produce vertical and horizontal bar charts.

63

Business Scenario

As part of its safety campaign to scrutinize older aircraft, International Airlines must determine how many aircraft have been put into service each year.

64

Business Scenario

Use a vertical bar chart to show how many aircraft have been put into service each year.

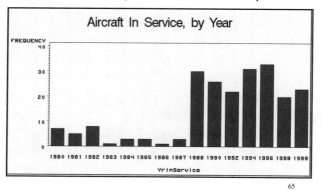

Business Scenario

Use a horizontal bar chart to show the average age of each aircraft model and the number of carriers in service for each model.

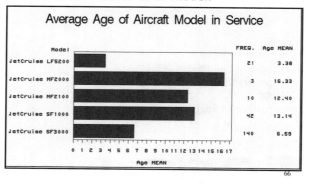

Creating a New Variable

To create a new variable, consider using

- an assignment statement
- a SAS function.

Aircraft Service Records

Model	AircraftID	InService	LastMaint
JetCruise LF5200	030003	12513	15045
JetCruise LF5200	030005	14290	15161
JetCruise LF5200	030008	13214	15432
JetCruise LF5200	030009	14166	15233
JetCruise LF5200	030011	14126	15218
JetCruise LF5200	030012	12420	15063

YrInService
1994
1999
1996
1998
1994
1994

Using an Assignment Statement

An assignment statement evaluates an expression and assigns the resulting value to a variable. Assignment statements are used in the DATA step.

General form of an assignment statement:

> *variable=expression;*

68

 You can also use an assignment statement to **modify** the values of an **existing** variable.

Using Operators

Selected operators for basic arithmetic calculations in an assignment statement:

Operator	Action	Example	Priority
+	Addition	sum=x+y;	III
-	Subtraction	diff=x-y;	III
*	Multiplication	mult=x*y;	II
/	Division	divide=x/y;	II
**	Exponentiation	raise=x**y;	I
-	Negative prefix	negative=-x;	I

69

Rules for Operators

- Operations of priority I are performed before operations of priority II, and so on.
- Consecutive operations with the same priority are performed
  - from right to left with priority I
  - from left to right within priority II and III.
- Parentheses can be used to control the order of operations.

70

 If any value used with an arithmetic operator is missing, the result is missing.

Using SAS Functions

A *SAS function* is a routine that returns a value that is determined from specified arguments.

General syntax of a SAS function:

$$\boxed{function\text{-}name(argument1,argument2, \ldots)}$$

71

Each argument is separated from other arguments by a comma. Most functions accept arguments that are

- constants
- variables
- expressions
- functions.

Using SAS Functions

SAS functions

- perform arithmetic operations

- compute statistics (for example, mean)

- manipulate SAS dates and process character values

- perform many other tasks.

72

Selected Date Functions

YEAR(*SAS-date*)   extracts the year from a SAS date and returns a four-digit value for year.

QTR(*SAS-date*)   extracts the quarter from a SAS date and returns a number from 1 to 4.

MONTH(*SAS-date*)   extracts the month from a SAS date and returns a number from 1 to 12.

continued...

73

Selected Date Functions

WEEKDAY(*SAS-date*)	extracts the day of the week from a SAS date and returns a number from 1 to 7, where 1 represents Sunday, and so on.
MDY(*month,day,year*)	uses the *month*, *day*, and *year* values to return the corresponding SAS date value.
TODAY()	obtains the date value from the system clock.

74

 The TODAY function has no arguments, but the parentheses are required.

Creating a New Variable

Add an assignment statement to the DATA step that

- identifies the new variable

```
data work.aircraft;
   infile 'aircraft.dat';
   input @1 Model $16. @18 AircraftID $6.
         @25 InService mmddyy10.
         @36 LastMaint mmddyy10.;
   YrInService=expression;
run;
```

continued...

75

Creating a New Variable

- applies the YEAR function to the values of INSERVICE and assigns those values to the new variable

```
data work.aircraft;
   infile 'aircraft.dat';
   input @1 Model $16. @18 AircraftID $6.
         @25 InService mmddyy10.
         @36 LastMaint mmddyy10.;
   YrInService=year(InService);
run;
```

76

Because the YEAR function is used to assign values, each bar is represented as a four-digit-year value.

Creating a Vertical Bar Chart

Use the GCHART procedure and the VBAR statement to create a vertical bar chart.

```
proc gchart data=work.aircraft;
   vbar YrInService;
   title 'Aircraft In Service, by Year';
run;
```

continued...

77

Creating a Vertical Bar Chart

Add the DISCRETE option to the VBAR statement so that the chart contains a bar for each year that new aircraft were put into service.

```
proc gchart data=work.aircraft;
   vbar YrInService / discrete;
   title 'Aircraft In Service, by Year';
run;
```

78

Chart Puts the bar at the mid Point OF the interval.

Use midpoints = 1980 to 1999 to show all bars for every year

Creating a New Variable and Reporting with Vertical Bar Charts

File: c4s4d1.sas

Create a new variable that indicates the start of service as a four-digit year. Report the results graphically.

- Use an assignment statement and a SAS function to create a new variable and assign its values.
- Use the GCHART procedure and the VBAR statement to create a vertical bar chart.
- Add the DISCRETE option.

Creating a New Variable

1. Include the DATA step that was used earlier to create the temporary data set WORK.AIRCRAFT. Add an assignment statement with the YEAR function.

```
data work.aircraft;
    infile 'aircraft.dat';
    input @1  Model $16. @18 AircraftID $6.
          @25 InService mmddyy10.
          @36 LastMaint mmddyy10.;
    YrInService=year(InService);
run;
```

2. Submit the program for execution and browse the messages in the SAS log.

    The log
    - does not contain any warnings or error messages
    - indicates that the data set WORK.AIRCRAFT was created with 216 observations and 5 variables.

Creating a Vertical Bar Chart

1. Write a PROC GCHART step that creates a vertical bar chart with the new variable YRINSERVICE as the chart variable.

```
proc gchart data=work.aircraft;
    vbar YrInService;
    title 'Aircraft In Service, by Year';
run;
quit;
```

2. Submit the program for execution and browse the results.

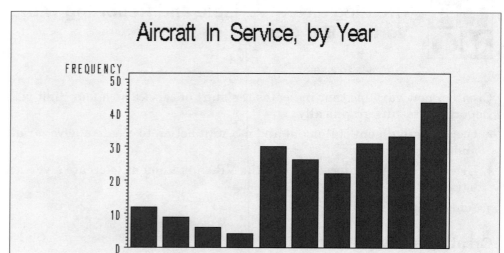

By default,

- the vertical bar chart is displayed with the name of the chart variable at the bottom of the chart
- each bar is displayed with a midpoint value based on the values of YRINSERVICE.

Because the YEAR function is used to assign the values, each bar is represented as a four-digit year value.

3. Add the DISCRETE option to the program so that the graph contains a bar for each year that aircraft were put into service.

```
proc gchart data=work.aircraft;
   vbar YrInService / discrete;
   title 'Aircraft In Service, by Year';
run;
```

4. Resubmit the program and browse the results. Note that during several
    years, no new aircraft were put into service.

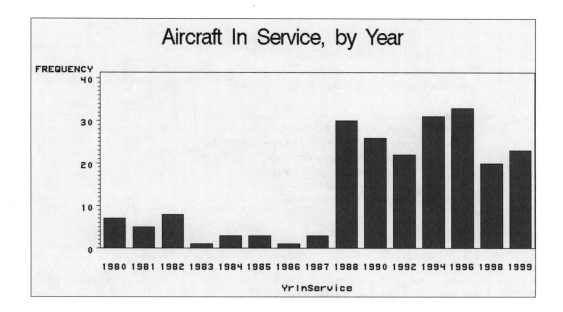

Creating a New Variable and a Horizontal Bar Chart of Its Values

Creating a New Variable

Add an assignment statement to the DATA step that

- applies the YEAR function to the TODAY function

```
data work.aircraft;
   infile 'work.aircraft';
   input @1 Model $16. @18 AircraftID $6.
         @25 InService mmddyy10.
         @36 LastMaint mmddyy10.;
   YrInService=year(InService);
   Age=year(today())-expression;
run;
```

continued... [80]

Creating a New Variable

- subtracts the returned values of YRINSERVICE from today's year and assigns the values to AGE

```
data work aircraft;
   infile 'work.aircraft';
   input @1 Model $16. @18 AircraftID $6.
         @25 InService mmddyy10.
         @36 LastMaint mmddyy10.;
   YrInService=year(InService);
   Age=year(today())-YrInService;
run;
```

[81]

There are many other methods for calculating age values. For example, you can subtract the two SAS date values to return the number of days in service and divide by the number of days in a year:

```
Age=(today()-InService)/365.25;
```

Customizing Your Graphic

You can gain reporting flexibility by using these options on the VBAR or HBAR statement:

TYPE=*statistic*   specifies the statistic to be calculated.

SUMVAR=*numeric-variable*   specifies the variable to be used for sum or mean calculations.

82

Valid values for TYPE= are
- FREQ (the default)
- CFREQ
- PERCENT
- CPERCENT
- SUM
- MEAN.

The SUMVAR= option is required with SUM and MEAN.

For SUMVAR=, the default statistic is SUM when the SUMVAR= option is used and the TYPE= option is omitted.

Customizing Your Graphic

How the value of the statistic is represented depends on the type of the chart. It can be the

- height of a vertical bar
- length of a horizontal bar
- height of a three-dimensional block
- relative size of a pie slice.

83

Creating a Horizontal Bar Chart

Write a PROC GCHART step that creates a horizontal bar chart with MODEL as the chart variable. Use the

- SUMVAR= option to specify that the values of AGE are to be used in the calculation
- TYPE= option to designate MEAN as the calculated statistic.

```
proc gchart data=work.aircraft;
   hbar Model / sumvar=Age type=mean;
   title 'Average Age of Aircraft Model '
         'in Service';
run;
```

84

Creating a New Variable and Reporting with Horizontal Bar Charts

File: c4s4d2.sas

Calculate the age of the aircraft and report the mean values by MODEL.

- Use an assignment statement and a SAS function to create a new variable and compute its values.
- Use the GCHART procedure and the HBAR statement with the SUMVAR= and TYPE= options to create a horizontal bar chart.

Creating a New Variable

1. Include the DATA step that was used earlier to create the temporary data set and to create the variable YRINSERVICE. Add an assignment statement to create a variable whose values represent the age of the aircraft.

```
data work.aircraft;
   infile 'aircraft.dat';
   input @1  Model $16. @18 AircraftID $6.
         @25 InService mmddyy10.
         @36 LastMaint mmddyy10.;
   YrInService=year(InService);
   Age=year(today())-YrInService;
run;
```

2. Submit the program for execution and browse the messages in the SAS log. The log

- does not contain any warnings or error messages
- indicates that WORK.AIRCRAFT was created with 216 observations and 6 variables.

Creating a Horizontal Bar Chart

1. Write a PROC GCHART step that creates a horizontal bar chart with the variable MODEL as the chart variable. Use the SUMVAR= option to specify that the values of AGE are to be used in the calculation and the TYPE= option to designate MEAN as the calculated statistic.

```
proc gchart data=work.aircraft;
   hbar Model / sumvar=Age type=mean;
   title 'Average Age of Aircraft Model in Service';
run;
quit;
```

2. Submit the program.

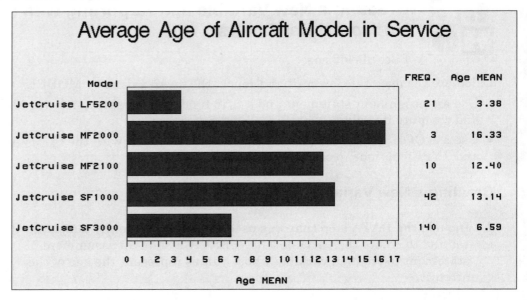

The graph

- contains a bar for each aircraft model
- indicates the number of airplanes in service for a particular model
- indicates the mean age for each aircraft model in service.

The average age of JetCruise Model LF5200 is the lowest, with an average age of 3.38 years in service and 21 aircraft flying.

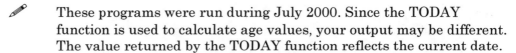 These programs were run during July 2000. Since the TODAY function is used to calculate age values, your output may be different. The value returned by the TODAY function reflects the current date.

Exercises

3. Assigning Day of the Week Values and Charting the Results

This exercise requires that you include a DATA step that is contained in a program file called SCHD2001. Use an INCLUDE command to read the file:

> **INCLUDE '_____'**

a. Include the DATA step contained in the program file. This DATA step reads in a raw data file and creates a SAS data set.

Examine the DATA step and complete the following table.

Name of the SAS data set created:	*Destination*
Name of the raw data file read:	*schd2001.dat*
Number of variables in the SAS data set	*7*
Names of the character variables in the SAS data set:	*4*
Names of the numeric variables in the SAS data set:	*1*
Name of the informat used to read in the DATE variable:	*1*
Name of the informat used to read in the DISTANCE variable:	*1*

b. When you have completed the table, submit the DATA step. Examine the log. Are there any errors?

c. Create a vertical bar chart of the resulting data set that displays the frequency of the values of the scheduled flight date. Display the values in this format: JAN2001. Use the DISCRETE option to produce the following chart.

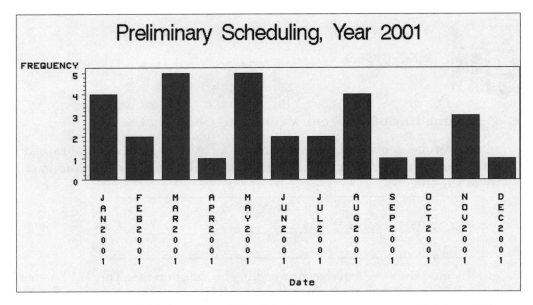

d. Recall the DATA step and modify it to create a new variable called DAYOFWEEK. The value of DAYOFWEEK should be equal to the day of the week for the scheduled flight.

e. Examine the data portion of the data set to make sure the new variable was created.

Partial SAS Output

Obs	Flight ID	RouteID	Origin	Destination	Tot Pass Cap	Date	Distance	Day Of Week
				WORK.DESTINATION				
1	IA03502	0000035	RDU	BNA	150	15028	453	5
2	IA01101	0000011	RDU	ORD	150	15296	645	7
3	IA00901	0000009	RDU	LAX	267	15035	2255	5
4	IA03700	0000037	RDU	MSY	150	15283	779	1
5	IA02302	0000023	RDU	BHM	150	15058	488	7
6	IA01901	0000019	RDU	BOS	150	15203	615	5

f. Recall the PROC GCHART step and modify it to create a vertical bar chart that displays the frequency of the day of the week for the scheduled flight. Make sure there is a bar for each day of the week.

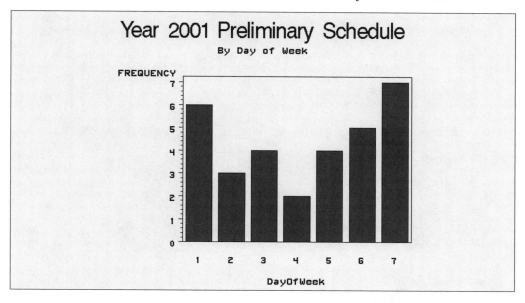

g. Recall the previous GCHART step and modify it to create the chart, below. Use the appropriate options on the VBAR statement to set the height of each bar equal to the sum of total passenger capacity for each day of the week. Assign an appropriate title.

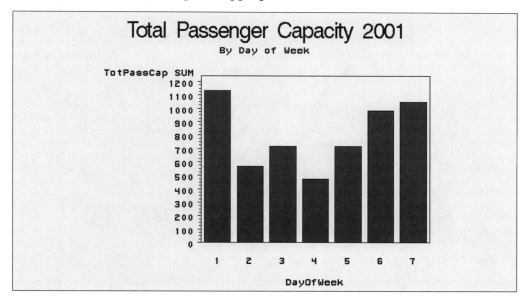

4.5   Subsetting Data Rows from a Raw Data File

Objectives

- Define the subsetting IF statement.
- Explain a subsetting IF expression.
- Use a subsetting IF statement to read selected rows from a raw data file based on the subsetting criteria and write them to a SAS data set.
- Use the GCHART procedure to present the subset in a horizontal bar chart.

88

Business Scenario

As part of its safety campaign, International Airlines will identify the number of carriers that have been in service 15 years or longer.

89

Business Scenario

Subset the data and report the results in a
horizontal bar chart.

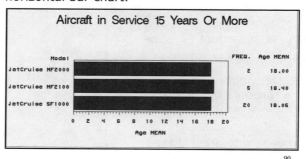

90

Selecting Rows Conditionally

You can use a subsetting IF statement to
determine which rows are written to the
SAS data set.

General form of the subsetting IF statement:

IF *expression*;

The *expression* can be any SAS expression.

91

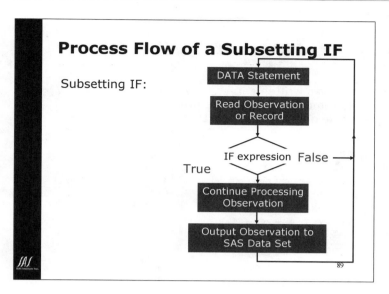

The subsetting IF statement
- returns control to the top of the DATA statement if the expression is false
- works like a gate; it enables a row to pass only when the expression is true.

Selecting Rows Conditionally

The subsetting IF statement is valid

- only in a DATA step

- when the variable that is used to select observations is

  - created from a raw data file when an INPUT statement is used

  - created by an assignment statement

  - obtained from an existing SAS data set.

93

Reading a Subset of Raw Data

Use the DATA step that was written earlier.
Add a subsetting IF statement to process only the
subset in which the value of AGE is at least 15.

```
data work.aircraft;
   infile 'aircraft.dat';
   input @1 Model $16. @18 AircraftID $6.
         @25 InService mmddyy10.
         @36 LastMaint mmddyy10.;
   YrInService=year(InService);
   Age=year(today())-YrInService;
   if Age>=15;
run;
```

9

Reading a Subset of Raw Data and Reporting the Results Graphically

File: c4s5d1.sas

Select a subset of the aircraft based on years in service and display the results in a horizontal bar chart.

- Use a subsetting IF statement to read selected rows from a raw data file and write the results to a SAS data set.
- Use the GCHART procedure and the HBAR statement with the SUMVAR= and TYPE= options to create a horizontal bar chart.

Subsetting Raw Data

1. Include the DATA step that was used earlier to create the temporary SAS data set. Add the subsetting IF statement with the desired expression.

```
data work.aircraft;
   infile 'aircraft.dat';
   input @1  Model $16. @18 AircraftID $6.
         @25 InService mmddyy10.
         @36 LastMaint mmddyy10.;
   YrInService=year(InService);
   Age=year(today())-YrInService;
   if Age>=15;
run;
```

2. Submit the program for execution and browse the log. The log

   - does not indicate any warnings or error message
   - indicates that 216 records were read
   - indicates that WORK.AIRCRAFT contains 27 observations and 6 variables.

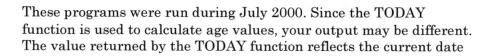 These programs were run during July 2000. Since the TODAY function is used to calculate age values, your output may be different. The value returned by the TODAY function reflects the current date

Creating a Horizontal Bar Chart

1. Write a GCHART step that creates a horizontal bar chart. Use the SUMVAR= option to specify that the values of AGE are to be used in the calculation and the TYPE= option to designate MEAN as the calculated statistic.

```
proc gchart data=work.aircraft;
   hbar Model / sumvar=Age type=mean;
      title 'Aircraft in Service 15 Years Or More';
run;
```

2. Submit the program.

    The graph shows that three different models and 27 planes have been in service an average of 15 years or more.

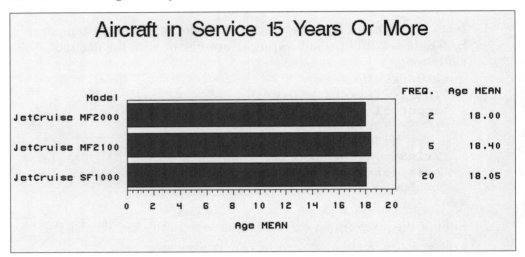

Changing the Subsetting Criteria

To cast a more positive light on the airline's aircraft, create a report that highlights the number of aircraft put into service within the last 5 years.

1. Modify the previous DATA step to include only data for aircraft that have been in service 5 years or less. Use the same PROC GCHART step to create the horizontal graph.

```
data work.aircraft;
   infile 'aircraft.dat';
   input @1  Model $16. @18 AircraftID $6.
         @25 InService mmddyy10.
         @36 LastMaint mmddyy10.;
   YrInService=year(InService);
   Age=year(today())-YrInService;
   if Age<=5;
run;

proc gchart data=work.aircraft;
   hbar Model / sumvar=Age type=mean;
   title 'Aircraft in Service 5 Years Or Less';
run;
quit;
```

2. Submit the program. The SAS log indicates that WORK.AIRCRAFT contains 76 observations and 6 variables.

    The graph shows that four different models and 76 carriers have been in service 5 years or less.

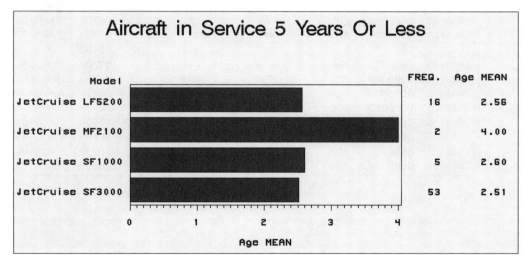

Exercises

4. Creating a Subset of Raw Data

This exercise requires that you include a DATA step that is contained in a program file called SCHEDULE. Use an INCLUDE command to read the file:

> INCLUDE '_____'

a. Include the DATA step that is contained in the program file. This DATA step reads in a raw data file and creates a SAS data set.

b. Submit this DATA step and then create a listing report. Browse the results.

Partial SAS Output

Flight Schedules							
Flight ID	RouteID	Origin	Destination	Distance	Tot Pass Cap	Cargo Cap	Date
IA06901	0000069	LHR	AMS	220	139	39700	13AUG1997
IA06903	0000069	LHR	AMS	220	139	39700	01AUG1998
IA03100	0000031	SFO	ANC	2025	267	77400	23AUG2001
IA03300	0000033	RDU	ANC	3502	207	82400	24AUG1999
IA06503	0000065	FRA	ARN	747	139	39700	10AUG2003
IA02302	0000023	RDU	BHM	488	150	36900	16AUG2003
IA02302	0000023	RDU	BHM	488	150	36900	15AUG2002
IA02305	0000023	RDU	BHM	488	150	36900	04AUG2000
IA03505	0000035	RDU	BNA	453	150	36900	06AUG2001
IA03501	0000035	RDU	BNA	453	150	36900	03AUG1999
IA03503	0000035	RDU	BNA	453	150	36900	21AUG1998
IA01904	0000019	RDU	BOS	615	150	36900	10AUG1999

c. The airline is interested in flights that travel at least 3000 miles. Recall your program and alter it to subset the raw data and write it to a temporary data set called WORK.MEDDIST. Alter the PROC PRINT to print the new data set with an appropriate title.

How many observations does this data set contain?

SAS Output

			Long Distance Flights			Tot Pass	Cargo	
Flight ID	RouteID	Origin	Destination	Distance		Cap	Cap	Date
IA03300	0000033	RDU	ANC	3502		207	82400	24AUG1999
IA07801	0000078	DXB	FRA	3024		238	105500	08AUG2002
IA08800	0000088	NBO	FRA	3945		207	82400	31AUG1999
IA07801	0000078	DXB	FRA	3024		238	105500	09AUG2002
IA10200	0000102	SYD	HKG	4608		255	105500	14AUG2001
IA10201	0000102	SYD	HKG	4608		255	105500	16AUG2002
IA11201	0000112	SFO	HND	5169		255	105500	07AUG2002
IA08301	0000083	LHR	JNB	5670		238	105500	02AUG1999
IA08700	0000087	FRA	NBO	3945		207	82400	15AUG2001
IA00400	0000004	FRA	RDU	4288		207	82400	02AUG1999
IA10101	0000101	HKG	SYD	4608		255	105500	10AUG1999

4.6 Chapter Summary

Data must be in the form of a SAS data set to be processed by many SAS procedures and some DATA step statements. You can use formatted input to read data that is stored in a fixed-field raw data file. Use an INPUT statement to read the data values by

- moving the input pointer to the starting position of the field
- specifying a column name
- specifying a SAS informat.

A SAS informat specifies the width of the input field and how to read the data values that are stored in the field.

Formatted input is appropriate for reading

- data in fixed columns
- standard and nonstandard character and numeric data
- date values and converting them to SAS date values.

You can imbed lines of data in a DATA step by

- placing the DATALINES statement after the last statement in the DATA step
- following the statement with rows of data
- ending with a RUN statement on a line alone.

Date values that are stored as SAS dates are special numeric values. A SAS date value is interpreted as the number of days between January 1, 1960, and a specific date. SAS uses date informats to **read** and convert dates to SAS date values. SAS uses formats to **write** values from columns that represent dates.

Use an assignment statement in the DATA step to create a new variable or to **modify** the values of an **existing** variable. Operators for basic arithmetic calculations in an assignment statement include the following:

- + (addition)
- − (subtraction)
- * (multiplication)
- / (division)
- ** (exponentiation)
- − (negative prefix).

You can also use a SAS function in an assignment statement to create a new variable. A SAS function is a routine that returns a value that is determined from specified arguments. SAS functions

- perform arithmetic operations
- compute statistics
- manipulate SAS dates and process character values.

For example, the YEAR function extracts a four-digit year value from a SAS date. The TODAY function obtains the current date from the system clock.

Use a subsetting IF statement in the DATA step to determine which rows from a raw data file are written to a SAS data set. The subsetting IF statement

- returns control to the top of the DATA statement if the expression is false
- works like a gate: it allows a row to pass only when the expression is true.

You can use the GCHART procedure to create presentation-quality graphs and charts. The GCHART procedure summarizes data and depicts the summarized information as

- bars within a vertical or horizontal bar chart
- blocks within a three-dimensional block chart
- slices within a pie chart
- spines or slices within a star chart.

Use the VBAR statement to create a vertical bar chart and the HBAR statement to create a horizontal bar chart.

You can use the TYPE= option on the VBAR and HBAR statements to specify the statistic to be calculated. Valid values include FREQ (the default), CFREQ, PERCENT, CPERCENT, SUM, and MEAN.

Use the SUMVAR= option to specify the numeric variable to be used for sum or mean calculations. The default statistic is SUM when the SUMVAR= option is used and the TYPE= option is omitted.

Use the DISCRETE option with the VBAR or HBAR statement to create a separate bar for each discrete value of a numeric chart variable.

General form of the INPUT statement with formatted input:

> **INPUT** *pointer-control variable informat ...;*

General form of an informat:

> *$informat-namew.d*

General form of a PROC GCHART step:

> **PROC GCHART** DATA=*SAS-data-set;*
>   **HBAR | VBAR | PIE** *chart-variable(s)*
>   *</option(s)>;*
> **RUN;**
> **QUIT;**

General form of the DATALINES statement:

> **DATALINES;**

General form of an assignment statement:

> *variable = expression;*

General form of a SAS function:

> *function-name(argument1,argument2, …)*

General form of the subsetting IF statement:

> **IF** *expression;*

4.7 Solutions

1. Reading a Raw Data File with Formatted Input

a. Fill out the table as follows:

Field Description	Character or numeric?	Starting Column	Informat
Date of hire	numeric	1	DATE9.
Last name	character	10	$16.
First name	character	26	$14.
Employee location	character	40	$10.
Telephone number	character	50	$4.
Employee number	character	55	$6.
Job code	character	62	$6.
Annual salary	numeric	68	comma7.

b. Write and submit the following DATA step program:

```
data work.employee;
   infile 'employe1.dat';
   input @1   HireDate date9.
         @10  LastName $16.
         @26  FirstName $14.
         @40  Location $10.
         @50  Phone $4.
         @55  EmpID $6.
         @62  JobCode $6.
         @68  Salary comma7.;
run;
```

In the raw data file, row 23 contains an invalid value for SALARY and row 59 contains an invalid value for HIREDATE.

c.

```
proc contents data=work.employee;
   title;
run;
```

d.

```
proc print data=work.employee;
   title 'Employee Database';
run;
```

These HIREDATE values represent SAS date values.

e.

```
proc print data=work.employee;
   format hiredate mmddyy10.;
   title 'Employee Database';
run;
```

The invalid data value for HIREDATE is represented as a missing value.

f.

```
data work.test;
   input @1   HireDate date9.
         @10  LastName $16.
         @26  FirstName $14.
         @40  Location $10.
         @50  Phone $4.
         @55  EmpID $6.
         @62  JobCode $6.
         @68  Salary comma7.;
datalines;
06SEP1993HOLLEMAN        JOHN W        CARY       1937
E03009 PILOT2$43,000
17MAR1981CAVILL          RODNEY        SYDNEY     1012
E03018 FINCLK$17,000
08MAY1982SEMMLER         BARBARA       FRANKFURT 1132
E03102 PILOT1$64,000
run;
proc print data=work.test;
   title 'Employee Database';
run;
```

The data lines will appear as single lines in your Program Editor. The lines are wrapped in the course notes because of the constraints of the page margins.

2. Creating Vertical and Horizontal Bar Charts

   a. Fill out the table as follows:

Name of the SAS data set created:	WORK.SCHEDULE
Name of the raw data file read:	schedule.dat
Number of variables in the SAS data set:	8
Names of the character variables in the SAS data set:	FLIGHTID ROUTEID DESTINATION ORIGIN
Names of the numeric variables in the SAS data set:	DISTANCE TOTPASSCAP CARGOCAP DATE
Name of the informat used to read in the DATE variable:	MMDDYY10.
Name of the informat used to read in the CARGOCAP variable:	COMMA8.

   b. The SAS log contains no errors.

c.

```
proc contents data=work.schedule;
    title;
run;
```

Partial SAS Output

```
                    The CONTENTS Procedure

Data Set Name: WORK.SCHEDULE        Observations:          200
Member Type:   DATA                 Variables:             8
Engine:        V8                   Indexes:               0
Created:       15:40 Monday, July 17, 2000   Observation Length:  56
Last Modified: 15:40 Monday, July 17, 2000   Deleted Observations: 0
Protection:                         Compressed:            NO
Data Set Type:                      Sorted:                NO
Label:


        -----Alphabetic List of Variables and Attributes-----


        #     Variable        Type     Len     Pos

        7     CargoCap        Num       8       16
        8     Date            Num       8       24
        4     Destination     Char      3       49
        5     Distance        Num       8        0
        1     FlightID        Char      7       32
        3     Origin          Char      3       46
        2     RouteID         Char      7       39
        6     TotPassCap      Num       8        8
```

d.

```
proc print data=work.schedule;
run;
```

Partial SAS Output

Obs	Flight ID	RouteID	Origin	Destination	Distance	Tot Pass Cap	Cargo Cap	Date
1	IA06901	0000069	LHR	AMS	220	139	39700	13739
2	IA06903	0000069	LHR	AMS	220	139	39700	14092
3	IA03100	0000031	SFO	ANC	2025	267	77400	15210
4	IA03300	0000033	RDU	ANC	3502	207	82400	14480
5	IA06503	0000065	FRA	ARN	747	139	39700	15927
6	IA02302	0000023	RDU	BHM	488	150	36900	15933
7	IA02302	0000023	RDU	BHM	488	150	36900	15567
8	IA02305	0000023	RDU	BHM	488	150	36900	14826
9	IA03505	0000035	RDU	BNA	453	150	36900	15193
10	IA03501	0000035	RDU	BNA	453	150	36900	14459
11	IA03503	0000035	RDU	BNA	453	150	36900	14112
12	IA01904	0000019	RDU	BOS	615	150	36900	13736
13	IA01905	0000019	RDU	BOS	615	150	36900	15927

e.

```
proc gchart data=work.schedule;
   format Date date9.;
   vbar Date;
   title 'Scheduled Flight Dates';
run;
quit;
```

Each vertical bar represents how many flights are scheduled during a range of dates, with the midpoints labeled on the graph.

f.

```
proc gchart data=work.schedule;
   format Date date9.;
   hbar Date;
run;
quit;
```

The horizontal bar includes the additional statistics.

3. Assigning Day of the Week Values and Charting the Results

a. Fill out the table as follows:

Name of the SAS data set created:	WORK.DESTINATION
Name of the raw data file read:	schd2001.dat
Number of variables in the SAS data set:	7
Names of the character variables in the SAS data set:	FLIGHTID ROUTEID ORIGIN DESTINATION
Names of the numeric variables in the SAS data set:	TOTPASSCAP DATE DISTANCE
Name of the informat used to read in the DATE variable:	DATE9.
Name of the informat used to read in the DISTANCE variable:	COMMA6.

b. The SAS log contains no errors.

c.

```
proc gchart data=work.destination;
   format Date monyy7.;
   vbar Date / discrete;
   title 'Preliminary Scheduling, Year 2001';
run;
quit;
```

d.

```
data work.destination;
   infile 'schd2001.dat';
   input @1  FlightID $7.
         @9  RouteID $7.
         @16 Origin $3.
         @19 Destination $3.
         @22 TotPassCap 3.
         @26 Date date9.
         @35 Distance comma6.;
   DayOfWeek=weekday(Date);
run;
```

e.

```
proc print data=work.destination;
   title 'WORK.DESTINATION';
run;
```

f.

```
proc gchart data=work.destination;
   format Date monyy7.;
   vbar DayOfWeek / discrete;
   title 'Year 2001 Preliminary Schedule';
   title2 'By Day of Week';
run;
quit;
```

g.

```
proc gchart data=work.destination;
   format Date monyy7.;
   vbar DayOfWeek / discrete sumvar=TotPassCap
                    type=sum;
   title 'Total Passenger Capacity 2001';
   title2 'By Day of Week';
run;
quit;
```

4. Creating a Subset of Raw Data

d.

```
data work.schedule;
   infile 'schedule.dat';
   input @1  FlightID $7.
         @9  RouteID  $7.
         @16 Origin $3.
         @20 Destination $3.
         @23 Distance comma5.
         @29 TotPassCap 3.
         @33 CargoCap comma8.
         @42 Date mmddyy10.;
   format Date date9.;
run;
```

e.

```
proc print data=work.schedule noobs;
   title 'Flight Schedules';
run;
```

f. .

```
data work.meddist;
   infile 'schedule.dat';
   input @1  FlightID $7.
         @9  RouteID  $7.
         @16 Origin $3.
         @20 Destination $3.
         @23 Distance comma5.
         @29 TotPassCap 3.
         @33 CargoCap comma8.
         @42 Date mmddyy10.;
   format Date date9.;
   if Distance ge 3000;
run;

proc print data=work.meddist noobs;
   title 'Long Distance Flights';
run;
```

WORK.MEDDIST contains 11 observations.

Chapter 5   Reading and Manipulating SAS® Data Sets and Creating Detailed Reports

5.1 Introduction

Business Scenario

International Airlines wants to analyze the capacity of its planes.

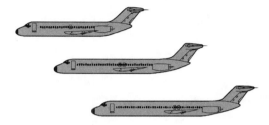

3

Business Scenario

The airline must

- write the relevant aircraft data to a SAS data set so that it can be processed further
- determine the minimum, maximum, and average passenger capacity of the planes
- assign each plane a size (small, medium, or large) based on passenger capacity, and the appropriate maximum flight range

continued...

4

Business Scenario

- determine the number of small, medium, and large planes
- determine the minimum, maximum, and average passenger capacity for each plane size
- create an enhanced report that lists all of the planes.

5

The SAS Data Set

Partial SAS Data Set

Model	AircraftID	FClassCap	BClassCap	EClassCap	InService
MF4000	010012	16	.	251	10890
LF5200	030006	14	30	163	10300
LF5200	030008	14	30	163	11389
LF5200	030015	14	30	163	12229
LF5200	030016	14	30	163	12746
LF5200	030025	14	30	163	10885
LF5200	030027	14	30	163	11354

6

Creating a Subset of a SAS Data Set

Model	AircraftID	FClassCap	BClassCap	EClassCap	InService
MF4000	010012	16	.	251	10890
LF5200	030006	14	30	163	10300
LF5200	030008	14	30	163	11389

New Variable

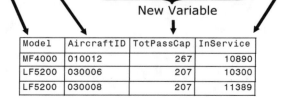

Model	AircraftID	TotPassCap	InService
MF4000	010012	267	10890
LF5200	030006	207	10300
LF5200	030008	207	11389

7

Calculating Summary Statistics for All Planes

Model	AircraftID	InService	TotPassCap
MF4000	010012	10890	267
LF5200	030006	10300	207
LF5200	030008	11389	207

```
                  The MEANS Procedure

              Analysis Variable : TotPassCap

  N        Mean        Std Dev      Minimum      Maximum

 64       163.47         47.22        97.00       290.00
```

8

Creating a New Variable Using Conditional Processing

Model	AircraftID	InService	TotPassCap	Size
LF5100	040010	10975	165	Medium
LF8100	100002	12757	255	Large
MF4000	010012	10890	267	Large
SF3000	130010	11433	139	Medium
SF7000	080003	11833	97	Small

9

Calculating Summary Statistics for Each Type of Plane

```
                  The MEANS Procedure
              Analysis Variable : TotPassCap

         N
Size    Obs    N    Mean   Std Dev    Minimum     Maximum

Large    16   16  230.13    32.39     207.00      290.00
Medium    9    9  178.56    11.40     165.00      188.00
Small    39   39  132.64    18.85      97.00      150.00
```

10

Creating an Enhanced List Report

```
                                   In      Total
Aircraft                 Aircraft  Service  Passenger
  Size    Aircraft Model    ID       Date    Capacity
  Small   JetCruise SF1000  070013  08/29/1976    150
          JetCruise SF1000  070017  12/26/1968    150
          JetCruise SF1000  070026  10/10/1985    150
          JetCruise SF1000  070032  02/25/1983    150
          JetCruise SF1000  070035  10/02/1983    150
          JetCruise SF1000  070040  04/29/1989    150
```

11

5.2   Creating a SAS Data Set

Objectives

- Create a SAS data set using another SAS data set as input.
- Read and create permanent SAS data sets.
- Select variables to store in a SAS data set.

13

Reading a SAS Data Set

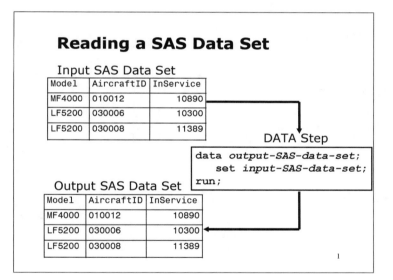

Input SAS Data Set

Model	AircraftID	InService
MF4000	010012	10890
LF5200	030006	10300
LF5200	030008	11389

DATA Step

```
data output-SAS-data-set;
   set input-SAS-data-set;
run;
```

Output SAS Data Set

Model	AircraftID	InService
MF4000	010012	10890
LF5200	030006	10300
LF5200	030008	11389

1

Reading a SAS Data Set

In order to create a SAS data set using a SAS data set as input, you must

- start a DATA step and name the SAS data set being created (DATA statement)
- identify the input SAS data set (SET statement).

1

The INFILE and INPUT statements are used to read external files. The SET statement is used to read SAS data sets.

Reading a SAS Data Set

General form of a DATA step:

```
DATA SAS-data-set;
    SET SAS-data-set;
    additional SAS statements
RUN;
```

Example:

```
data ia.aircraftcap;
    set ia.aircraftdata;
run;
```

16

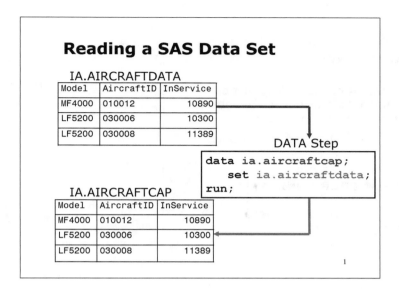

The DATA statement serves as the beginning of the DATA step and identifies
IA.AIRCRAFTCAP as the output data set. The SET statement instructs the
DATA step to read from IA.AIRCRAFTDATA.

Reading a SAS Data Set

By default, the SET statement reads

- all of the observations from the input
  SAS data set

- all of the variables from the input
  SAS data set.

1

Selecting Variables to Store in a SAS Data Set

You can use a DROP= or KEEP= data set option in a DATA statement to control what variables are **written to** the new SAS data set.

General form of the DROP= and KEEP= data set options:

> *SAS-data-set*(**DROP=***variables*)
> or
> *SAS-data-set*(**KEEP=***variables*)

1

Use the DROP= data set option to specify the variables that are not to be written to the output data set. Use the KEEP= data set option to specify the variables that are to be written to the output data set.

 As a time-saver, use the option that requires the least amount of typing. You never use both options; they are mutually exclusive.

Selecting Variables to Store in a SAS Data Set

General form of the DROP= and KEEP= data set options in a DATA statement:

> **DATA** *output-SAS-data-set*(KEEP=*variables*);
> **SET** *input-SAS-data-set*;
> **RUN;**

Example:
```
data ia.aircraftcap(keep=Model AircraftID InService);
   set ia.aircraftdata;
run;
```

20

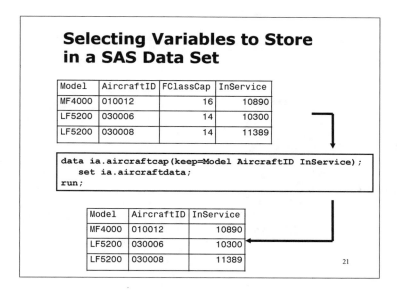

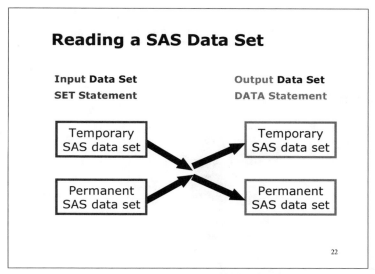

You can use the DATA step to read and write any combination of temporary and permanent SAS data sets.

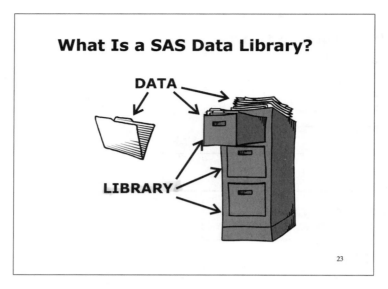

Each SAS file resides in a SAS data library.

A *SAS data library* is a collection of SAS files that are recognized as a unit by the SAS System.

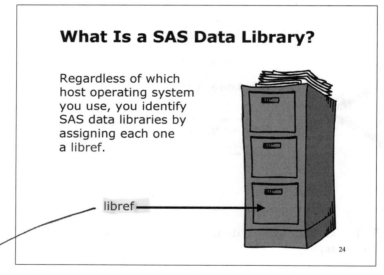

8 Characters or less

The *libref* is a nickname for the physical location of the SAS data library.

What Is a SAS Data Library?

By default, SAS creates
two SAS data libraries:

- a temporary library
  called WORK

- a permanent library
  called SASUSER.

25

The temporary SAS data library WORK is

- assigned the libref WORK
- deleted at the end of your SAS session or job.

What Is a SAS Data Library?

Host Operating System	SAS Data Library Organized As
directory-based	directory
OS/390	specially formatted operating system file

26

Assigning a Libref

You can use the LIBNAME statement to assign a libref to a SAS data library.

General form of the LIBNAME statement:

> **LIBNAME** *libref 'SAS-data-library'* *<options>*;

Example:
Windows

```
libname mydata 'c:\company\datalib';
```

27

Assigning a Libref

More examples:

UNIX
```
libname mydata '/users/company/datalib';
```

OS/390
```
libname mydata 'edc.company.datalib';
```

Selected option:

DISP=OLD|SHR   specifies the disposition of the file. The default is OLD.

28

 A disposition of SHR allows you and others simultaneous read-only access to the data library. This is adequate for browsing, reporting, and so on. A disposition of OLD, the default value of this option, gives you exclusive read-write access to the library. Exclusive access is required to create, delete, or update data sets.

Assigning a Libref

```
libname ia 'SAS-data-library';
```

IA

Must be created before defining in SAS

29

The LIBNAME statement is a global SAS statement. It is not part of a DATA or PROC step.

By default, the libref remains assigned until the end of your SAS session or job.

 Each time you start a SAS session or job, you must reassign a libref to the host operating system name for **each** SAS data library that will be accessed.

You cannot use an operating system editor to edit a file stored in a SAS data library.

What Is a SAS Filename?

General form of a SAS filename:

libref.SAS-data-set-name

libref   refers to the SAS data
                      library (library reference).

SAS-data-set-name   refers to a SAS data set
                      in the library.

30

What Is a SAS Filename?

The data set
EMPLOYEE is a SAS
file in the IA
data library.

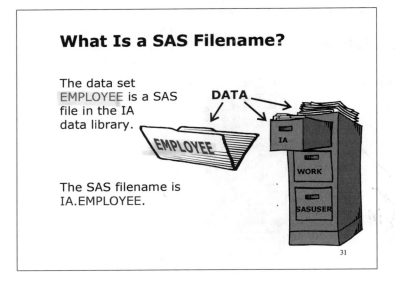

The SAS filename is
IA.EMPLOYEE.

31

What Is a SAS Filename?

The libref WORK can be omitted when you
refer to a file in the WORK library.

Example:

```
work.employee <-----> employee
```

32

Examining a SAS Data Library

Generate a listing of
all SAS files in a SAS
data library.

33

Examining a SAS Data Library

General form of the CONTENTS procedure to access the contents of a data library:

```
PROC CONTENTS DATA=libref._ALL_  NODS;
RUN;
```

ALL   requests a listing of all the files in the library

NODS   suppresses the printing of detailed information about each file.

34

Name of Data Set

*Blank before NODS
Says it is a sas request, not
name of a file*

Examining the IA Data Library

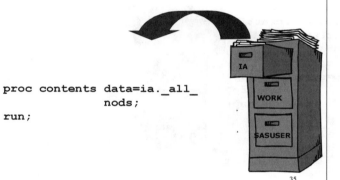

```
proc contents data=ia._all_
               nods;
run;
```

35

Reading and Creating Permanent SAS Data Sets

```
data ia.aircraftcap
     (keep=Model AircraftID
           InService);
   set ia.aircraftdata;
run;
```

3

Creating a New Column

The SUM function adds the values of the arguments and ignores missing values.

General form of the SUM function to create a new variable:

$$variable = \textbf{SUM}(argument1, argument2);$$

variable   variable you want to create

argument   variables, literals, or expressions to be summed.

3

Reading and Creating Permanent SAS Data Sets

```
data ia.aircraftcap
     (keep=Model AircraftID
           TotPassCap
           InService);
  set ia.aircraftdata;
  TotPassCap=sum(FClassCap,
                 BClassCap,
                 EClassCap);
run;
```

3

Assigning Librefs, Examining a SAS Data Library, and Creating a SAS Data Set Using Another SAS Data Set as Input

File: c5s2d1.sas

- Use the LIBNAME statement to assign the IA libref to the appropriate SAS data library.
- Use the CONTENTS procedure to examine the contents of the IA data library.
- Use the CONTENTS procedure to examine the descriptor portion of the IA.AIRCRAFTDATA input data set.
- Use the DATA step to read from a permanent SAS data set and create a new permanent SAS data set.

Assigning a Libref

1. Assign the IA libref to the permanent SAS library where the International Airlines data sets are stored.

   Windows:
   ```
   libname ia '.';
   ```

   UNIX:
   ```
   libname ia '.';
   ```

   OS/390:
   ```
   libname ia '.prog1.sasdata';
   ```

   SAS Log
   ```
   1     libname ia 'c:\workshop\winsas\prog1';
   NOTE: Libref IA was successfully assigned as follows:
         Engine:        V8
         Physical Name: c:\ workshop\winsas\prog1
   ```

Examining Contents of a SAS Data Library

1. Examine the contents of the IA SAS data library using PROC CONTENTS.
   ```
   proc contents data=ia._all_ nods;
      title 'IA Library Contents';
   run;
   ```

   Partial SAS Output
   ```
                        IA Library Contents

                      The CONTENTS Procedure

                      -----Directory-----

              Libref:        IA
   ```

```
            Engine:          V8
            Physical Name: C:\workshop\winsas\prog1
            File Name:      C:\workshop\winsas\prog1


                             File
      #  Name          Memtype size  Last modified

      1  AIRCRAFTDATA  DATA    9216  10JUL2000:11:03:39
      2  AIRPLANES     DATA    25600 10JUL2000:13:38:29
      3  AIRPLANESMF   DATA    25600 10JUL2000:13:38:36
```

2. Display the descriptor portion of the input SAS data set.

```
proc contents data=ia.aircraftdata;
   title 'IA.AIRCRAFTDATA Contents';
run;
```

Partial SAS Output

```
     -----Alphabetic List of Variables and Attributes-----

      #     Variable   Type   Len   Pos   Format   Informat

      2     AircraftID Char    6    76    $6.      $6.
      4     BClassCap  Num     8     8    8.       8.
      6     CargoCap   Num     8    24    8.       8.
      5     EClassCap  Num     8    16    8.       8.
      3     FClassCap  Num     8     0    8.       8.
      7     InService  Num     8    32    8.       8.
      8     LastMaint  Num     8    40    8.       8.
      1     Model      Char   20    56    $20.     $20.
      9     Speed      Num     8    48
```

Creating a New SAS Data Set

1. Read the permanent SAS data set, keep only the desired variables, and create a new variable that is the total of all passenger capacities.

```
data ia.aircraftcap(keep=Model AircraftID TotPassCap
                         InService);
   set ia.aircraftdata;
   TotPassCap=sum(FClassCap,BClassCap,EClassCap);
run;
```

 Instead of using the KEEP= data set option on the DATA statement, you can use the DROP= data set option. The syntax for this example is

```
data ia.aircraft(drop=FClassCap BClassCap EClassCap
                      CargoCap LastMaint Speed);
```

Partial SAS Log

```
116  data ia.aircraftcap(keep=Model AircraftID TotPassCap
117                      InService);
118     set ia.aircraftdata;
119     TotPassCap=sum(FClassCap,BClassCap,EClassCap);
```

```
120  run;

NOTE: There were 64 observations read from the dataset IA.AIRCRAFTDATA.
NOTE: The data set IA.AIRCRAFTCAP has 64 observations and 4 variables.
```

2. Examine the descriptor portion of the new SAS data set.

```
proc contents data=ia.aircraftcap;
    title 'IA.AIRCRAFTCAP Contents';
run;
```

Partial SAS Output

```
        -----Alphabetic List of Variables and Attributes-----

           #    Variable     Type    Len   Pos    Format
Informat


           2    AircraftID   Char     6    36     $6.      $6.
           3    InService    Num      8     0     8.       8.
           1    Model        Char    20    16     $20.     $20.
           4    TotPassCap   Num      8     8
```

3. Examine the data portion of the new SAS data set.

```
proc print data=ia.aircraftcap;
   title 'IA.AIRCRAFTCAP Listing';
run;
```

Partial SAS Output

```
                        IA.AIRCRAFTCAP Listing

                                                         Tot
                                    Aircraft      In    Pass
      Obs    Model                     ID      Service   Cap

        1    JetCruise MF4000        010012     10890    267
        2    JetCruise LF5200        030006     10300    207
        3    JetCruise LF5200        030008     11389    207
        4    JetCruise LF5200        030015     12229    207
        5    JetCruise LF5200        030016     12746    207
        6    JetCruise LF5200        030025     10885    207
        7    JetCruise LF5200        030027     11354    207
        8    JetCruise LF5200        030028     10483    207
        9    JetCruise LF5200        030031     12576    207
       10    JetCruise LF5200        030037     10546    207
       11    JetCruise LF5200        030041     11670    207
       12    JetCruise LF5100        040008     10655    165
       13    JetCruise LF5100        040010     10975    165
       14    JetCruise LF5100        040022     11012    165
       15    JetCruise LF5000        050001     12851    172
       16    JetCruise MF6000        060002     11322    188
```

Exercises

1. **Making Data Sets Available to the System**

   a. Issue a LIBNAME statement to make the airline data sets available to your SAS session:

      libname ia '_____**';**

      Use the LOG window to confirm that the libref IA was successfully assigned.

      Issue a null TITLE statement to clear any existing titles.

   b. Use the CONTENTS procedure to view the available data sets in the IA library. Based on the data set names listed in the resulting report, which data sets appear to contain schedule data?

      Hint: Use the NODS option to avoid printing the individual contents of each data set.

   c. Look specifically at the information pertaining to the IA.FROMRDUSCHEDULE data set. What are the name, type, and length of each variable in the data set?

Name	Type	Length

2. Creating a List Report of Flights

a. Use the IA.FROMRDUSCHEDULE data set to create a new data set named WORK.FROMRDUSHORT with the following characteristics:

- WORK.FROMRDUSHORT should contain a new variable DURATION that stores the length of the flight in **minutes**.

  Hint: A SAS time value is the number of seconds that have elapsed since midnight of the current day. Therefore, DURATION will represent the number of seconds between two SAS time values. To convert DURATION from seconds to minutes, you must divide the difference between the two SAS time values by 60.

- Use a subsetting IF statement to ensure that WORK.FROMRDUSHORT contains only those observations that pertain to flights less than two hours (120 minutes) long.

- WORK.FROMRDUSHORT should contain only the variables AIRCRAFTID, FLIGHTID, ORIGIN, DESTINATION, DEPARTTIME, DURATION, and DATE.

  🖉 The arrival time is unnecessary because the departure time and length of the flight will be stored in WORK.FROMRDUSHORT.

b. Use PROC PRINT to produce a list report of WORK.FROMRDUSHORT. Create and display an appropriate label for DURATION, and use the appropriate format to display the values of DATE in the form Friday, January 1, 1960.

3. Working with Functions (Optional)

In the previously created report, the values of DURATION contain decimal places.

Using the Help facility, find a SAS function that takes a numeric argument and returns the largest integer that is less than or equal to the argument.

Use this function in the expression that assigns the value of DURATION, and eliminate the decimal places from the value.

Use PROC PRINT to verify the modifications.

5.3   Calculating Simple Descriptive Statistics

Objectives

- Generate simple descriptive statistics using the MEANS procedure.
- Restrict the variables processed by the MEANS procedure using the VAR statement.
- Group observations of a SAS data set for analysis using the CLASS statement in the MEANS procedure.

Business Scenario

International Airlines wants to determine the minimum, maximum, and average passenger capacity of its planes.

Minimum capacity:	97.00
Maximum capacity:	290.00
Average capacity:	163.47

3

Calculating Summary Statistics

The MEANS procedure displays simple descriptive statistics for the numeric variables in a SAS data set.

General form of a simple PROC MEANS step:

PROC MEANS DATA=*SAS-data-set*;
RUN;

Example:

```
proc means data=ia.aircraftcap;
run;
```

Calculating Summary Statistics

Model	AircraftID	InService	TotPassCap
MF4000	010012	10890	267
LF5200	030006	10300	207
LF5200	030008	11389	207

```
proc means data=ia.aircraftcap;
run;
```

```
                    The MEANS Procedure

Variable      N         Mean      Std Dev      Minimum      Maximum
────────────────────────────────────────────────────────────────────
InService    64      10647.97      1966.95      3282.00      13125.00
TotPassCap   64   163.4687500   47.2208485   97.0000000   290.0000000
```

5

Calculating Summary Statistics

By default, PROC MEANS

- analyzes every numeric variable in the SAS data set
- prints the statistics N, MEAN, STD, MIN, and MAX
- excludes missing values before calculating statistics.

Default statistics are

N   number of rows with nonmissing values

MEAN   arithmetic mean (or average)

STD   standard deviation

MIN   minimum value

MAX   maximum value.

Selecting Variables

The VAR statement restricts the variables processed by PROC MEANS. Variables that are included in the statistical analysis are listed in the VAR statement.

General form of the VAR statement:

VAR *SAS-variables*;

Selecting Variables

General form of the VAR statement in a
PROC MEANS step:

PROC MEANS DATA=*SAS-data-set*;
    VAR *variables*;
RUN;

Example:

```
proc means data=ia.aircraftcap;
   var TotPassCap;
run;
```

Selecting Variables

Model	AircraftID	InService	TotPassCap
MF4000	010012	10890	267
LF5200	030006	10300	207
LF5200	030008	11389	207

```
proc means data=ia.aircraftcap;
   var TotPassCap;
run;
```

```
                  The MEANS Procedure

              Analysis Variable : TotPassCap

   N        Mean       Std Dev       Minimum       Maximum
  ─────────────────────────────────────────────────────────
  64    163.4687500   47.2208485   97.0000000   290.0000000
  ─────────────────────────────────────────────────────────
```

The MAXDEC= Option

The PROC MEANS statement option MAXDEC=
gives the maximum number of decimal places for
PROC MEANS to use in printing results.

General form of PROC MEANS with the MAXDEC=
option:

PROC MEANS DATA=*SAS-data-set*
             MAXDEC=*number*;
RUN;

5

The MAXDEC= Option

Model	AircraftID	InService	TotPassCap
MF4000	010012	10890	267
LF5200	030006	10300	207
LF5200	030008	11389	207

```
proc means data=ia.aircraftcap maxdec=2;
  var TotPassCap;
run;
```

```
                  The MEANS Procedure

             Analysis Variable : TotPassCap

    N        Mean       Std Dev      Minimum      Maximum

   64       163.47        47.22        97.00       290.00
```

5

Grouping Observations

The CLASS statement in the MEANS procedure
groups the observations of the SAS data set for
analysis.

General form of the CLASS statement:

CLASS *SAS-variables*;

5

Grouping Observations

General form of a CLASS statement in a
PROC MEANS step:

PROC MEANS DATA=*SAS-data-set*;
    CLASS *SAS-variables*;
RUN;

Example:

```
proc means data=ia.aircraftcap;
   class Model;
run;
```

53

Grouping Observations

Model	AircraftID	InService	TotPassCap
MF4000	010012	10890	267
LF5200	030006	10300	207
LF5200	030008	11389	207

```
proc means data=ia.aircraftcap maxdec=2;
   var TotPassCap;
   class Model;
run;
```

continued...

5

Grouping Observations

Partial SAS Output

```
              The MEANS Procedure

         Analysis Variable : TotPassCap

            N
Model     Obs    N     Mean   Std Dev   Minimum   Maximum

LF5000      1    1   172.00         .    172.00    172.00
LF5100      3    3   165.00         0    165.00    165.00
LF5200     10   10   207.00         0    207.00    207.00
LF8100      3    3   255.00         0    255.00    255.00
MF2000      2    2   290.00         0    290.00    290.00
```

55

Creating Simple Descriptive Statistical Reports

File: c5s3d1.sas

Use the MEANS procedure to calculate default statistics.

- Use the VAR statement to select which variables to analyze.
- Use the MAXDEC= option to limit the number of decimal places in the displayed statistics to 2.
- Use the CLASS statement to group the observations in the data set by MODEL for analysis.

1. Create a default statistical report using PROC MEANS.

```
proc means data=ia.aircraftcap;
    title 'Passenger Capacities Analysis';
run;
```

SAS Output

```
                  Passenger Capacities Analysis

                       The MEANS Procedure

Variable      N          Mean        Std Dev       Minimum        Maximum

InService    64      10647.97       1966.95       3282.00       13125.00
TotPassCap   64     163.4687500    47.2208485    97.0000000    290.0000000
```

2. Create a statistical report and analyze only the TOTPASSCAP variable.

```
proc means data=ia.aircraftcap;
    var TotPassCap;
run;
```

SAS Output

```
                  Passenger Capacities Analysis

                       The MEANS Procedure

                  Analysis Variable : TotPassCap

   N          Mean          Std Dev         Minimum         Maximum

  64      163.4687500      47.2208485      97.0000000      290.0000000
```

3. Create a statistics report, analyze only the TOTPASSCAP variable, and limit the statistics to two decimal places.

```
proc means data=ia.aircraftcap maxdec=2;
   var TotPassCap;
run;
```

SAS Output

```
                     Passenger Capacities Analysis

                        The MEANS Procedure

                   Analysis Variable : TotPassCap

     N          Mean         Std Dev        Minimum        Maximum
    ─────────────────────────────────────────────────────────────
    64        163.47           47.22          97.00         290.00
```

4. Create a statistics report that analyzes only the TOTPASSCAP variable, limit the statistics to two decimal places, and group the observations by MODEL.

```
proc means data=ia.aircraftcap maxdec=2;
   var TotPassCap;
   class Model;
run;
```

Partial SAS Output

```
                     Passenger Capacities Analysis

                        The MEANS Procedure

                   Analysis Variable : TotPassCap

                       N
    Model            Obs    N         Mean      Std Dev      Minimum
    ──────────────────────────────────────────────────────────────
    JetCruise LF5000   1    1       172.00         .          172.00
    JetCruise LF5100   3    3       165.00       0.00         165.00
    JetCruise LF5200  10   10       207.00       0.00         207.00
    JetCruise LF8100   3    3       255.00       0.00         255.00
    JetCruise MF2000   2    2       290.00       0.00         290.00
    JetCruise MF4000   1    1       267.00         .          267.00
    JetCruise MF6000   5    5       188.00       0.00         188.00
    JetCruise SF1000   8    8       150.00       0.00         150.00
    JetCruise SF3000  23   23       139.00       0.00         139.00
    JetCruise SF7000   8    8        97.00       0.00          97.00
```

Exercises

4. **Creating a Report Containing Summary Statistics about Airplanes**

   a. Generate a simple PROC MEANS report using the IA.AIRPLANES data set.

   By default, PROC MEANS reports statistics on **all** numeric variables, including those that store SAS date values. Identify the two rows on the report that contain SAS date values.

   b. Recall the program from part A. Modify it to produce a PROC MEANS report that displays statistics for the variables TOTPASSCAP, CARGOCAP, and RANGE only.

   Limit the number of decimal plasces in the output to two.

   Add the title `Summary Statistics of IA Airplanes`.

5. **Requesting Specific Statistics through PROC MEANS (Optional)**

   a. Specific statistics can be requested by listing their names in a PROC MEANS statement. For example, to request N (the frequency of non-missing values), and only N, use the following PROC MEANS step:

   ```
   proc means data=SAS-data-set-name n;
   run;
   ```

   Recall the PROC MEANS step from part **4.b.**, and alter the PROC MEANS statement to request only the minimum (MIN), maximum (MAX), and mean (MEAN) statistics for the three variables listed in part B. Change the title to `MIN, MAX, and MEAN Statistics of IA Airplanes`.

5.4 Creating Variables through Conditional Processing

Objectives

- Execute statements conditionally using IF-THEN logic.
- Control the length of character variables explicitly with the LENGTH statement.

59

Business Scenario

International Airlines wants to identify each plane as small, medium, or large based on passenger capacity.

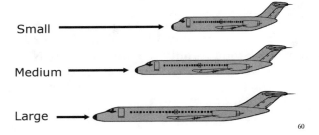

Small

Medium

Large

60

Business Scenario

International Airlines then wants to calculate descriptive statistics for each type of plane.

```
                    The MEANS Procedure

                 Analysis Variable : TotPassCap

                N
Size          Obs    N    Mean   Std Dev   Minimum   Maximum

Large          16   16  230.13    32.39    207.00    290.00
Medium          9    9  178.56    11.40    165.00    188.00
Small          39   39  132.64    18.85     97.00    150.00
```

61

Conditionally Executing Statements

General form of IF-THEN and ELSE statements:

```
IF expression THEN statement;
ELSE statement;
```

62

IF-THEN and ELSE statements are used only in the DATA step.

Only one statement can follow THEN.

The ELSE statement is optional.

Conditionally Executing Statements

Expression contains operands and operators that form a set of instructions that produce a resulting value.

Operands are

- variable names
- functions
- constants.

63

Conditionally Executing Statements

Operators are symbols that request

- a comparison
- a logical operation
- an arithmetic calculation.

64

Comparison is Case Sensitive

Conditionally Executing Statements

Example:

```
if AirportCode='JFK' then City='New York';
else if AirportCode='CDG' then
     City='Paris';
```

AirportCode		City
JFK	→	New York
CDG	→	Paris
CDG	→	Paris
JFK	→	New York

65

Conditionally Creating a New Variable

···

TotPassCap
100
207
98
188

Size

```
if TotPassCap<=150 then Size='Small';
else if 150<TotPassCap<=200 then
     Size='Medium';
  else if 200<TotPassCap then
       Size='Large';
```

66

Conditionally Creating a New Variable

···

TotPassCap
100
207
98
188

100<=150?

Size

```
if TotPassCap<=150 then Size='Small';
else if 150<TotPassCap<=200 then
     Size='Medium';
  else if 200<TotPassCap then
       Size='Large';
```

67

Conditionally Creating a New Variable

···

TotPassCap
100
207
98
188

TRUE

100<=150?

Size

```
if TotPassCap<=150 then Size='Small';
else if 150<TotPassCap<=200 then
     Size='Medium';
  else if 200<TotPassCap then
       Size='Large';
```

68

Conditionally Creating a New Variable

TotPassCap
100
207
98
188

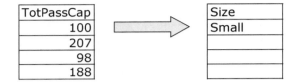

Size
Small

```
if TotPassCap<=150 then Size='Small';
else if 150<TotPassCap<=200 then
     Size='Medium';
   else if 200<TotPassCap then
       Size='Large';
```

69

Conditionally Creating a New Variable

TotPassCap
100
207
98
188

207<=150?

Size
Small

```
if TotPassCap<=150 then Size='Small';
else if 150<TotPassCap<=200 then
     Size='Medium';
   else if 200<TotPassCap then
       Size='Large';
```

70

Conditionally Creating a New Variable

TotPassCap
100
207
98
188

FALSE

207<=150?

Size
Small

```
if TotPassCap<=150 then Size='Small';
else if 150<TotPassCap<=200 then
     Size='Medium';
   else if 200<TotPassCap then
       Size='Large';
```

71

Conditionally Creating a New Variable

TotPassCap
100
207
98
188

`150<207<=200?`

Size
Small

```
if TotPassCap<=150 then Size='Small';
else if 150<TotPassCap<=200 then
     Size='Medium';
  else if 200<TotPassCap then
       Size='Large';
```

72

Conditionally Creating a New Variable

TotPassCap
100
207
98
188

FALSE

`150<207<=200?`

Size
Small

```
if TotPassCap<=150 then Size='Small';
else if 150<TotPassCap<=200 then
     Size='Medium';
  else if 200<TotPassCap then
       Size='Large';
```

73

Conditionally Creating a New Variable

TotPassCap
100
207
98
188

`200<=207?`

Size
Small

```
if TotPassCap<=150 then Size='Small';
else if 150<TotPassCap<=200 then
     Size='Medium';
  else if 200<TotPassCap then
       Size='Large';
```

74

···

Conditionally Creating a New Variable

TotPassCap
100
207
98
188

TRUE

200<=207?

Size
Small

```
if TotPassCap<=150 then Size='Small';
else if 150<TotPassCap<=200 then
    Size='Medium';
  else if 200<TotPassCap then
      Size='Large';
```

75

···

Conditionally Creating a New Variable

TotPassCap
100
207
98
188

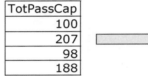

Size
Small
Large

```
if TotPassCap<=150 then Size='Small';
else if 150<TotPassCap<=200 then
    Size='Medium';
  else if 200<TotPassCap then
      Size='Large';
```

76

···

Conditionally Creating a New Variable

TotPassCap
100
207
98
188

98<=150?

Size
Small
Large

```
if TotPassCap<=150 then Size='Small';
else if 150<TotPassCap<=200 then
    Size='Medium';
  else if 200<TotPassCap then
      Size='Large';
```

77

Conditionally Creating a New Variable

...

TotPassCap
100
207
98
188

TRUE

Size
Small
Large

```
if TotPassCap<=150 then Size='Small';
else if 150<TotPassCap<=200 then
    Size='Medium';
  else if 200<TotPassCap then
      Size='Large';
```

78

Conditionally Creating a New Variable

...

TotPassCap
100
207
98
188

⟹

Size
Small
Large
Small

```
if TotPassCap<=150 then Size='Small';
else if 150<TotPassCap<=200 then
    Size='Medium';
  else if 200<TotPassCap then
      Size='Large';
```

79

Conditionally Creating a New Variable

...

TotPassCap
100
207
98
188

188<=150?

Size
Small
Large
Small

```
if TotPassCap<=150 then Size='Small';
else if 150<TotPassCap<=200 then
    Size='Medium';
  else if 200<TotPassCap then
      Size='Large';
```

80

Conditionally Creating a New Variable

TotPassCap
100
207
98
188

FALSE

$188<=150?$

Size
Small
Large
Small

```
if TotPassCap<=150 then Size='Small';
else if 150<TotPassCap<=200 then
    Size='Medium';
  else if 200<TotPassCap then
      Size='Large';
```

81

Conditionally Creating a New Variable

TotPassCap
100
207
98
188

$150<188<=200?$

Size
Small
Large
Small

```
if TotPassCap<=150 then Size='Small';
else if 150<TotPassCap<=200 then
    Size='Medium';
  else if 200<TotPassCap then
      Size='Large';
```

82

Conditionally Creating a New Variable

TotPassCap
100
207
98
188

TRUE

$150<188<=200?$

Size
Small
Large
Small

```
if TotPassCap<=150 then Size='Small';
else if 150<TotPassCap<=200 then
    Size='Medium';
  else if 200<TotPassCap then
      Size='Large';
```

83

Conditionally Creating
a New Variable

TotPassCap
100
207
98
188

Size
Small
Large
Small
Mediu

```
if TotPassCap<=150 then Size='Small';
else if 150<TotPassCap<=200 then
     Size='Medium';
  else if 200<TotPassCap then
       Size='Large';
```

84

Conditionally Executing Statements

File: c5s4d1.sas

- Use conditional logic to create a new variable.
- Examine the data portion of the new data set using PROC PRINT.
- Examine the descriptor portion of the new data set using PROC CONTENTS.

Creating a New Variable Using Conditional Logic

Create a new variable SIZE based on the values of TOTPASSCAP.

```
data ia.aircraftcap(keep=Model AircraftID
                         TotPassCap InService Size);
   set ia.aircraftdata;
   TotPassCap=sum(FClassCap,BClassCap,EClassCap);
   if TotPassCap<=150 then Size='Small';
   else if 150<TotPassCap<=200 then
         Size='Medium';
      else if 200<TotPassCap then
         Size='Large';
run;
```

Examining the Data Portion of a Data Set Using PROC PRINT

Generate a list report of the TOTPASSCAP and SIZE variables.

```
proc print data=ia.aircraftcap;
   title 'IA.AIRCRAFTCAP';
   var TotPassCap Size;
run;
```

The value for SIZE is MEDIU instead of MEDIUM.

Partial SAS Output

Obs	Tot Pass Cap	Size
	IA.AIRCRAFTCAP	
1	267	Large
2	207	Large
3	207	Large
4	207	Large
5	207	Large
6	207	Large
7	207	Large
8	207	Large
9	207	Large
10	207	Large
11	207	Large
12	165	Mediu
13	165	Mediu
14	165	Mediu
15	172	Mediu
16	188	Mediu
17	188	Mediu
18	188	Mediu
19	188	Mediu
20	188	Mediu
21	150	Small
22	150	Small
23	150	Small
24	150	Small
25	150	Small
26	150	Small
27	150	Small
28	150	Small
29	97	Small
30	97	Small

Examining the Descriptor Portion of a Data Set Using PROC CONTENTS

Examine the descriptor portion of the new SAS data set.

```
proc contents data=ia.aircraftcap;
run;
```

Notice that the length of the variable SIZE is 5.

Partial SAS Output

```
        -----Alphabetic List of Variables and Attributes-----

    #    Variable      Type    Len    Pos    Format    Informat

    2    AircraftID    Char      6     36    $6.       $6.
    3    InService     Num       8      0    8.        8.
    1    Model         Char     20     16    $20.      $20.
    5    Size          Char      5     42
    4    TotPassCap    Num       8      8
```

The LENGTH Statement

You can use the LENGTH statement to define the length of a variable explicitly.

General form of the LENGTH statement:

> **LENGTH** *variable(s)* $ *length*;

Example:

```
length Size $ 6;
```

86

The LENGTH Statement

```
data ia.aircraftcap(keep=Model AircraftID
                         TotPassCap InService Size);
   set ia.aircraftdata;
   TotPassCap=sum(FClassCap,BClassCap,EClassCap);
   length Size $ 6;
   if TotPassCap<=150 then Size='Small';
   else if 150<TotPassCap<=200 then
       Size='Medium';
     else if 200<TotPassCap then
         Size='Large';
run;
```

87

Calculating Capacity Statistics for Each Type of Plane

Model	AircraftID	InService	TotPassCap	Size
MF4000	010012	10890	267	Large
LF5200	030006	10300	207	Large
LF5200	030008	11389	207	Large

```
proc means data=ia.aircraftcap maxdec=2;
   var TotPassCap;
   class Size;
run;
```

88

Calculating Capacity Statistics for Each Type of Plane

```
                      The MEANS Procedure
                 Analysis Variable : TotPassCap

           N
Size      Obs    N     Mean   Std Dev   Minimum    Maximum

Large      16   16   230.13     32.39    207.00     290.00
Medium      9    9   178.56     11.40    165.00     188.00
Small      39   39   132.64     18.85     97.00     150.00
```

89

Explicitly Assigning a Length to a Variable and Calculating Summary Statistics

File: c5s4d2.sas

- Use a LENGTH statement to set the length of the SIZE variable explicitly.
- Use PROC CONTENTS to verify that the new length is stored in the descriptor portion of the data set.
- Use PROC MEANS to calculate capacity statistics for each type of plane.

1. Define the length of the new variable SIZE to be 6.

```
data ia.aircraftcap(keep=Model AircraftID
                         TotPassCap InService Size);
   set ia.aircraftdata;
   TotPassCap=sum(FClassCap,BClassCap,EClassCap);
   length size $ 6;
   if TotPassCap<=150 then Size='Small';
   else if 150<TotPassCap<200 then
        Size='Medium';
      else if 200<TotPassCap then
           Size='Large';
run;
```

✎ The SIZE variable has been added to the KEEP= data set option.

2. Examine the descriptor portion of the IA.AIRCRAFTCAP SAS data set.

```
proc contents data=ia.aircraftcap;
run;
```

The length of the SIZE variable is now 6.

Partial SAS Output

```
      -----Alphabetic List of Variables and Attributes-----

   #    Variable     Type    Len    Pos    Format    Informat

   2    AircraftID   Char     6     36     $6.       $6.
   3    InService    Num      8      0     8.        8.
   1    Model        Char    20     16     $20.      $20.
   5    Size         Char     6     42
   4    TotPassCap   Num      8      8
```

3. Generate descriptive statistics for the variable TOTPASSCAP grouped by the values of the variable SIZE.

```
proc means data=ia.aircraftcap maxdec=2;
   title 'Passenger Capacities';
   var TotPassCap;
   class Size;
run;
```

The second value for SIZE is now MEDIUM.

SAS Output

```
                        Passenger Capacities

                         The MEANS Procedure

                    Analysis Variable : TotPassCap

            N
 Size      Obs    N        Mean       Std Dev       Minimum       Maximum

 Large      16   16      230.13         32.39        207.00        290.00
 Medium      9    9      178.56         11.40        165.00        188.00
 Small      39   39      132.64         18.85         97.00        150.00
```

Conditionally Executing Multiple Statements

You can use DO and END statements to execute a group of statements based on a condition.

General form of DO and END statements:

```
IF expression THEN
    DO;
            executable statements
    END;
ELSE
    DO;
            executable statements
    END;
```

91

Every DO statement must have a matching END statement.

...

Conditionally Creating New Variables

TotPassCap
100
207
98
188

100<=150?

Size	MaxRange

```
if TotPassCap<=150 then
    do;
        Size='Small';
        MaxRange=1300;
    end;
```

92

···

Conditionally Creating New Variables

TotPassCap		Size	MaxRange
100	**TRUE** `100<=150?`		
207			
98			
188			

```
if TotPassCap<=150 then
   do;
      Size='Small';
      MaxRange=1300;
   end;
```

93

Conditionally Creating New Variables

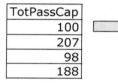

TotPassCap	Size	MaxRange
100	Small	1300
207		
98		
188		

```
if TotPassCap<=150 then
   do;
      Size='Small';
      MaxRange=1300;
   end;
```

94

Conditionally Executing Multiple Statements

File: c5s4d3.sas

- Use DO-END groups to create both the SIZE and MAXRANGE variables.
- Use PROC PRINT to display the values of TOTPASSCAP, SIZE, and MAXRANGE.

Creating New Variables Using DO-END Groups

Create two new variables conditionally.

```
data ia.aircraftcap(keep=Model AircraftID
                         TotPassCap InService
                         Size MaxRange);
   set ia.aircraftdata;
   TotPassCap=sum(FClassCap,BClassCap,EClassCap);
   length Size $ 6;
   if TotPassCap<=150 then
      do;
         Size='Small';
         MaxRange=1300;
      end;
   else if 150<TotPassCap<=200 then
      do;
         Size='Medium';
         MaxRange=5000;
      end;
      else if 200<TotPassCap then
         do;
            Size='Large';
            MaxRange=7000;
         end;
run;
```

✎ The MAXRANGE variable was added to the KEEP= data set option.

Displaying Values

Use the PRINT procedure to display the values of TOTPASSCAP, SIZE, and MAXRANGE.

```
proc print data=ia.aircraftcap;
    title 'Aircraft Data';
    var TotPassCap Size MaxRange;
run;
```

Partial SAS Output

Obs	Tot Pass Cap	Size	Max Range
		Aircraft Data	
1	267	Large	7000
2	207	Large	7000
3	207	Large	7000
4	207	Large	7000
5	207	Large	7000
6	207	Large	7000
7	207	Large	7000
8	207	Large	7000
9	207	Large	7000
10	207	Large	7000
11	207	Large	7000
12	165	Medium	5000
13	165	Medium	5000
14	165	Medium	5000
15	172	Medium	5000
16	188	Medium	5000
17	188	Medium	5000
18	188	Medium	5000
19	188	Medium	5000
20	188	Medium	5000
21	150	Small	1300

IF JobCode = 'FLTAT1' or JobCode = 'Pilot1' then do;

or

IF JobCode in ('FLTAT1', 'Pilot1') then do;

Exercises

6. Creating Variables Conditionally

a. Using the IA.CREW data set, create a new temporary data set named WORK.LEVELS. WORK.LEVELS must contain a character variable named JOBLEVEL. The values of JOBLEVEL are based on the value of the existing variable JOBCODE.

JOBCODE	Value of new variable JOBLEVEL to be assigned
FLTAT1	
PILOT1	LEVEL I
FLTAT2	
PILOT2	LEVEL II
FLTAT3	
PILOT3	LEVEL III

Use PROC CONTENTS or the VAR command to examine the descriptor portion of the WORK.LEVELS data set. Use a null TITLE statement to clear any existing titles.

b. Use PROC PRINT to display the data portion of the WORK.LEVELS data set. Make sure the displayed values of JOBLEVEL appear as above. If not, make the necessary corrections to your DATA step.

Show only the variables EMPID, FIRSTNAME, LASTNAME, JOBCODE, JOBLEVEL, and SALARY.

Display the values of SALARY with dollar signs, commas, and no decimal places.

7. Creating Variables Conditionally Using DO-END Groups

a. Modify the previous DATA step to create a second variable RAISE, based on the value of JOBCODE. RAISE stores the salary increase that each crew member receives, as indicated in the table below:

Existing value of JOBCODE	Raise amount
FLTAT1	
PILOT1	6% of current salary
FLTAT2	
PILOT2	8% of current salary
FLTAT3	
PILOT3	10% of current salary

b. Use PROC PRINT to create a list report of the resulting data set. Specify a title `Salary Increases for Crew Members`, and format the values of SALARY and RAISE with dollar signs, commas, and two decimal places. Display only the variables EMPID, LASTNAME, SALARY, JOBLEVEL, and RAISE.

8. Analyzing and Modifying Values

a. Use PROC MEANS to generate summary statistics about the IA.AIRPLANESMF data set. Analyze only the variables TOTPASSCAP, RANGE, and SPEED.

Group the observations so that the TOTPASSCAP, RANGE, and SPEED statistics are calculated for each value of MODEL.

Add a null TITLE statement to clear any existing titles.

b. Notice that the last two values of MODEL are invalid. What are these invalid values?

Look at the section of the report pertaining to JetCruise MF2000, and examine the N statistic. How many values of TOTPASSCAP are missing?

c. Correct the invalid values of MODEL and the missing TOTPASSCAP values by using a DATA step to create an WORK.AIRPLANES2 data set.

Use IF-THEN logic to correct the two invalid values of MODEL.

Similarly, use IF-THEN logic to determine the total passenger capacity when necessary. TOTPASSCAP is equal to the sum of FCLASSCAP, BCLASSCAP, and ECLASSCAP.

🖉   The IF-THEN logic guarantees that every observation has a non-missing value for TOTPASSCAP.

d. Create a new PROC MEANS report with the corrected model names and total passenger capacities. The report must generate summary statistics for the three variables listed in part **a** and group together the observations based on MODEL.

Use the appropriate option on the PROC MEANS statement to display all the statistics with no decimal places.

Add three titles to the report. The top title contains the text `Summary Statistics of`, the middle title is blank, and the third title is `Airplanes Owned by International Airlines`.

5.5   Creating a Detail Report with the REPORT Procedure

Objectives

- Create a list report using the REPORT procedure in a nonwindowing environment.
- Select variables to include in a list report using the COLUMN statement.
- Enhance a report using the DEFINE statement.

98

Business Scenario

International Airlines wants to create an enhanced list report that details the passenger capacity of its planes.

```
                                      In       Total
Aircraft                   Aircraft  Service  Passenger
  Size    Aircraft Model     ID       Date    Capacity
 Small   JetCruise SF1000   070013  08/29/1976    150
         JetCruise SF1000   070017  12/26/1968    150
         JetCruise SF1000   070026  10/10/1985    150
         JetCruise SF1000   070032  02/25/1983    150
```

99

PROC REPORT Features

In addition to creating list reports, PROC REPORT enables you to

- create custom reports
- request separate subtotals and grand totals
- calculate columns
- create and store report definitions
- generate reports in windowing or nonwindowing environments.

100

Creating a List Report

General form of a simple PROC REPORT step:

PROC REPORT DATA=*SAS-data-set <options>*;
RUN;

Selected options:

WINDOWS|WD   invokes the procedure in a
                    windowing mode (default).

NOWINDOWS|NOWD displays a listing of the
                    report in the OUTPUT
                    window.

101

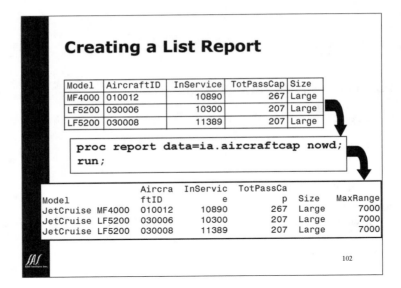

Creating a List Report

Model	AircraftID	InService	TotPassCap	Size
MF4000	010012	10890	267	Large
LF5200	030006	10300	207	Large
LF5200	030008	11389	207	Large

```
proc report data=ia.aircraftcap nowd;
run;
```

		Aircra	InServic	TotPassCa		
Model		ftID	e	p	Size	MaxRange
JetCruise	MF4000	010012	10890	267	Large	7000
JetCruise	LF5200	030006	10300	207	Large	7000
JetCruise	LF5200	030008	11389	207	Large	7000

102

By default, PROC REPORT displays all observations and all variables.

Printing Selected Variables

You can use a COLUMN statement to

- select the variables to appear in the report
- select the order in which the variables appear in the report.

General form of the COLUMN statement:

COLUMN *SAS-variables;*

103

Creating a List Report

Model	AircraftID	InService	TotPassCap	Size
MF4000	010012	10890	267	Large
LF5200	030006	10300	207	Large
LF5200	030008	11389	207	Large

```
proc report data=ia.aircraftcap nowd;
   column AircraftID Size TotPassCap;
run;
```

```
Aircra              TotPassCa
ftID     Size               p
010012   Large             267
030006   Large             207
030008   Large             207
```

104

Creating a List Report

File: c5s5d1.sas

- Use PROC REPORT in the nonwindowing mode to generate a default listing of IA.AIRCRAFTCAP.
- Use the COLUMN statement to select the variables AIRCRAFTID, SIZE, and TOTPASSCAP.

Generating a Default List Report

Create a default list report of the aircraft capacity data.

```
proc report data=ia.aircraftcap nowd;
   title 'Aircraft Data';
run;
```

Partial SAS Output

```
                             Aircraft Data

                   Aircra  InServic  TotPassCa
Model              ftID           e          p  Size      MaxRange
JetCruise MF4000   010012     10890        267  Large         7000
JetCruise LF5200   030006     10300        207  Large         7000
JetCruise LF5200   030008     11389        207  Large         7000
JetCruise LF5200   030015     12229        207  Large         7000
JetCruise LF5200   030016     12746        207  Large         7000
JetCruise LF5200   030025     10885        207  Large         7000
JetCruise LF5200   030027     11354        207  Large         7000
JetCruise LF5200   030028     10483        207  Large         7000
JetCruise LF5200   030031     12576        207  Large         7000
JetCruise LF5200   030037     10546        207  Large         7000
JetCruise LF5200   030041     11670        207  Large         7000
JetCruise LF5100   040008     10655        165  Medium        5000
JetCruise LF5100   040010     10975        165  Medium        5000
JetCruise LF5100   040022     11012        165  Medium        5000
JetCruise LF5000   050001     12851        172  Medium        5000
JetCruise MF6000   060002     11322        188  Medium        5000
JetCruise MF6000   060016     11888        188  Medium        5000
JetCruise MF6000   060018     12122        188  Medium        5000
JetCruise MF6000   060066     12279        188  Medium        5000
JetCruise MF6000   060090     10964        188  Medium        5000
JetCruise SF1000   070013      6085        150  Small         1300
JetCruise SF1000   070017      3282        150  Small         1300
JetCruise SF1000   070026      9414        150  Small         1300
```

Selecting Variables for the Report

Use the COLUMN statement to select certain variables for the report.

```
proc report data=ia.aircraftcap nowd;
   column AircraftID Size TotPassCap;
run;
```

Partial SAS Output

```
                          Aircraft Data

              Aircra             TotPassCa
              ftID     Size          p
              010012   Large        267
              030006   Large        207
              030008   Large        207
              030015   Large        207
              030016   Large        207
              030025   Large        207
              030027   Large        207
              030028   Large        207
              030031   Large        207
              030037   Large        207
              030041   Large        207
              040008   Medium       165
              040010   Medium       165
              040022   Medium       165
              050001   Medium       172
              060002   Medium       188
              060016   Medium       188
              060018   Medium       188
              060066   Medium       188
              060090   Medium       188
              070013   Small        150
              070017   Small        150
              070026   Small        150
```

The REPORT Procedure

The listing displays

- each data value as it is stored in the data set
- variable names as report column headings
- a default width for the report columns
- character values left-justified
- numeric values right-justified
- observations in the order in which they are stored in the data set.

106

The DEFINE Statement

You can enhance the report by using DEFINE statements to

- define how each variable is used in the report
- assign formats to variables
- specify report column headers and column widths
- justify the variable values and column headings within the report columns
- change the order of the rows in the report.

107

The DEFINE Statement

General form of the DEFINE statement:

DEFINE *variable /<usage> <attribute-list>*;

You can define options (usage and attributes) in the DEFINE statement in any order.

Default usage for character variables is DISPLAY.

- The report lists all of the variable's values from the data set.

108

You can list DEFINE statements in any order.

The DEFINE Statement

Default usage for numeric variables is ANALYSIS.

- If the report contains at least one display variable and no group variables, the report lists all of the values of the numeric variable.

- If the report contains only numeric variables, the report displays grand totals for the numeric variables.

- If the report contains group variables, the report displays the sum of the numeric variables' values for each group.

109

The DEFINE Statement

Other available statistics include

N	number of nonmissing values
MEAN	average
MAX	maximum value
MIN	minimum value

110

The DEFINE Statement

Order in the "Column" Superceeds the order in "define" Statement

Additional usage:

ORDER	determines the order of the rows in the report.
	• The default order is ascending.
	• To force the order to be descending, include the DESCENDING option on the DEFINE statement.
	• Repetitious printing of values is suppressed.

111

The DEFINE Statement

Selected attributes:

FORMAT=	assigns a format to a variable.
	• If there is a format stored in the descriptor portion of the data set it is the default format.
WIDTH=	controls the width of a report column.
	• The default width is the variable length.

continued...
112

The DEFINE Statement

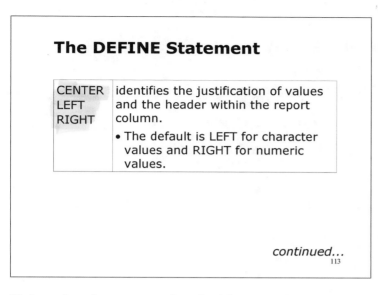

CENTER LEFT RIGHT	identifies the justification of values and the header within the report column. • The default is LEFT for character values and RIGHT for numeric values.

continued...
113

If there is a format associated with a variable, the formatted value is justified within the report column width.

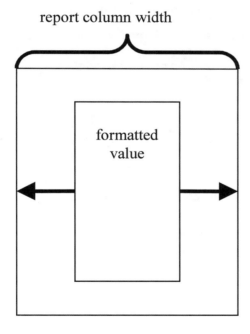

The DEFINE Statement

'report-column-header'	defines the report column header. • If there is a label stored in the descriptor portion of the data set it is the default header.

114

The default split character is /.

To define a different split character, use the SPLIT= option in the PROC REPORT statement, for example:

```
proc report data=ia.aircraftcap nowd split='*';
   column Model InService;
   define Model      / 'Aircraft*Model';
   define InService / 'In*Service*Date';
run;
```

Creating an Enhanced List Report

The enhanced aircraft capacity list report includes

- appropriate report column headings
- formatted values for the INSERVICE variable
- column widths wide enough for the headings
- values and headings centered within the columns
- rows of the report ordered by descending values of the variable SIZE.

115

Enhancing a List Report

File: c5s5d2.sas

- Use the COLUMN statement to select the variables and their order for the report.
- Use a DEFINE statement to format the values of INSERVICE. Use DEFINE statements to give all of the report columns informative headings.
- Modify the DEFINE statements to assign a width large enough for the headings and center all of the values and headers within the report columns.
- Modify the appropriate DEFINE statement to assign a standard numeric format to the TOTPASSCAP variable and assign a width large enough for the report column heading.
- Modify the appropriate DEFINE statement to assign the ORDER usage to the SIZE variable.
- Modify the DEFINE statement that assigns the ORDER usage to the SIZE variable and request a DESCENDING sequence.

Selecting Variables for a List Report

Use the COLUMN statement to select the following variables in this order: SIZE, MODEL, AIRCRAFTID, INSERVICE, TOTPASSCAP.

```
proc report data=ia.aircraftcap nowd;
   title 'Aircraft Data';
   column Size Model AircraftID InService TotPassCap;
run;
```

Partial SAS Output

```
                          Aircraft Data

                             Aircra  InServic  TotPassCa
          Size   Model       ftID           e          p
          Large  JetCruise MF4000  010012   10890        267
          Large  JetCruise LF5200  030006   10300        207
          Large  JetCruise LF5200  030008   11389        207
          Large  JetCruise LF5200  030015   12229        207
          Large  JetCruise LF5200  030016   12746        207
          Large  JetCruise LF5200  030025   10885        207
          Large  JetCruise LF5200  030027   11354        207
          Large  JetCruise LF5200  030028   10483        207
          Large  JetCruise LF5200  030031   12576        207
          Large  JetCruise LF5200  030037   10546        207
```

Formatting Values with the DEFINE Statement

Use a DEFINE statement to assign the MMDDYY10. format to the INSERVICE variable. Use DEFINE statements to give all of the report columns informative headings.

```
proc report data=ia.aircraftcap nowd;
   column Size Model AircraftID InService TotPassCap;
   define Size       / 'Aircraft Size';
   define Model      / 'Aircraft Model';
   define AircraftID / 'Aircraft ID';
   define InService  / format=mmddyy10.
                       'In Service Date';
   define TotPassCap / 'Total Passenger Capacity';
run;
```

Partial SAS Output

```
                           Aircraft Data

    Aircra                              In     Total
    ft                        Aircra  Service  Passenger
    Size    Aircraft Model    ft ID    Date    Capacity
    Large   JetCruise MF4000  010012  10/25/1989    267
    Large   JetCruise LF5200  030006  03/14/1988    207
    Large   JetCruise LF5200  030008  03/08/1991    207
    Large   JetCruise LF5200  030015  06/25/1993    207
    Large   JetCruise LF5200  030016  11/24/1994    207
    Large   JetCruise LF5200  030025  10/20/1989    207
    Large   JetCruise LF5200  030027  02/01/1991    207
    Large   JetCruise LF5200  030028  09/13/1988    207
    Large   JetCruise LF5200  030031  06/07/1994    207
```

Modifying the DEFINE Statement

1. Modify the DEFINE statements to assign a width large enough for the headings and center all of the values and headers within the report columns.

```
proc report data=ia.aircraftcap nowd;
   column Size Model AircraftID InService TotPassCap;
   define Size        / 'Aircraft Size' width=8 center;
   define Model       / 'Aircraft Model' center;
   define AircraftID  / 'Aircraft ID' width=8 center;
   define InService   / format=mmddyy10.
                        'In Service Date' center;
   define TotPassCap  / 'Total Passenger Capacity'
                        center;
run;
```

Partial SAS Output

```
                              Aircraft Data

                                         In      Total
     Aircraft                 Aircraft  Service  Passenger
       Size     Aircraft Model   ID      Date    Capacity
       Large    JetCruise MF4000  010012  10/25/1989    267
       Large    JetCruise LF5200  030006  03/14/1988    207
       Large    JetCruise LF5200  030008  03/08/1991    207
       Large    JetCruise LF5200  030015  06/25/1993    207
       Large    JetCruise LF5200  030016  11/24/1994    207
       Large    JetCruise LF5200  030025  10/20/1989    207
       Large    JetCruise LF5200  030027  02/01/1991    207
       Large    JetCruise LF5200  030028  09/13/1988    207
       Large    JetCruise LF5200  030031  06/07/1994    207
       Large    JetCruise LF5200  030037  11/15/1988    207
```

2. Modify the appropriate DEFINE statement to assign the 3. format and a width of 9 to the TOTPASSCAP variable. The report centers the formatted values in a report column with a width of 9.

```
proc report data=ia.aircraftcap nowd;
   column Size Model AircraftID InService TotPassCap;
   define Size        / 'Aircraft Size' width=8 center;
   define Model       / 'Aircraft Model' center;
   define AircraftID  / 'Aircraft ID' width=8 center;
   define InService   / format=mmddyy10.
                        'In Service Date' center;
   define TotPassCap  / 'Total Passenger Capacity'
                        center format=3. width=9;
run;
```

Partial SAS Output

```
                                Aircraft Data

                                          In      Total
   Aircraft                     Aircraft  Service Passenger
     Size    Aircraft Model       ID      Date    Capacity
   Large     JetCruise MF4000   010012  10/25/1989   267
   Large     JetCruise LF5200   030006  03/14/1988   207
   Large     JetCruise LF5200   030008  03/08/1991   207
   Large     JetCruise LF5200   030015  06/25/1993   207
   Large     JetCruise LF5200   030016  11/24/1994   207
   Large     JetCruise LF5200   030025  10/20/1989   207
   Large     JetCruise LF5200   030027  02/01/1991   207
   Large     JetCruise LF5200   030028  09/13/1988   207
   Large     JetCruise LF5200   030031  06/07/1994   207
   Large     JetCruise LF5200   030037  11/15/1988   207
```

3. Modify the appropriate DEFINE statement to assign the ORDER usage
   to the SIZE variable. This orders the rows in the report in ascending
   order according to the values of the variable SIZE. The report also
   suppresses the repetitious printing of the values of the variable SIZE.

```
proc report data=ia.aircraftcap nowd;
   column Size Model AircraftID InService TotPassCap;
   define Size       / order 'Aircraft Size' width=8
                       center;
   define Model      / 'Aircraft Model' center;
   define AircraftID / 'Aircraft ID' width=8 center;
   define InService  / format=mmddyy10.
                       'In Service Date' center;
   define TotPassCap / 'Total Passenger Capacity'
                       center format=3. width=9;
run;
```

Partial SAS Output

```
                              Aircraft Data

                                          In        Total
     Aircraft                   Aircraft  Service   Passenger
       Size    Aircraft Model     ID      Date      Capacity
     Large     JetCruise MF4000  010012  10/25/1989   267
               JetCruise LF5200  030006  03/14/1988   207
               JetCruise LF5200  030008  03/08/1991   207
               JetCruise LF5200  030015  06/25/1993   207
               JetCruise LF5200  030016  11/24/1994   207
               JetCruise LF5200  030025  10/20/1989   207
               JetCruise LF5200  030027  02/01/1991   207
               JetCruise LF5200  030028  09/13/1988   207
               JetCruise LF5200  030031  06/07/1994   207
               JetCruise LF5200  030037  11/15/1988   207
               JetCruise LF5200  030041  12/14/1991   207
               JetCruise LF8100  100002  12/05/1994   255
               JetCruise LF8100  100003  05/10/1994   255
               JetCruise LF8100  100008  05/13/1993   255
               JetCruise MF2000  110002  08/15/1974   290
               JetCruise MF2000  110005  09/09/1977   290
     Medium    JetCruise LF5100  040008  03/04/1989   165
               JetCruise LF5100  040010  01/18/1990   165
               JetCruise LF5100  040022  02/24/1990   165
               JetCruise LF5000  050001  03/09/1995   172
               JetCruise MF6000  060002  12/31/1990   188
               JetCruise MF6000  060016  07/19/1992   188
               JetCruise MF6000  060018  03/10/1993   188
               JetCruise MF6000  060066  08/14/1993   188
               JetCruise MF6000  060090  01/07/1990   188
     Small     JetCruise SF1000  070013  08/29/1976   150
               JetCruise SF1000  070017  12/26/1968   150
               JetCruise SF1000  070026  10/10/1985   150
               JetCruise SF1000  070032  02/25/1983   150
```

4. Modify the DEFINE statement that assigns the ORDER usage to the SIZE variable and request a DESCENDING sequence.

```
proc report data=ia.aircraftcap nowd;
   column Size Model AircraftID InService TotPassCap;
   define Size        / order descending 'Aircraft Size'
                        width=8 center ;
   define Model       / 'Aircraft Model' center;
   define AircraftID / 'Aircraft ID' width=8 center;
   define InService  / format=mmddyy10.
                        'In Service Date' center;
   define TotPassCap / 'Total Passenger Capacity'
                        center format=3. width=9;
run;
```

Partial SAS Output

```
                              Aircraft Data

                                           In      Total
                                         Service  Passenger
Aircraft                       Aircraft  Service  Passenger
  Size     Aircraft Model        ID       Date    Capacity
Small      JetCruise SF1000    070013   08/29/1976    150
           JetCruise SF1000    070017   12/26/1968    150
           JetCruise SF1000    070026   10/10/1985    150
           JetCruise SF1000    070032   02/25/1983    150
           JetCruise SF1000    070035   10/02/1983    150
           JetCruise SF1000    070040   04/29/1989    150
           JetCruise SF1000    070055   10/25/1977    150
           JetCruise SF1000    070074   06/21/1990    150
           JetCruise SF7000    080003   05/25/1992     97
           JetCruise SF7000    080004   12/29/1992     97
           JetCruise SF7000    080013   09/27/1992     97
           JetCruise SF7000    080019   12/08/1995     97
           JetCruise SF7000    080025   07/05/1991     97
           JetCruise SF7000    080051   03/23/1991     97
           JetCruise SF7000    080053   04/28/1995     97
           JetCruise SF7000    080068   01/23/1994     97
           JetCruise SF3000    130010   04/21/1991    139
           JetCruise SF3000    130023   05/25/1985    139
           JetCruise SF3000    130070   11/23/1988    139
           JetCruise SF3000    130072   03/04/1993    139
           JetCruise SF3000    130079   11/16/1983    139
           JetCruise SF3000    130092   07/11/1984    139
           JetCruise SF3000    130096   05/17/1983    139
           JetCruise SF3000    130102   11/23/1988    139
           JetCruise SF3000    130105   12/29/1994    139
           JetCruise SF3000    130109   08/18/1991    139
           JetCruise SF3000    130114   02/22/1988    139
           JetCruise SF3000    130133   01/13/1990    139
```

Exercises

9. Using the REPORT Procedure to Create a List Report

Use PROC REPORT and the IA.MIASCHEDULE data set to produce a list report with the following characteristics:

- The report should display only the variables AIRCRAFTID, FLIGHTID, DEPARTTIME, ARRIVALTIME, and DATE.
- Each variable displayed should have a descriptive report column heading.
- DATE should be displayed in the form *mmddyy* with a four-digit year.
- The columns of the report should be wide enough so that individual words in each column heading are not split onto multiple lines. (Different words can appear on different lines, but a single word must appear on a single line.)
- The values of AIRCRAFTID, FLIGHTID, and DATE should be centered.
- The observations on the report should be ordered by the values of AIRCRAFTID.
- Title the report `Flights from RDU to MIA`.

Partial PROC REPORT Output

```
                    Flights from RDU to MIA

                                             Scheduled
    Aircraft    Flight   Departure   Arrival   Flight
       ID         ID       Time       Time      Date
    070018     IA02702      13:50     15:44   07/11/2001
               IA02702      13:50     15:44   03/19/1997
               IA02700       7:50      9:44   12/13/1997
               IA02702      13:50     15:44   05/16/2001
               IA02702      13:50     15:44   12/13/2002
               IA02704      19:50     21:44   12/16/2001
               IA02702      13:50     15:44   11/25/1998
               IA02702      13:50     15:44   08/04/1999
               IA02702      13:50     15:44   03/28/2000
               IA02702      13:50     15:44   07/13/2003
```

5.6   Chapter Summary

In order to create a SAS data set using a SAS data set as input, you must
- start a DATA step and name the SAS data set being created (DATA statement)
- identify the input SAS data set (SET statement).

You can use a DROP= or a KEEP= data set option in a DATA statement to control what variables are written to the new SAS data set.

Each SAS file resides in a SAS data library. A SAS data library is a collection of SAS files that are recognized as a unit by the SAS System. You can identify SAS data libraries by assigning each one a libref.

By default, SAS creates a temporary library and assigns the libref WORK to it. This library is deleted at the end of your SAS session of job.

SAS data libraries are organized differently on each host operating system. Regardless of your host operating system, you can use the LIBNAME statement to assign a libref to a SAS data library. By default the libref remains assigned until the end of your SAS session or job.

A SAS filename is comprised of two parts: the libref and the file name.

You can use the CONTENTS procedure to generate a listing of all SAS files in a SAS data library. You can use the NODS option to suppress the printing of detailed information about each file.

You can use the MEANS procedure to display simple descriptive statistics for the numeric variables in a data set. The default statistics are N, MEAN, STD, MIN, and MAX. The MEANS procedure excludes missing values before calculating statistics. The VAR statement enables you to select which variables to include in the statistical analysis. The MAXDEC= option on the PROC MEANS statement gives the maximum number of decimal places to be used in printing the statistics. The CLASS statement groups the observations of the SAS data set for analysis.

IF-THEN and ELSE statements can be used to conditionally execute other SAS statements. IF-THEN and ELSE statements are used only in the DATA step. Only one statement can follow THEN. The ELSE statement is optional. You can add DO and END statements to execute a group of statements.

You can use the LENGTH statement to explicitly define the length of a variable.

You can use the REPORT procedure to generate detailed list reports in both windowing and nonwindowing environments. By default, the REPORT procedure lists all of the variables and observations in the data set. You can use a WHERE statement to select the observations and a COLUMN statement to select the variables and their order.

In the REPORT procedure you can use DEFINE statements to enhance your report by

- defining how each variable is used in the report
- assigning formats to variables
- specifying report column headers and widths
- justifying values and column headings within report columns
- changing the order of the rows in the report.

General form of a SET statement:

SET *SAS-data-set(s)*;

General form of a DROP= data set option:

SAS-data-set(**DROP=***variables*)

General form of a KEEP= data set option:

SAS-data-set(**KEEP=***variables*)

General form of a LIBNAME statement:

LIBNAME *libref 'SAS-data-library' <options>*;

General form of a CONTENTS procedure to access the contents of a SAS data library:

PROC CONTENTS DATA=*libref._ALL_* NODS;
RUN;

General form of a PROC MEANS step:

PROC MEANS DATA=*SAS-data-set*;
RUN;

General form of a VAR statement:

VAR *SAS-variables*;

General form of a MAXDEC= option:

PROC MEANS DATA=*data-set*
                MAXDEC=*number*;
RUN;

General form of a CLASS statement:

CLASS *SAS-variables*;

General form of IF-THEN and ELSE statements:

> **IF** *expression* **THEN** *statement*;
> **ELSE** *statement*;

General form of DO and END statements:

> **IF** *expression* **THEN**
>   **DO;**
>   *statements*
>   **END;**
> **ELSE**
>   **DO;**
>   *statements*
>   **END;**

General form of a LENGTH statement:

> **LENGTH** *variable(s) $ length*;

General form of a nonwindowing mode PROC REPORT step:

> **PROC REPORT** DATA=*SAS-data-set* NOWD;
> **RUN;**

General form of a COLUMN statement:

> **COLUMN** *SAS-variables*;

General form of a DEFINE statement:

> **DEFINE** *variable </usage> <attribute-list>*;

5.7 Solutions

1. **Making Data Sets Available to the System**

    a.

    ```
    libname ia 'operating-system-specific-information';

    title;
    ```

    b.

    ```
    proc contents data=ia._all_ nods;
    run;
    ```

Partial Output

#	Name	Memtype	File Size	Last Modified
1	AIRCRAFTDATA	DATA	9216	05JUL2000:10:04:00
2	AIRPLANES	DATA	25600	10JUL2000:13:38:29
3	AIRPLANESMF	DATA	25600	10JUL2000:13:38:36
4	ALLGOALS	DATA	5120	06JUL2000:09:43:16
5	ALLGOALS2	DATA	5120	06JUL2000:10:43:26
6	ALLSALES	DATA	5120	21JUN2000:10:33:12
7	ALLSALES2	DATA	5120	21JUN2000:10:32:12
8	APRBUDGETV	DATA	25600	10JUL2000:13:38:42
9	BUDGET121999	DATA	115712	10JUL2000:13:38:48
10	CREW	DATA	17408	10JUL2000:13:40:33
11	EGOALS	DATA	5120	05JUL2000:16:34:46
12	EGOALS2	DATA	5120	06JUL2000:10:53:23
13	ESALES	DATA	5120	20JUN2000:15:07:27
14	FROMRDUSCHEDULE	DATA	9216	10JUL2000:13:39:07
15	GOALS	DATA	5120	06JUL2000:09:21:49
16	JUNBUDGETV	DATA	25600	10JUL2000:13:39:13
17	MAYBUDGETV	DATA	25600	10JUL2000:13:39:20
18	MIASCHEDULE	DATA	9216	10JUL2000:13:39:27
19	SALES	DATA	5120	06JUL2000:09:21:50
20	SALES1	DATA	37888	12JUL2000:14:40:19
21	SALES121999	DATA	115712	10JUL2000:13:39:32
22	SALES2	DATA	37888	12JUL2000:14:40:26

The FROMRDUSCHEDULE and MIASCHEDULE data sets appear
to contain schedule data.

c.

```
proc contents data=ia.fromrduschedule;
run;
```

Name	Type	Length
AIRCRAFTID	Char	6
ARRIVALTIME	Num	8
DATE	Num	8
DEPARTTIME	Num	8
DESTINATION	Char	3
FLIGHTID	Char	7
ORIGIN	Char	3

2. **Creating a List Report of Flights**

a.

```
data work.fromrdushort(keep=AircraftID FlightID Origin
                            Destination DepartTime
                            Date Duration);
    set ia.fromrduschedule;
    Duration=(ArrivalTime-DepartTime)/60;
    if Duration le 120;
run;
```

b.
```
proc print data=work.fromrdushort label;
   label Duration='Length of Flight';
   format Date weekdate.;
run;
```

Partial Output

Obs	Aircraft ID	Flight ID	Origin	Destination	Depart Time
1	070008	IA02003	RDU	BOS	15:55
2	070009	IA02000	RDU	BOS	6:55
3	070008	IA02003	RDU	BOS	15:55
4	070009	IA02002	TDU	BOS	12:55
5	070009	IA02000	RDU	BOS	6:55
6	070009	IA02004	RDU	BOS	18:55
7	070008	IA02003	RDU	BOS	15:55
8	070005	IA01402	RDU	IAD	13:05
9	070004	IA01403	RDU	IAD	15:35
10	070005	IA01400	RDU	IAD	6:05
11	070004	IA01403	RDU	IAD	15:35
12	070005	IA01400	RDU	IAD	6:05
13	070005	IA01404	RDU	IAD	18:05
14	070004	IA01405	RDU	IAD	20:35
15	070005	IA01404	RDU	IAD	18:05
16	070005	IA01404	RDU	IAD	18:05
17	070016	IA02601	RDU	IND	9:55
18	070017	IA02600	RDU	IND	6:55
19	070016	IA02605	RDU	IND	21:55
20	070016	IA02603	RDU	IND	15:55
21	070016	IA02601	RDU	IND	9:55
22	070016	IA02605	RDU	IND	21:55

Obs	Date	Length of Flight
1	Friday, November 19, 1999	102.917
2	Tuesday, December 24, 2002	102.917
3	Wednesday, March 11, 1998	102.917
4	Wednesday, June 2, 1999	102.917
5	Saturday, October 21, 2000	102.917
6	Monday, June 29, 1998	102.917
7	Wednesday, October 29, 1997	102.917
8	Thursday, February 20, 1997	51.417

3. Working with Functions (Optional)

```
data work.fromrdushort(keep=AircraftID FlightID Origin
                            Destination DepartTime
                            Date Duration);
   set ia.fromrduschedule;
   Duration=floor((ArrivalTime-DepartTime)/60);
   if Duration le 120;
run;

proc print data=work.fromrdushort label;
   label Duration='Length of Flight';
   format Date weekdate.;
run;
```

Partial Output

Obs	Aircraft ID	Flight ID	Origin	Destination	Depart Time
1	070008	IA02003	RDU	BOS	15:55
2	070009	IA02000	RDU	BOS	6:55
3	070008	IA02003	RDU	BOS	15:55
4	070009	IA02002	TDU	BOS	12:55
5	070009	IA02000	RDU	BOS	6:55
6	070009	IA02004	RDU	BOS	18:55
7	070008	IA02003	RDU	BOS	15:55
8	070005	IA01402	RDU	IAD	13:05
9	070004	IA01403	RDU	IAD	15:35
10	070005	IA01400	RDU	IAD	6:05
11	070004	IA01403	RDU	IAD	15:35
12	070005	IA01400	RDU	IAD	6:05
13	070005	IA01404	RDU	IAD	18:05
14	070004	IA01405	RDU	IAD	20:35
15	070005	IA01404	RDU	IAD	18:05
16	070005	IA01404	RDU	IAD	18:05
17	070016	IA02601	RDU	IND	9:55
18	070017	IA02600	RDU	IND	6:55
19	070016	IA02605	RDU	IND	21:55
20	070016	IA02603	RDU	IND	15:55
21	070016	IA02601	RDU	IND	9:55
22	070016	IA02605	RDU	IND	21:55

Obs	Date	Length of Flight
1	Friday, November 19, 1999	102
2	Tuesday, December 24, 2002	102
3	Wednesday, March 11, 1998	102
4	Wednesday, June 2, 1999	102
5	Saturday, October 21, 2000	102
6	Monday, June 29, 1998	102
7	Wednesday, October 29, 1997	102
8	Thursday, February 20, 1997	51
9	Thursday, July 22, 1999	51
10	Thursday, January 16, 2003	51

4. **Creating a Report Containing Summary Statistics about Airplanes**

   a.
   ```
   proc means data=ia.airplanes;
   run;
   ```

   ```
                         The MEANS Procedure

   Variable      N        Mean      Std Dev      Minimum      Maximum
   ─────────────────────────────────────────────────────────────────
   FClassCap    109   15.6146789    3.2257880   14.0000000   22.0000000
   BClassCap      9   30.0000000            0   30.0000000   30.0000000
   EClassCap    109  136.4128440   18.2016539  125.0000000  166.0000000
   TotPassCap   109  154.5045872   25.1357882  139.0000000  207.0000000
   CargoCap     109     46293.58     12454.99     39700.00     82400.00
   Range        109      2221.54      1051.35      1661.00      5250.00
   InService    109     11059.96      1354.12      8453.00     13123.00
   LastMaint    109     13552.52  209.9598990     13150.00     13873.00
   Speed        109  515.6880734    9.0642738  510.0000000  530.0000000
   ─────────────────────────────────────────────────────────────────
   ```

   LASTMAINT and INSERVICE contain SAS date values.

   b.
   ```
   proc means data=ia.airplanes maxdec=2;
       var TotPassCap CargoCap Range;
       title 'Summary Statistics of IA Airplanes';
   run;
   ```

   ```
              Summary Statistics of IA Airplanes

                     The MEANS Procedure

   Variable      N        Mean      Std Dev    Minimum     Maximum
   ──────────────────────────────────────────────────────────────
   TotPassCap   109      154.50        25.14     139.00      207.00
   CargoCap     109    46293.58     12454.99   39700.00    82400.00
   Range        109     2221.54      1051.35    1661.00     5250.00
   ──────────────────────────────────────────────────────────────
   ```

5. **Requesting Specific Statistics through PROC MEANS (Optional)**
   ```
   proc means data=ia.airplanes min max mean maxdec=2;
       var TotPassCap CargoCap Range;
       title 'MIN, MAX and MEAN Statistics of IA Airplanes';
   run;
   ```

   ```
            MIN, MAX and MEAN Statistics of IA Airplanes

                     The MEANS Procedure

   Variable        Minimum      Maximum         Mean
   ──────────────────────────────────────────────────
   TotPassCap       139.00       207.00       154.50
   CargoCap       39700.00     82400.00     46293.58
   Range           1661.00      5250.00      2221.54
   ──────────────────────────────────────────────────
   ```

6. Creating Variables Conditionally

a.

```
data work.levels;
   set ia.crew;
   length JobLevel $9;
   if JobCode='FLTAT1' then JobLevel='LEVEL I';
   else if JobCode='PILOT1' then
        JobLevel='LEVEL I';
      else if JobCode='FLTAT2' then
           JobLevel='LEVEL II';
         else if JobCode='PILOT2' then
              JobLevel='LEVEL II';
            else if JobCode='FLTAT3' then
                 JobLevel='LEVEL III';
               else if JobCode='PILOT3' then
                    JobLevel='LEVEL III';
run;

proc contents data=work.levels;
   title;
run;
```

Partial Output

```
                         The CONTENTS Procedure

Data Set Name: WORK.LEVELS                    Observations:          69
Member Type:   DATA                           Variables:             11
Engine:        V8                             Indexes:               0
Created:       11:03 Thursday, July 13, 2000  Observation Length:    184
Last Modified: 11:03 Thursday, July 13, 2000  Deleted Observations:  0
Protection:                                   Compressed:            NO
Data Set Type:                                Sorted:                NO
Label:


-----Alphabetic List of Variables and Attributes-----

    #    Variable    Type    Len    Pos    Format      Informat

    5    Country     Char     25    110    $25.        $25.
    1    Division    Char     30     16    $30.        $30.
    8    EmpID       Char      6    159    $6.         $6.
    4    FirstName   Char     32     78    $32.        $32.
    2    HireDate    Num       8      0    DATE9.      DATE9.
    9    JobCode     Char      6    165    $6.         $6.
   11    JobLevel    Char      9    171
    3    LastName    Char     32     46    $32.        $32.
    6    Location    Char     16    135    $16.        $16.
    7    Phone       Char      8    151    $8.         $8.
   10    Salary      Num       8      8    DOLLAR10.   DOLLAR10.
```

b.

```
proc print data=work.levels;
   var EmpID FirstName LastName JobCode JobLevel
Salary;
   format Salary dollar10.;
run;
```

Partial Ouput

Obs	EmpID	FirstName
1	E00525	SALLY T.
2	E02466	CHRISTOPHER
3	E00802	BARBARA ANN
4	E00565	ROBERT M.
5	E01457	SUSAN B.
6	E04296	TERESA L.
7	E03631	JOANN H.
8	E04219	ANNETTE M.
9	E01146	JOHN G.
10	E02158	DOUGLAS G.
11	E02789	JOHN C.
12	E01132	WILLIAM
13	E01886	DANIEL R.
14	E02306	JOANNE
15	E02035	KENNETH R.
16	E01093	ANITA M.

Obs	LastName	JobCode	JobLevel	Salary
1	BEAUMONT	PILOT1	LEVEL I	$65,000
2	BERGAMASCO	FLTAT1	LEVEL I	$30,000
3	BETHEA	FLTAT2	LEVEL II	$31,000
4	BJURSTROM	FLTAT3	LEVEL III	$45,000
5	BONDS	FLTAT3	LEVEL III	$26,000
6	CHANG	PILOT3	LEVEL III	$45,000
7	CHOPRA	FLTAT2	LEVEL II	$31,000
8	CHRISTENSEN	FLTAT2	LEVEL II	$44,000
9	CHRISTIAN	FLTAT2	LEVEL II	$18,000
10	CIAMPA	FLTAT2	LEVEL II	$38,000
11	CLAYTON	FLTAT3	LEVEL III	$17,000
12	DIELEMAN	PILOT1	LEVEL I	$61,000
13	DOWELL	PILOT3	LEVEL III	$31,000
14	DOWTY	PILOT3	LEVEL III	$17,000
15	EATON	FLTAT3	LEVEL III	$38,000
16	EHRISMAN	FLTAT3	LEVEL III	$45,000

7. Creating Variables Conditionally Using DO-END Groups

a.

```
data work.levels;
    set ia.crew;
    length JobLevel $9;
    if JobCode='FLTAT1' then
        do;
            JobLevel='LEVEL I';
            Raise=Salary*.06;
        end;
    else if JobCode='PILOT1' then
        do;
            JobLevel='LEVEL I';
            Raise=Salary*.06;
        end;
        else if JobCode='FLTAT2' then
            do;
                JobLevel='LEVEL II';
                Raise=Salary*.08;
            end;
            else if JobCode='PILOT2' then
                do;
                    JobLevel='LEVEL II';
                    Raise=Salary*.08;
                end;
                else if JobCode='FLTAT3' then
                    do;
                        JobLevel='LEVEL III';
                        Raise=Salary*.10;
                    end;
                    else if JobCode='PILOT3' then
                        do;
                            JobLevel='LEVEL III';
                            Raise=Salary*.10;
                        end;
run;
```

b.

```
proc print data=work.levels;
    var EmpID LastName Salary JobLevel Raise;
    title 'Salary Increases for Crew Members';
    format Raise Salary dollar10.2;
run;
```

Partial SAS Output

```
                    Salary Increases for Crew Members

        Obs     EmpID       LastName

         1      E00525      BEAUMONT
         2      E02466      BERGAMASCO
         3      E00802      BETHEA
         4      E00565      BJURSTROM
         5      E01457      BONDS
         6      E04296      CHANG
         7      E03631      CHOPRA
         8      E04219      CHRISTENSEN
         9      E01146      CHRISTIAN
        10      E02158      CIAMPA


        Obs        Salary      JobLevel          Raise

         1      $65,000.00     LEVEL I        $3,900.00
         2      $30,000.00     LEVEL I        $1,800.00
         3      $31,000.00     LEVEL II       $2,480.00
         4      $45,000.00     LEVEL III      $4,500.00
         5      $26,000.00     LEVEL III      $2,600.00
         6      $45,000.00     LEVEL III      $4,500.00
         7      $31,000.00     LEVEL II       $2,480.00
         8      $44,000.00     LEVEL II       $3,520.00
         9      $18,000.00     LEVEL II       $1,440.00
        10      $38,000.00     LEVEL II       $3,040.00
```

8. Analyzing and Modifying Values

a.
```
proc means data=ia.airplanesmf;
   var TotPassCap Range Speed;
   class Model;
   title;
run;
```

Partial Output

```
                          The MEANS Procedure

                       N
Model                 Obs  Variable     Minimum          Maximum

JetCruise MF6000       87  TotPassCap   188.0000000      188.0000000
                           Range           2970.00          2970.00
                           Speed        530.0000000      530.0000000

jc mf4000               3  TotPassCap   267.0000000      267.0000000
                           Range           2880.00          2880.00
                           Speed        530.0000000      530.0000000

jetcruise mf6000        3  TotPassCap   188.0000000      188.0000000
                           Range           2970.00          2970.00
                           Speed        530.0000000      530.0000000
```

🖉   The order of the report varies among operating environments due to the collating sequences used by each environment.

b.   The values `jc mf4000` and `jetcruise mf6000` are invalid.

There are two missing values of TOTPASSCAP. The N statistic for TOTPASSCAP is three, and N Obs for the value JetCruise MF2000 is five.

c.
```
data work.airplanes2;
   set ia.airplanesmf;
   if Model='jc mf4000' then
      Model='JetCruise MF4000';
   else if Model='jetcruise mf6000' then
       Model='JetCruise MF6000';
   if TotPassCap=. then
      TotPassCap=sum(FClassCap,BClassCap,EClassCap);
run;
```

d.

```
proc means data=work.airplanes2 maxdec=0;
   var TotPassCap Range Speed;
   class Model;
   title 'Summary Statistics of';
   title2;
   title3 'Airplanes Owned by International Airlines';
run;
```

Partial Output

```
                        Summary Statistics of

              Airplanes Owned by International Airlines

                        The MEANS Procedure

                    N
Model             Obs   Variable       N        Mean      Std Dev
------------------------------------------------------------------
JetCruise MF2000    5   TotPassCap     5         290            0
                        Range          5        2878            0
                        Speed          5         540            0

JetCruise MF2100   13   TotPassCap    13         237            0
                        Range         13        2878            0
                        Speed         13         540            0

JetCruise MF4000   27   TotPassCap    27         267            0
                        Range         27        2880            0
                        Speed         27         530            0

JetCruise MF4100    8   TotPassCap     8         198            0
                        Range          8        2880            0
                        Speed          8         530            0

JetCruise MF6000   90   TotPassCap    90         188            0
                        Range         90        2970            0
                        Speed         90         530            0
------------------------------------------------------------------
```

9. Using the REPORT Procedure to Create a List Report

a.

```
proc report data=ia.miaschedule nowd;
   column AircraftID FlightID DepartTime
          ArrivalTime Date;
   define AircraftID  / order width=10
                        center 'Aircraft ID';
   define FlightID    / display width=8
                        center 'Flight ID';
   define DepartTime  / display width=10
                        right 'Departure Time';
   define ArrivalTime / display width=10
                        right 'Arrival Time';
   define Date        / display format=mmddyy10.
                        center 'Scheduled Flight Date';
   title 'Flights from RDU to MIA';
run;
```

Chapter 6 Concatenating SAS® Data Sets and Creating Summary Reports

6.1 Introduction

Business Scenario

For its annual meeting, International Airlines needs to

- combine two data sets to create a detailed annual sales report
- report sales and passenger data by day of the week
- subset the data to create a report for the holiday season.

3

Concatenating SAS Data Sets

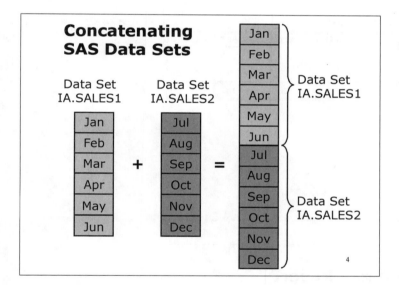

4

Creating New Variables

Sales and Passenger Data for 1999

Date	FlightID	FClassAct	BClassAct	EClassAct
01JAN1999	IA00100	12	47	148
02JAN1999	IA00100	13	28	125
03JAN1999	IA00201	13	26	147

TotPass
207
166
186

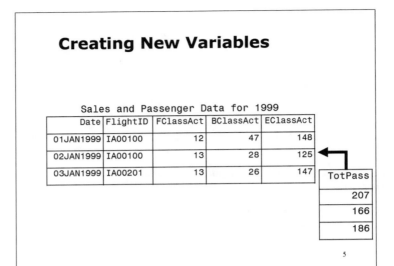

5

Eliminating Variables

Sales and Passenger Data for 1999

Date	FlightID	FClassAct	BClassAct	EClassAct	TotPass
01JAN1999	IA00100	12	47	148	207
02JAN1999	IA00100	13	28	125	166
03JAN1999	IA00201	13	26	147	186

cut

6

Writing a Detail Report

Sales and Passenger Data for 1999			
Sales Date	Flight	Total Passengers	Total Revenue
01JAN1999	IA00100	207	$123,948.00
02JAN1999	IA00100	166	$117,695.00
03JAN1999	IA00201	186	$127,197.00
04JAN1999	IA00300	186	$140,170.00
05JAN1999	IA00400	194	$141,826.00
06JAN1999	IA00502	230	$15,110.00
07JAN1999	IA00504	237	$15,516.00
08JAN1999	IA00500	227	$14,700.00
09JAN1999	IA00502	253	$16,326.00
10JAN1999	IA00604	267	$15,570.00

7

Writing a Summary Report

```
                Sales and Passenger Data, by Day of Week
                       Sunday through Saturday

Day of                     Total
  Week                   Passengers              Total Revenue


     1                     8,806                 $4,019,906.00
     2                     8,627                 $4,038,376.00
     3                     8,673                 $4,054,418.00
     4                     8,640                 $3,932,574.00
     5                     8,493                 $3,982,091.00
     6                     8,794                 $4,103,601.00
     7                     8,649                 $4,033,889.00
```

8

Subsetting a Report

```
    Date| FlightID | TotPassCap| TotPass |       TotRev
04JAN1999| IA00300  |       207 |     186 | $140,170.00
26NOV1999| IA00300  |       207 |     176 | $133,704.00
31DEC1999| IA00401  |       207 |     171 | $129,491.00
```

where Date between '24nov1999'd and '03jan2000'd;

```
    Date FlightID TotPassCap  TotPass        TotRev
26NOV1999 IA00300        207      176   $133,704.00
31DEC1999 IA00401        207      171   $129,491.00
```

9

6.2   Concatenating SAS Data Sets

Objectives

- Define concatenation.
- Use the SET statement in a DATA step to concatenate two SAS data sets.
- Use the WEEKDAY function and the SUM function in an assignment statement to create new variables.
- Use the KEEP= option to write only selected variables to the output data set.
- Use the REPORT procedure to create a detail report.

11

Business Scenario

For its 1999 sales report, International Airlines must include the sales data both for the first six months and for the second six months.

12

Business Scenario

It will be necessary to

- combine the two SAS data sets
- create new variables based on calculated values
- eliminate unwanted variables from the newly created data set
- create a presentation-quality list report.

13

Business Scenario

```
              Sales and Passenger Data for 1999

Sales                           Total              Total
Date            Flight      Passengers           Revenue


01JAN1999       IA00100            207       $123,948.00
02JAN1999       IA00100            166       $117,695.00
03JAN1999       IA00201            186       $127,197.00
04JAN1999       IA00300            186       $140,170.00
05JAN1999       IA00400            194       $141,826.00
06JAN1999       IA00502            230        $15,110.00
07JAN1999       IA00504            237        $15,516.00
08JAN1999       IA00500            227        $14,700.00
09JAN1999       IA00502            253        $16,326.00
10JAN1999       IA00604            267        $15,570.00
```

14

Concatenating SAS Data Sets

A *concatenation*

- combines two or more SAS data sets one after the other, into a single SAS data set
- uses the SET statement
- is one of several methods for combining SAS data sets.

15

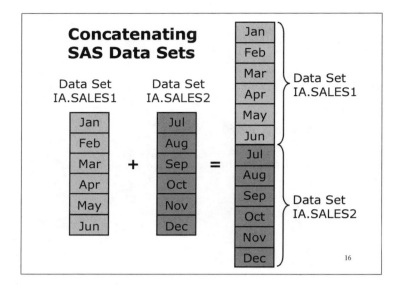

Think of concatenation as a stacking operation in which SAS data sets are appended to each other in the order that they are listed.

Concatenating SAS Data Sets

Use the SET statement in a DATA step to concatenate SAS data sets.

General form of a DATA step concatenation:

```
DATA SAS-data-set;
    SET SAS-data-set-1 SAS-data-set-2;
RUN;
```

17

   In addition to concatenation, you can combine SAS data sets by merging them with a MERGE statement in a DATA step. The MERGE statement is used to join corresponding observations from two or more SAS data sets.

Concatenating SAS Data Sets

Example program to concatenate **two**
SAS data sets:

```
data ia.personnel;
   set ia.employees ia.departments;
run;
```

Example program to concatenate **several**
SAS data sets:

```
data ia.airlines;
   set ia.airport ia.aircraft ia.schedule
       ia.budget ia.sales ia.personnel;
run;
```

18

Any number of SAS data sets can be read with a single SET statement.

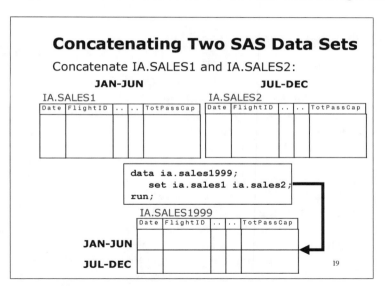

Variables in IA.SALES1 and IA.SALES2

#	Variable	Type	Len	Pos	Format	Informat
12	BClassAct	Num	8	56		
7	BClassCap	Num	8	16	8.	8.
15	BClassRev	Num	8	80	DOLLAR15.2	
10	CargoCap	Num	8	40	8.	8.
18	CargoRev	Num	8	104	DOLLAR15.2	
17	CargoWt	Num	8	96		
1	Date	Num	8	0	DATE9.	
5	Destination	Char	3	129		
13	EClassAct	Num	8	64		
8	EClassCap	Num	8	24	8.	8.
16	EClassRev	Num	8	88	DOLLAR15.2	
11	FClassAct	Num	8	48		
6	FClassCap	Num	8	8	8.	8.
14	FClassRev	Num	8	72	DOLLAR15.2	
2	FlightID	Char	7	112		
4	Origin	Char	3	126		
3	RouteID	Char	7	119		
9	TotPassCap	Num	8	32	8.	8.

[20]

IA.SALES1 and IA.SALES2 contain the same variables with the same variable attributes.

 Most of the variables have been assigned labels:

BCLASSACT	Number of Business Passengers
BCLASSCAP	Aircraft Capacity – Business Class Passengers
BCLASSREV	Revenue from Business Passengers
CARGOCAP	Aircraft Capacity – Total Payload in Pounds
CARGOREV	Revenue from Cargo
CARGOWT	Weight of Cargo in Pounds
DATE	
DESTINATION	Destination
ECLASSACT	Number of Economy Passengers
ECLASSCAP	Aircraft Capacity – Economy Class Passengers
ECLASSREV	Revenue from Economy Passengers
FCLASSACT	Number of First Class Passengers
FCLASSCAP	Aircraft Capacity – First Class Passengers
FCLASSREV	Revenue from First Class Passengers
FLIGHTID	Flight Number
ORIGIN	Start Point
ROUTEID	Route Number
TOTPASSCAP	Aircraft Capacity – Total Passengers

Concatenating Two SAS Data Sets

Use the SET statement in a DATA step to perform the concatenation. Name the new data set IA.SALES1999.

```
data ia.sales1999;
   set ia.sales1 ia.sales2;
   more SAS statements
run;
```

21

 It is important to list the SAS data sets in the SET statement in the order that you want them concatenated.

Using the WEEKDAY Function in an Assignment Statement

Use the WEEKDAY function in an assignment statement to return a value for each day of the week based on the date values. Assign those values to the new variable DAY.

```
data ia.sales1999;
   set ia.sales1 ia.sales2;
   Day=weekday(Date);
   more SAS statements
run;
```

22

The WEEKDAY function returns the day of the week (1 = Sunday) of the value of the variable DATE. DATE must be a numeric variable representing a SAS date value.

Using the SUM Function in an Assignment Statement

Use the SUM function in an assignment statement to sum the values of FCLASSACT, ECLASSACT, and BCLASSACT to create the new variable TOTPASS.

```
data ia.sales1999;
   set ia.sales1 ia.sales2;
   Day=weekday(Date);
   TotPass=sum(FClassAct,EClassAct,BClassAct);
   more SAS statements
run;
```

23

The SUM function adds the values of the variables FCLASSACT, ECLASSACT, and BCLASSACT, ignoring any missing values.

Using the SUM Function in an Assignment Statement

Use the SUM function in an assignment statement to sum the values of BCLASSREV, ECLASSREV, and FCLASSREV to create the new variable TOTREV.

```
data ia.sales1999;
   set ia.sales1 ia.sales2;
   Day=weekday(Date);
   TotPass=sum(FClassAct,EClassAct,BClassAct);
   TotRev=sum(BClassRev,EClassRev,FClassRev);
run;
```

24

Eliminating Variables with the KEEP= Option

Use the KEEP= option to write only the newly created variables, as well as FLIGHTID, DATE, and TOTPASSCAP to the output data set.

```
data ia.sales1999(keep=FlightID Date TotPass
                       Day TotPassCap TotRev);
   set ia.sales1 ia.sales2;
   Day=weekday(Date);
   TotPass=sum(FClassAct,EClassAct,BClassAct);
   TotRev=sum(BClassRev,EClassRev,FClassRev);
run;
```

25

Of the variables to be dropped, three are needed to

- create the variable that reflects the total number of passengers
- compute total revenues.

When the DROP= and KEEP= options are specified in the DATA statement, all variables are available for processing but some variables are not written to the output data set.

   When the DROP= and KEEP= options are specified in the SET statement, the variables that are being eliminated are **not** available for processing.

Adding Options to Enhance Report Appearance

Selected PROC REPORT options:

HEADLINE   underlines all column headers and the spaces between them.

HEADSKIP   writes a blank line beneath all column headers.

26

Writing a PROC REPORT Step

Write a PROC REPORT step. Use the

- HEADLINE and HEADSKIP options to underline the column headers and insert a blank line
- COLUMN statement to specify which variables to include.

```
proc report data=ia.sales1999 nowd headline
            headskip;
   column Date FlightID TotPass TotRev;
   more SAS statements
run;
```

27

Writing a PROC REPORT Step

Use DEFINE statements to define the variables as display variables.

- Add column headers and specify column width.
- Add formats and specify alignment. Add titles.

```
proc report data=ia.sales1999 nowd headline
            headskip;
   column Date FlightId TotPass TotRev;
   define Date     / display center 'Sales Date';
   define FlightId / display center 'Flight';
   define TotPass  / display format=3. width=10
                     center 'Total Passengers';
   define TotRev   / display format=dollar11.2
                     center 'Total Revenue';
   title 'Sales and Passenger Data for 1999';
run;
```

28

Concatenating Two Data Sets to Create a New Data Set and Reporting the Results

File: c6s2d1.sas

Combine the two sets of 1999 sales data, eliminating and creating variables as needed.

- Concatenate IA.SALES1 and IA.SALES2.
- Use the WEEKDAY and SUM functions in assignment statements.
- Use the KEEP= option to eliminate unnecessary variables.
- Create a detail report.

Concatenating Data Sets, Computing New Variables, and Dropping Unwanted Variables

1. Use the SET statement to concatenate IA.SALES1 and IA.SALES2.

2. Write an assignment statement using the WEEKDAY function on the variable DATE to return a numeric value to reflect the day of the week.

3. Use the SUM function in two assignment statements: one to compute the total number of passengers and one to compute total revenues.

4. Use the KEEP= option to write only selected variables to the new data set.

```
data ia.sales1999(keep=FlightID Date Day
                  TotPassCap TotPass TotRev);
   set ia.sales1 ia.sales2;
   Day=weekday(Date);
   TotPass=sum(FClassAct,EClassAct,BClassAct);
   TotRev=sum(BClassRev,EClassRev,FClassRev);
run;
```

5. Submit the program for execution and browse the log.

SAS Log

```
25    data ia.sales1999(keep=FlightID Date Day
26                      TotPassCap TotPass TotRev);
27      set ia.sales1 ia.sales2;
28      Day=weekday(Date);
29      TotPass=sum(FClassAct,EClassAct,BClassAct);
30      TotRev=sum(BClassRev,EClassRev,FClassRev);
31    run;

NOTE: There were 181 observations read from the dataset
IA.SALES1.
NOTE: There were 184 observations read from the dataset
IA.SALES2.
NOTE: The data set IA.SALES1999 has 365 observations and 6
variables.
```

The log indicates that

- 181 observations were read from IA.SALES1 and that 184 observations were read from IA.SALES2
- the data set IA.SALES1999 was successfully created with 365 observations and six variables.

Creating a Detail Report

Use the REPORT procedure with the NOWD option and the HEADLINE and HEADSKIP options.

1. Use the COLUMN statement to specify the variables to be included and their order.

2. Use the DEFINE statement to
   - define all columns as display columns
   - add appropriate column headers and center the column values
   - add formats and increase the column width, as needed.

```
proc report data=ia.sales1999 nowd headline headskip;
   column Date FlightID TotPass TotRev;
   define Date     / display center 'Sales Date';
   define FlightID / display center 'Flight';
   define TotPass  / display format=3. width=10 center
                     'Total Passengers';
   define TotRev   / display format=dollar11.2 center
                     'Total Revenue';
   title 'Sales and Passenger Data for 1999';
run;
```

3. Submit the program for execution and browse the results.

Partial Output

```
           Sales and Passenger Data for 1999

          Sales              Total        Total
          Date     Flight   Passengers   Revenue
          ──────────────────────────────────────

        01JAN1999  IA00100      207    $123,948.00
        02JAN1999  IA00100      166    $117,695.00
        03JAN1999  IA00201      186    $127,197.00
        04JAN1999  IA00300      186    $140,170.00
        05JAN1999  IA00400      194    $141,826.00
        06JAN1999  IA00502      230     $15,110.00
        07JAN1999  IA00504      237     $15,516.00
        08JAN1999  IA00500      227     $14,700.00
        09JAN1999  IA00502      253     $16,326.00
        10JAN1999  IA00604      267     $15,570.00
        11JAN1999  IA00600      231     $15,168.00
        12JAN1999  IA00602      226     $14,996.00
        13JAN1999  IA00604      220     $14,648.00
        14JAN1999  IA00700      205     $77,595.00
        15JAN1999  IA00800      267     $80,235.00
        16JAN1999  IA00902      226     $77,429.00
        17JAN1999  IA00900      262     $88,481.00
        18JAN1999  IA00902      210     $74,374.00
        19JAN1999  IA01000      267     $74,988.00
        20JAN1999  IA01002      241     $82,034.00
        21JAN1999  IA01102      138     $13,914.00
        22JAN1999  IA01104      124     $12,859.00
        23JAN1999  IA01100      118     $12,331.00
```

Exercises

1. **Concatenating SAS Data Sets, Keeping Selected Variables, and Creating a Presentation-quality Report**

   The goal is to create a second-quarter budgetary report for International Airline's Vienna hub.

   One of the first steps is to combine budget information for April, May, and June into one data set. This data is currently stored in separate data sets by month as follows:

   - IA.APRBUDGETV
   - IA.MAYBUDGETV
   - IA.JUNBUDGETV

   a. As a first step, browse the descriptor portion of each data set to determine the number of observations, as well as the number of variables and their attributes.

      How many observations does each data set contain?
      IA.APRBUDGETV   _____
      IA.MAYBUDGETV   _____
      IA.JUNBUDGETV   _____

      How many variables does each data set contain?
      IA.APRBUDGETV   _____
      IA.MAYBUDGETV   _____
      IA.JUNBUDGETV   _____

   b. Concatenate the three data sets and create a new data set called IA.Q2VIENNA. Keep only the variables FLIGHTID, DESTINATION, DATE, FCLASSBUD, ECLASSBUD, FCLASSBUDREV, and ECLASSBUDREV.

   c. Browse the SAS log. There should be no warning or error messages.
      - How many observations are written to the new data set?
      - How many variables does the new data set contain?

   d. Create the following default detail report, and include a descriptive title.

Partial PROC REPORT Output

```
                    Second Quarter Budget Report, Vienna Hub

                                Target    Target
                                Number    Number
                    Des         of First    of      Target Revenue
                    tin  Scheduled   Class  Economy    from First
           Flight   ati  Date of  Passenger Passenger     Class
           Number   on   Flight      s        s       Passengers
           IA06100  CDG  01APR2000    8       85       $3,328.00
           IA05900  CDG  01APR2000    8       85       $2,392.00
           IA07200  FRA  01APR2000   10       97       $1,720.00
           IA04700  LHR  01APR2000   14      120       $2,576.00
           IA06100  CDG  02APR2000    8       85       $3,328.00
           IA05900  CDG  02APR2000    8       85       $2,392.00
           IA07200  FRA  02APR2000   10       97       $1,720.00


                    Second Quarter Budget Report, Vienna Hub


                          Target Revenue
                          from Economy
                           Passengers
                          $11,730.00
                           $8,415.00
                           $5,432.00
                           $7,320.00
                          $11,730.00
                           $8,415.00
                           $5,432.00
```

e. Recall the DATA step and modify it to create two new variables: TOTBUDPASS and TOTBUDREV.

- TOTBUDPASS is the total number of economy and first class passengers projected to fly out of Vienna for the second quarter.

- TOTBUDREV is the total revenue expected from economy and first class passengers who fly out of Vienna for the second quarter.

Do not write the unsummed passenger or revenue values to the new data set; it contains only five variables.

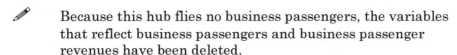 Because this hub flies no business passengers, the variables that reflect business passengers and business passenger revenues have been deleted.

f. Create the final report, shown below. Add the following enhancements as needed:

- Increase column widths and center values.
- Format data values.
- Assign descriptive column headers to the new variables.
- Change the report title as shown.

Partial PROC REPORT Output

		Second Quarter Budget Summary, Vienna Hub		
Flight Number	Destination	Scheduled Date of Flight	Total Budgeted Passengers	Total Budgeted Revenues
IA06100	CDG	01APR2000	93	$15,058.00
IA05900	CDG	01APR2000	93	$10,807.00
IA07200	FRA	01APR2000	107	$7,152.00
IA04700	LHR	01APR2000	134	$9,896.00
IA06100	CDG	02APR2000	93	$15,058.00
IA05900	CDG	02APR2000	93	$10,807.00
IA07200	FRA	02APR2000	107	$7,152.00
IA04700	LHR	02APR2000	134	$9,896.00
IA06100	CDG	03APR2000	93	$15,058.00
IA05900	CDG	03APR2000	93	$10,807.00
IA07200	FRA	03APR2000	107	$7,152.00
IA04700	LHR	03APR2000	134	$9,896.00
IA06100	CDG	04APR2000	93	$15,058.00
IA05900	CDG	04APR2000	93	$10,807.00
IA07200	FRA	04APR2000	107	$7,152.00
IA04700	LHR	04APR2000	134	$9,896.00
IA06100	CDG	05APR2000	93	$15,058.00
IA05900	CDG	05APR2000	93	$10,807.00

6.3 Creating a Summary Report with the REPORT Procedure

Objectives

- Explain the GROUP option used in the DEFINE statement in a PROC REPORT step.

- Explain the SUM option used in the DEFINE statement in a PROC REPORT step.

- Use the SUM and GROUP options and other PROC REPORT features to create a summary report of presentation quality.

32

Business Scenario

International Airlines has already created the following detail report for its annual meeting.

```
           Sales and Passenger Data for 1999

   Sales                      Total         Total
   Date         Flight     Passengers      Revenue

01JAN1999      IA00100        207       $123,948.00
02JAN1999      IA00100        166       $117,695.00
03JAN1999      IA00201        186       $127,197.00
04JAN1999      IA00300        186       $140,170.00
05JAN1999      IA00400        194       $141,826.00
06JAN1999      IA00502        230        $15,110.00
07JAN1999      IA00504        237        $15,516.00
08JAN1999      IA00500        227        $14,700.00
09JAN1999      IA00502        253        $16,326.00
10JAN1999      IA00604        267        $15,570.00
```

33

Business Scenario

International Airlines wants to scrutinize total passengers and revenues by day of the week.

SUNDAY
MONDAY
TUESDAY
WEDNESDAY
THURSDAY
FRIDAY
SATURDAY

34

Business Scenario

Goal Report

Sales and Passenger Data, by Day of Week Sunday through Saturday		
Day of Week	Total Passengers	Total Revenue
1	8,806	$4,019,906.00
2	8,627	$4,038,376.00
3	8,673	$4,054,418.00
4	8,640	$3,932,574.00
5	8,493	$3,982,091.00
6	8,794	$4,103,601.00
7	8,649	$4,033,889.00

35

The Goal Report contains the summed values of selected variables from IA.SALES1999.

Defining Group Variables

Use the REPORT procedure to create a summary report by defining variables as **group** variables.

All observations whose group variables have the same values are collapsed into a single observation in the report.

36

Display = show data
order = order data
Group = collaps data

✎ All of the variables in a summary report must be defined as GROUP, ANALYSIS, COMPUTED, or ACROSS because PROC REPORT must be able to summarize all variables across an observation in order to collapse observations.

Defining Group Variables

DAY as Group Variable			
Before Grouping		**After Grouping**	
DAY	PASSENGERS	DAY	PASSENGERS
SUNDAY	186	SUNDAY	8,806
SUNDAY	267	MONDAY	8,627
MONDAY	210		
MONDAY	150		

37

Defining Group Variables

You can define more than one variable as a group variable, but all group variables must precede other types of variables.

Nesting is determined by the order of the variables in the COLUMN statement.

38

Each analysis variable is summarized based on the statistic that is defined for it. SUM is the default statistic.

Using PROC REPORT to Create a Summary Report

Selecting the Variables

Use the COLUMN statement in a PROC REPORT step to specify the variables to be included in the report.

```
proc report data=ia.sales1999 nowd;
    column Day TotPass TotRev;
    other SAS statements
run;
```

39

Defining the Variable Attributes

Use the DEFINE statement to define DAY as a group variable and assign it a column header.

```
proc report data=ia.sales1999 nowd;
   column Day TotPass TotRev;
   define Day / group 'Day of Week';
   other SAS statements

run;
```

40

Defining the Variable Attributes

Use the DEFINE statement to define TOTPASS and TOTREV as sum variables and assign their attributes.

```
proc report data=ia.sales1999 nowd;
   column Day TotPass TotRev;
   define Day      / group 'Day of Week';
   define TotPass / sum format=comma5.
                    width=10 center
                    'Total Passengers';
   define TotRev  / sum format=dollar13.2
                    width=10 center
                    'Total Revenue';
run;
```

41

Controlling Report Appearance

Use the HEADLINE option to underline the column headers and the HEADSKIP option to add a blank line between the column headers. Add titles.

```
title1 'Sales and Passenger Data, by Day of Week';
title2 'Sunday through Saturday';
proc report data=ia.sales1999 headline headskip
            nowd;
   column Day TotPass TotRev;
   define Day      / group 'Day of Week';
   define TotPass / sum format=comma5.
                    width=10 center
                    'Total Passengers';
   define TotRev  / sum format=dollar13.2
                    center 'Total Revenue';
run;
```

42

Creating a Summary Report

File: c6s3d1.sas

Create a report that summarizes passengers and revenues by day of the week.

- Create a summary report by using the GROUP and SUM options.
- Use other PROC REPORT features to create a presentation-quality summary report.

1. Use the COLUMN statement to specify the variables to be included.

2. Use the DEFINE statement to specify variable usage and attributes.

3. Use the HEADLINE and HEADSKIP options to make the report more readable and add TITLE statements.

```
proc report data=ia.sales1999 headline headskip nowd;
   column Day TotPass TotRev;
   define Day      / group 'Day of Week';
   define TotPass / sum format=comma5. width=10 center
                    'Total Passengers';
   define TotRev  / sum format=dollar13.2 center
                    'Total Revenue';
   title1 'Sales and Passenger Data, by Day of Week';
   title2 'Sunday through Saturday';
run;
```

4. Submit the program for execution.

SAS Output

```
                 Sales and Passenger Data, by Day of Week
                         Sunday through Saturday

            Day of      Total
            Week     Passengers   Total Revenue
            _____

               1        8,806      $4,019,906.00
               2        8,627      $4,038,376.00
               3        8,673      $4,054,418.00
               4        8,640      $3,932,574.00
               5        8,493      $3,982,091.00
               6        8,794      $4,103,601.00
               7        8,649      $4,033,889.00
```

The 1999 passenger counts and revenues are summed by day of the week, starting with Sunday. The values are very similar across days of the week.

Exercises

2. Creating a Summary Report

The following second-quarter report has already been created for
International Airline's Vienna hub.

Partial PROC REPORT Output

```
                Second Quarter Budget Summary, Vienna Hub

                             Scheduled     Total        Total
        Flight                Date of    Budgeted     Budgeted
        Number   Destination   Flight    Passengers   Revenues


        IA06100     CDG      01APR2000       93      $15,058.00
        IA05900     CDG      01APR2000       93      $10,807.00
        IA07200     FRA      01APR2000      107       $7,152.00
        IA04700     LHR      01APR2000      134       $9,896.00
        IA06100     CDG      02APR2000       93      $15,058.00
        IA05900     CDG      02APR2000       93      $10,807.00
        IA07200     FRA      02APR2000      107       $7,152.00
        IA04700     LHR      02APR2000      134       $9,896.00
        IA06100     CDG      03APR2000       93      $15,058.00
        IA05900     CDG      03APR2000       93      $10,807.00
        IA07200     FRA      03APR2000      107       $7,152.00
        IA04700     LHR      03APR2000      134       $9,896.00
        IA06100     CDG      04APR2000       93      $15,058.00
        IA05900     CDG      04APR2000       93      $10,807.00
        IA07200     FRA      04APR2000      107       $7,152.00
        IA04700     LHR      04APR2000      134       $9,896.00
        IA06100     CDG      05APR2000       93      $15,058.00
        IA05900     CDG      05APR2000       93      $10,807.00
        IA07200     FRA      05APR2000      107       $7,152.00
```

a. Use the REPORT procedure to create a summary report based on IA.Q2VIENNA. The report should show the total number of passengers and the total passenger revenues expected for each flight for the quarter.

- Include the variables as shown in the report below and define them to achieve the desired results.
- Apply column formats and widths as needed.
- Supply descriptive column headers.
- Add a report title as shown.

PROC REPORT Output

```
               Second Quarter Budget Summary, Vienna Hub
                              By Flight

                        Total              Total
            Flight     Budgeted          Budgeted
            Number    Passengers          Revenues


            IA04700     9,225           $677,115.00
            IA05900     7,240           $856,760.00
            IA06100     7,340         $1,210,300.00
            IA07200     9,737           $650,832.00
```

6.4   Subsetting Observations from a SAS Data Set

Objectives

- Subset data using the WHERE statement with comparison and logical operators.

- Define special operators and explain how they are used in the WHERE statement.

- Define SAS date constants.

- Define the YEARCUTOFF= option.

- Use a WHERE statement with a special operator to subset a SAS table.

46

Business Scenario

International Airlines wants to create a separate report for the holiday travel season.

```
               Holiday Sales Report
                            Total        Total
Flight    Seats    Passengers    Revenue

IA00300    207       186        $143,754.00
IA00301    207       190        $143,070.00
IA00300    207       176        $133,704.00
IA00301    207       194        $145,354.00
IA00300    207       191        $142,983.00
IA00301    207       169        $133,809.00
IA00300    207       193        $142,977.00
IA00301    207       167        $130,231.00
IA00300    207       207        $156,039.00
```

47

Business Scenario

```
                       Holiday Sales Report

      Sales                           Total          Total
      Date        Flight    Seats    Passengers      Revenue


     24NOV1999    IA00300     207       186        $143,754.00
     25NOV1999    IA00301     207       190        $143,070.00
     26NOV1999    IA00300     207       176        $133,704.00
     27NOV1999    IA00301     207       194        $145,354.00
     28NOV1999    IA00300     207       191        $142,983.00
     29NOV1999    IA00301     207       169        $133,809.00
     30NOV1999    IA00300     207       193        $142,977.00
     01DEC1999    IA00301     207       167        $130,231.00
     02DEC1999    IA00300     207       207        $156,039.00
     03DEC1999    IA00301     207       190        $146,094.00
     04DEC1999    IA00300     207       175        $136,143.00
                                                              48
```

Subsetting Your Data with the WHERE Statement

The WHERE statement enables you to select observations that meet a certain condition before SAS brings the observation into the PROC REPORT step.

Date	FlightID	TotPassCap	TotPass	TotRev
04JAN1999	IA00300	207	186	$140,170.00
26NOV1999	IA00300	207	176	$133,704.00
31DEC1999	IA00401	207	171	$129,491.00

```
proc report data=ia.sales1999 nowd;
   where Date between '24nov1999'd
         and '03jan2000'd;
run;
```

```
      Date  FlightID TotPassCap  TotPass        TotRev
  26NOV1999  IA00300        207      176   $133,704.00
  31DEC1999  IA00401        207      171   $129,491.00
                                                     49
```

Caution: Because the WHERE statement is applied directly to your SAS data set, you must use the variables from the SAS data set.

Subsetting Data with the WHERE Statement

General syntax of the WHERE statement:

WHERE *where-expression*;

where-expression is a sequence of operands and operators. Operands include

- variables
- functions
- constants.

50

Subsetting Your Data with the WHERE Statement

The WHERE statement can be used with

- comparison operators
- logical operators.

You can also use the WHERE statement with special operators.

51

Comparison Operators

Mnemonic	Symbol	Definition
EQ	=	equal to
NE	^=	not equal to
GT	>	greater than
LT	<	less than
GE	>=	greater than or equal to
LE	<=	less than or equal to
IN		equal to one of a list

52

Comparison Operators

Examples:

```
where Salary>25000;
where EmpID='0082';
where Salary=.;
where LastName=' ';
```

Numeric
character
Missing number
missing Character

53

Comparison Operator

You can use the IN comparison operator to see if a variable is equal to one of the values in a list.

Example:

```
where JobCode in ('PILOT1'
                  'PILOT2'
                  'PILOT3');
```

✎ Character comparisons are case sensitive.

54

Logical Operators

Logical operators include

AND if both expressions are true, then the compound expression is true

OR   if either expression is true, then the compound expression is true

NOT can be combined with other operators to reverse the logic of a comparison.

55

Logical Operators

Examples:

```
where JobCode='FLTAT3' and
      Salary>50000;
```

} *Both have to be true*

```
where JobCode='PILOT1' or
      JobCode='PILOT2' or
      JobCode='PILOT3';
```

} *only one may be true*

56

Special Operators

The following are special operators :

- LIKE selects observations by comparing character values to specified patterns. A percent sign (%) replaces any number of characters and an underscore (_) replaces one character.

```
where Code like 'E_U%';
```

(E, a single character, U, followed by any characters.)

continued...
57

Special Operators

- The sounds-like (=*) operator selects observations that contain a spelling variation of the word or words specified.

```
where Name=*'SMITH';
```

(Selects the names Smythe, Smitt, and so on.)

- CONTAINS or ? selects observations that include the specified substring.

```
where Word ? 'LAM';
```

(BLAME, LAMENT, and BEDLAM are selected.)

continued...
58

numeric

Special Operators

character

- IS NULL or IS MISSING selects observations in which the value of the variable is missing.

  ```
  where Flight is missing;
  ```

- BETWEEN-AND selects observations in which the value of the variable falls within a range of values.

  ```
  where Date between '01mar1999'd
                and '01apr1999'd;
  ```

59

The values `'01mar1999'd` and `'01apr1999'd` are SAS date constants.

Using SAS Date Constants

The constant **'ddMMMyyyy'd** creates a SAS date value from the dates enclosed in quotes where

dd   is a one- or two-digit value for the day

MMM   is a three-letter abbreviation for the month (JAN, FEB, MAR, and so on)

yyyy   is a two- or four-digit value for the year.

60

Using the YEARCUTOFF= Option

If you use a two-digit value for year, SAS will use the value of the YEARCUTOFF= system option to determine the complete year value.

YEARCUTOFF= specifies the first year of a 100-year span used to determine the century of a two-digit year.

```
options yearcutoff=1930;
```

...**1900**...**1930**...**1980**...**2029**.**2030**...**2050**...

100 year span

61

Subsetting a Report

Use a WHERE statement with the special operator BETWEEN-AND to create a subset based on dates.

```
proc report data=ia.sales1999 nowd headline
            headskip;
   column Date FlightID TotPassCap TotPass TotRev;
   where Date between '24nov1999'd and '03jan2000'd;
   define Date       / display center 'Sales Date';
   define FlightID   / display center 'Flight';
   define TotPassCap / display format=3. width=5
                       center 'Seats';
   define TotPass    / display format=3. width=10
                       center 'Total Passengers';
   define TotRev     / display format=dollar11.2
                       center 'Total Revenue';
   title 'Holiday Sales Report';
run;
```

62

WHERE or Subsetting IF?

Step and Usage	WHERE Statement	IF Statement
PROC step	Yes	No
DATA step (source of variable)		
INPUT statement	No	Yes
Assignment statement	No	Yes
SET statement (single data set)	Yes	Yes
SET/MERGE (multiple data sets)		
Variable in ALL data sets	Yes	Yes
Variable not in ALL data sets	No	Yes

63

Subsetting Report Data with a WHERE Statement

File: c6s4d1.sas

Use date constants in a WHERE statement to select a subset of data beginning with the 1999 Thanksgiving (late-November US holiday) travel rush and ending after New Years Day 2000.

- Use a special operator in a WHERE statement.
- Use date constants that correspond to the holiday time period.

1. Use the BETWEEN-AND operator in a WHERE statement.

2. Use `'24nov1999'd` and `'03jan2000'd` to reflect the range to be included.

3. Add a title.

```
proc report data=ia.sales1999 nowd headline headskip;
   column Date FlightID TotPassCap TotPass TotRev;
   where Date between '24nov1999'd and '03jan2000'd;
   define Date       / display center 'Sales Date';
   define FlightID   / display center 'Flight';
   define TotPassCap / display format=3. width=5
                       center 'Seats';
   define TotPass    / display format=3. width=10 center
                       'Total Passengers';
   define TotRev     / display format=dollar11.2 center
                       'Total Revenue';
   title 'Holiday Sales Report';
run;
```

4. Submit the program for execution and browse the results.

SAS Output

```
                            Holiday Sales Report

          Sales                         Total          Total
          Date       Flight    Seats   Passengers      Revenue


          24NOV1999  IA00300    207       186        $143,754.00
          25NOV1999  IA00301    207       190        $143,070.00
          26NOV1999  IA00300    207       176        $133,704.00
          27NOV1999  IA00301    207       194        $145,354.00
          28NOV1999  IA00300    207       191        $142,983.00
          29NOV1999  IA00301    207       169        $133,809.00
          30NOV1999  IA00300    207       193        $142,977.00
          01DEC1999  IA00301    207       167        $130,231.00
          02DEC1999  IA00300    207       207        $156,039.00
          03DEC1999  IA00301    207       190        $146,094.00
          04DEC1999  IA00300    207       175        $136,143.00
          05DEC1999  IA00301    207       176        $135,440.00
          06DEC1999  IA00300    207       165        $127,157.00
          07DEC1999  IA00301    207       202        $153,114.00
          08DEC1999  IA00300    207       183        $139,647.00
          09DEC1999  IA00301    207       161        $124,817.00
          10DEC1999  IA00300    207       176        $132,416.00
          11DEC1999  IA00301    207       170        $130,250.00
          12DEC1999  IA00300    207       174        $133,654.00
          13DEC1999  IA00301    207       169        $128,321.00
          14DEC1999  IA00300    207       173        $129,485.00
          15DEC1999  IA00301    207       199        $150,183.00
          16DEC1999  IA00400    207       201        $151,297.00
          17DEC1999  IA00401    207       189        $140,133.00
          18DEC1999  IA00400    207       194        $145,410.00
          19DEC1999  IA00401    207       202        $150,706.00
          20DEC1999  IA00400    207       165        $124,861.00
          21DEC1999  IA00401    207       188        $140,668.00
          22DEC1999  IA00400    207       195        $144,259.00
          23DEC1999  IA00401    207       182        $135,422.00
          24DEC1999  IA00400    207       174        $135,502.00
          25DEC1999  IA00401    207       192        $140,600.00
          26DEC1999  IA00400    207       190        $139,486.00
          27DEC1999  IA00401    207       179        $133,051.00
          28DEC1999  IA00400    207       183        $140,823.00
          29DEC1999  IA00401    207       190        $141,278.00
          30DEC1999  IA00400    207       183        $137,183.00
          31DEC1999  IA00401    207       171        $129,491.00
```

Exercises

3. Using Special Operators in a WHERE Statement for Subsetting

International Airlines has used the following PROC REPORT step to create a budget report for the second quarter.

```
proc report data=ia.q2vienna nowd headline headskip;
   column FlightID Destination Date TotBudPass
          TotBudRev;
   define FlightID    / display;
   define Destination / display width=11 center;
   define Date        / display center;
   define TotBudPass  / display width=10 center
                        'Total Budgeted Passengers';
   define TotBudRev   / display format=dollar10.2
                        'Total Budgeted Revenues';
   title 'Second Quarter Budget Summary, Vienna Hub';
run;
```

a. Modify this program to report only the observations from April 21 through April 30, when a scheduled major music festival will draw more travelers. Change the report title to `Projected Data--Music Festival 2000`. Make other adjustments as needed. You can recall this program from a previous exercise, or you can include the BKUP63 file as a starting point.

Directory-based   `include 'bkup63.sas'`

OS/390   `include '.prog1.sascode(bkup63)'`

The final report is displayed below.

PROC REPORT Output

```
                Projected Data -- Music Festival 2000

                     Scheduled     Total         Total
      Flight         Date of       Budgeted      Budgeted
      Number  Destination  Flight  Passengers    Revenues


      IA06100    CDG     21APR2000      93      $15,058.00
      IA05900    CDG     21APR2000      93      $10,807.00
      IA07200    FRA     21APR2000     107       $7,152.00
      IA04700    LHR     21APR2000     134       $9,896.00
      IA06100    CDG     22APR2000      93      $15,058.00
      IA05900    CDG     22APR2000      93      $10,807.00
      IA07200    FRA     22APR2000     107       $7,152.00
      IA04700    LHR     22APR2000     134       $9,896.00
      IA06100    CDG     23APR2000      93      $15,058.00
      IA05900    CDG     23APR2000      93      $10,807.00
      IA07200    FRA     23APR2000     107       $7,152.00
      IA04700    LHR     23APR2000     134       $9,896.00
      IA06100    CDG     24APR2000      93      $15,058.00
      IA05900    CDG     24APR2000      93      $10,807.00
      IA07200    FRA     24APR2000     107       $7,152.00
      IA04700    LHR     24APR2000     134       $9,896.00
      IA06100    CDG     25APR2000      93      $15,058.00
      IA05900    CDG     25APR2000      93      $10,807.00
      IA07200    FRA     25APR2000     107       $7,152.00
      IA04700    LHR     25APR2000     134       $9,896.00
      IA06100    CDG     26APR2000      93      $15,058.00
      IA05900    CDG     26APR2000      93      $10,807.00
      IA07200    FRA     26APR2000     107       $7,152.00
      IA04700    LHR     26APR2000     134       $9,896.00
      IA06100    CDG     27APR2000      93      $15,058.00
      IA05900    CDG     27APR2000      93      $10,807.00
      IA07200    FRA     27APR2000     107       $7,152.00
      IA04700    LHR     27APR2000     134       $9,896.00
      IA06100    CDG     28APR2000      93      $15,058.00
      IA05900    CDG     28APR2000      93      $10,807.00
      IA07200    FRA     28APR2000     107       $7,152.00
      IA04700    LHR     28APR2000     134       $9,896.00
      IA06100    CDG     29APR2000      93      $15,058.00
      IA05900    CDG     29APR2000      93      $10,807.00
      IA07200    FRA     29APR2000     107       $7,152.00
      IA04700    LHR     29APR2000     134       $9,896.00
      IA06100    CDG     30APR2000      93      $15,058.00
      IA05900    CDG     30APR2000      93      $10,807.00
      IA07200    FRA     30APR2000     107       $7,152.00
      IA04700    LHR     30APR2000     134       $9,896.00
```

6.5 Chapter Summary

Concatenation is one of several methods for combining SAS data sets. Two or more SAS data sets are combined one after the other in a stacking operation. Use the SET statement to perform a concatenation. The data sets are appended in the order in which they are listed.

You can use an assignment statement and SAS functions to create new variables.

- Use the WEEKDAY function in an assignment statement to return a value for each day of the week based on the date values.
- Use the SUM function in an assignment statement to sum the values of the selected arguments.

Use the KEEP= or DROP= option to prevent SAS variables from being written to a SAS data set. When the DROP= and KEEP= options are specified on the DATA statement, the variables are available for processing but are not written to the output data set. However, when these options are specified on the SET statement, the variables that are eliminated are **not** available for processing.

You can use the REPORT procedure to create detail or summary reports of presentation quality. Use the COLUMN statement to specify which variables are to be included. Use the DEFINE statement to specify the usage as DISPLAY, GROUP, or SUM. You can create a summary report by adding the GROUP option to define a group variable and by adding the SUM option to add variable values for all like values of the group variable. All observations whose group variables have the same values are collapsed into a single observation in the report. You can define more than one variable as a group variable, but group variables must precede other types of variables. Nesting is determined by the order of the variables in the COLUMN statement.

You can use PROC REPORT to determine variable attributes, such as column width, column headers, formats, and alignment. Add the following options to improve the report's appearance:

- HEADLINE underlines all column headers and the spaces between them
- HEADSKIP writes a blank line beneath all column headers.

Use the WHERE statement with comparison operators, logical operators, and special operators to subset the observations that are written to an output data set. The following are examples of special operators:

- LIKE selects rows by comparing character values to specified patterns
- sounds_LIKE (=*) selects observations that contain a spelling variation of the word(s) specified
- IS NULL or IS MISSING selects observations where the variable value is missing
- BETWEEN-AND selects observations where the variable value falls within a range of values.

You can use SAS date constants to generate a SAS date value from a specific date that has been entered in SAS code. The date constant '*ddMMMyyyy*'d creates a SAS date value from the dates enclosed in quotes, for example, `'01mar1999'd`.

Using four digits for the year value is strongly recommended. However, if you use a two-digit value, you can use the value of the SAS system option YEARCUTOFF= to determine the first two digits of the year of a four-digit year value, for example,

```
options yearcutoff=1920;
```

General form of a DATA step concatenation:

DATA *SAS-data-set*;
    SET *SAS-data-set-1 SAS-data-set-2*;
RUN;

General form of the SET statement:

SET *SAS-data-set*;

General form of the WEEKDAY function:

WEEKDAY(*date*)

General form of the SUM function:

SUM(*argument1,argument2,…*)

General form of the DROP= and KEEP= data set options:

SAS-data-set (**DROP**=*variable(s)*)

SAS-data-set(**KEEP**=*variable(s)*)

General form of a PROC REPORT step in nonwindowing mode:

PROC REPORT DATA=*SAS-data-set* <*options*>;
    COLUMN *variable-list*;
    DEFINE *report-item* </*usage*> <*attribute-list*>;
RUN;

General form of the WHERE statement:

WHERE *where-expression*;

General form of the YEARCUTOFF= option in an OPTIONS statement:

OPTIONS YEARCUTOFF=*four-digit-year*;

6.6 Solutions

1. **Concatenating SAS Data Sets, Keeping Selected Variables, and Creating a Presentation-quality Report**

    a. Write and submit PROC CONTENTS steps for each of the three data sets. Browse the output.

    ```
    proc contents data=ia.aprbudgetv;
    run;
    ```

    Partial PROC CONTENTS for IA.APRBUDGETV

    ```
                          The CONTENTS Procedure

    Data Set Name: IA.APRBUDGETV              Observations:          120
    Member Type:   DATA                       Variables:             19
    Engine:        V8                         Indexes:               0
    Created:       15:49 Monday, January 24, 2000   Observation Length:    144
    Last Modified: 15:49 Monday, January 24, 2000   Deleted Observations: 0
    Protection:                               Compressed:            NO
    Data Set Type:                            Sorted:                NO
    Label:
    ```

    The data set IA.APRBUDGETV contains 120 observations and 19 variables.

    ```
    proc contents data=ia.maybudgetv;
    run;
    ```

    Partial PROC CONTENTS for IA.MAYBUDGETV

    ```
                          The CONTENTS Procedure

    Data Set Name: IA.MAYBUDGETV              Observations:          67
    Member Type:   DATA                       Variables:             19
    Engine:        V8                         Indexes:               0
    Created:       15:50 Monday, January 24, 2000   Observation Length:    144
    Last Modified: 15:50 Monday, January 24, 2000   Deleted Observations: 0
    Protection:                               Compressed:            NO
    Data Set Type:                            Sorted:                NO
    Label:
    ```

    The data set IA.MAYBUDGETV contains 67 observations and 19 variables.

```
proc contents data=ia.junbudgetv;
run;
```

Partial PROC CONTENTS for IA.JUNBUDGETV

```
                          The CONTENTS Procedure

Data Set Name: IA.JUNBUDGETV              Observations:          120
Member Type:   DATA                       Variables:             19
Engine:        V8                         Indexes:               0
Created:       15:50 Monday, January 24, 2000   Observation Length:    144
Last Modified: 15:50 Monday, January 24, 2000   Deleted Observations: 0
Protection:                               Compressed:            NO
Data Set Type:                            Sorted:                NO
Label:
```

The data set IA.JUNBUDGETV contains 120 observations and 19 variables.

b. Write and submit the following DATA step:
```
data ia.q2vienna(keep=FlightID Destination Date
                      FClassBud EClassBud
                      FClassBudRev EClassBudRev);
   set ia.aprbudgetv ia.maybudgetv ia.junbudgetv;
run;
```

c. The new data set contains 307 observations and 7 variables.

d. Write and submit the following PROC REPORT step:
```
proc report data=ia.q2vienna nowd;
   title 'Second Quarter Budget Report, Vienna Hub';
run;
```

e. Recall the DATA step and change the program accordingly:
```
data ia.q2vienna(keep=FlightID Destination Date
                      TotBudPass TotBudRev);
   set ia.q2vienna;
   TotBudPass=sum(FClassBud,EClassBud);
   TotBudRev=sum(FClassBudRev,EClassBudRev);
run;
```

f. Write and submit the following PROC REPORT step:

```
proc report data=ia.q2vienna nowd headline headskip;
   column FlightID Destination Date TotBudPass
          TotBudRev;
   define FlightID    / display;
   define Destination / display width=11 center;
   define Date        / display center;
   define TotBudPass  / display width=10 center
                        'Total Budgeted Passengers';
   define TotBudRev   / display format=dollar10.2
                        'Total Budgeted Revenues';
   title 'Second Quarter Budget Summary, Vienna Hub';
run;
```

2. **Creating a Summary Report**

a. Write and submit the following PROC REPORT step:

```
proc report data=ia.q2vienna nowd headline headskip;
   column FlightID TotBudPass TotBudRev;
   define FlightID   / group;
   define TotBudPass / sum width=10 format=comma6.
                       center
                       'Total Budgeted Passengers';
   define TotBudRev  / sum format=dollar13.2
                       'Total Budgeted Revenues';
   title 'Second Quarter Budget Summary, Vienna Hub';
   title2 'By Flight';
run;
```

3. **Using Special Operators in a WHERE Statement for Subsetting**

a. Add the WHERE statement to the program and change the title as shown. Submit the program.

```
proc report data=ia.q2vienna nowd headline headskip;
   column FlightID Destination Date TotBudPass
          TotBudRev;
   where Date between '21apr2000'd and '30apr2000'd;
   define FlightID    / display;
   define Destination / display width=11 center;
   define Date        / display center;
   define TotBudPass  / display width=10 center
                        'Total Budgeted Passengers';
   define TotBudRev   / display format=dollar10.2
                        'Total Budgeted Revenues';
   title 'Projected Data -- Music Festival 2000';
run;
```

Chapter 7   Merging SAS® Data Sets and Creating HTML Reports

7.1   Introduction

Objectives

- Merge SAS data sets using the DATA step.
- Prepare data for merging using the SORT procedure and data set options.
- Create HTML reports using the Output Delivery System.
- Use the SQL procedure to join data sets, create reports, and create data sets.

3

Use "merge" Statement
to Put the data
Side-by-Side for a
Particular Variable
instead of a
"Set" Statement

Business Scenario

International Airlines is comparing monthly sales performance to monthly sales goals.

The sales and goal information is stored in two SAS data sets.

4

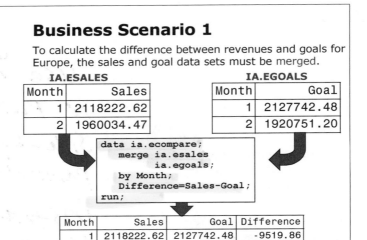

Business Scenario 1

To calculate the difference between revenues and goals for Europe, the sales and goal data sets must be merged.

IA.ESALES

Month	Sales
1	2118222.62
2	1960034.47

IA.EGOALS

Month	Goal
1	2127742.48
2	1920751.20

```
data ia.ecompare;
  merge ia.esales
        ia.egoals;
  by Month;
  Difference=Sales-Goal;
run;
```

Month	Sales	Goal	Difference
1	2118222.62	2127742.48	-9519.86
2	1960034.47	1920751.20	39283.27

5

Business Scenario 2

To calculate the difference between revenues and goals for multiple regions, the sales and goal data sets must be manipulated and then merged.

Match on MONTH and REGION

SaleMon	Region	FSales
1	Europe	2118222.62
1	North America	3135765.34
2	Europe	1960034.47
2	North America	2926929.91

Month	Region	FGoal
1	North America	2934441.72
1	Europe	2127742.48
2	North America	2747787.49
2	Europe	1920758.20

Rename to MONTH

Sort by REGION within MONTH

6

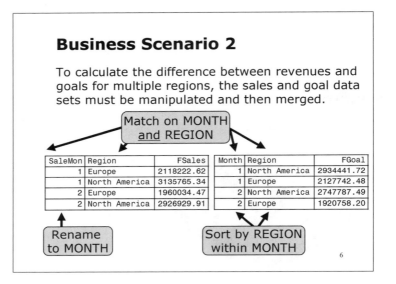

Business Scenario

Present the information as HTML reports.

HTML List Report

Month	Region	First Class	Business Class	Economy Class
1	Europe	$-9,519.86	$49,696.80	$69,953.42
1	North America	$201,323.62	$55,122.24	$265,783.52
2	Europe	$39,283.27	$95,708.98	$346,825.71
2	North America	$179,142.42	$117,457.44	$567,062.79
3	Europe	$-30,892.40	$78,634.66	$396,138.11
3	North America	$55,779.15	$97,362.38	$349,177.00
4	Europe	$71,851.76	$69,358.33	$110,510.24
4	North America	$29,880.04	$62,558.06	$615,186.80
5	Europe	$-27,530.75	$71,733.95	$499,819.92
5	North America	$127,052.96	$131,867.46	$317,823.87

7

7.2   Merging SAS Data Sets

Objectives

- Merge SAS data sets on a single common variable.
- Sort a data set, rename variables, and perform a merge using multiple common variables.

9

The two data Sets must be Sorted the Same before merge

Merging SAS Data Sets

IA.ESALES

Month	Sales
1	2118222.62
2	1960034.47
3	2094220.35

IA.EGOALS

Month	Goal
1	2127742.48
2	1920751.20
3	2125112.75

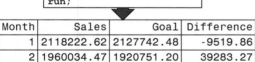

```
data ia.ecompare;
   merge ia.esales
         ia.egoals;
   by Month;
   Difference=Sales-Goal;
run;
```

Month	Sales	Goal	Difference
1	2118222.62	2127742.48	-9519.86
2	1960034.47	1920751.20	39283.27
3	2094220.35	2125112.75	-30892.40

Merging SAS Data Sets

General form of a DATA step match-merge:

```
DATA SAS-data-set;
    MERGE SAS-data-sets;
    BY by-variable(s);
    other statements
RUN;
```

11

"By" statement Checks for Sorting, if not sorted the
by the month ("by" variable) two data sets are
same, it gives errors.

Coding the DATA Step

Use the DATA statement to begin the DATA step and name the new data set.

```
data ia.ecompare;
```

Use the MERGE statement to identify the input data sets to be combined.

```
data ia.ecompare;
   merge ia.esales ia.egoals;
```

12

Any number of SAS data sets can be combined with the MERGE statement.

Coding the DATA Step

Use the BY statement to identify the matching or key variable.

```
data ia.ecompare;
   merge ia.esales ia.egoals;
   by Month;
```

13

The input SAS data sets must be ordered by (sorted) or indexed on the matching variable(s) used in the BY statement.

Coding the DATA Step

Add other statements to manipulate the combined data.

```
data ia.ecompare;
   merge ia.esales ia.egoals;
   by Month;
   Difference=Sales-Goal;
run;
```

14

Performing a Merge

IA.ESALES

Month	Sales
1	2118222.62
2	1960034.47
3	2094220.35

IA.EGOALS

Month	Goal
1	2127742.48
2	1920751.20
3	2125112.75

```
data ia.ecompare;
   merge ia.esales
         ia.egoals;
   by Month;
   Difference=Sales-Goal;
run;
```

IA.ECOMPARE

Month	Sales	Goal	Difference
1	2118222.62	2127742.48	-9519.86
2	1960034.47	1920751.20	39283.27
3	2094220.35	2125112.75	-30892.40

15

1. The value of MONTH is compared in both data sets.

2. If the MONTH value is the same, then the observation is read from each data set to create a composite observation.

3. Once the data is read, the DIFFERENCE value is calculated and a new observation is written to IA.ECOMPARE.

4. The value of MONTH is compared in the next observation of both data sets.

Performing a Merge

File: c7s2d1.sas

Compare the monthly sales performance for the European first class revenue with the monthly sales goals. Merge the IA.ESALES and IA.EGOALS data sets, and use MONTH as the variable to match the appropriate observation from each data set.

```
data ia.ecompare;
   merge ia.esales ia.egoals;
   by Month;
   Difference=Sales-Goal;
run;

proc print data=ia.ecompare;
   title 'Sales Performance';
run;
```

SAS Output

		Sales Performance		
Obs	Month	Sales	Goal	Difference
1	1	2118222.62	2127742.48	-9519.86
2	2	1960034.47	1920751.20	39283.27
3	3	2094220.35	2125112.75	-30892.40
4	4	2130248.76	2058397.00	71851.76
5	5	2100211.73	2127742.48	-27530.75
6	6	2164796.68	2056301.92	108494.76
7	7	2252662.24	2127230.78	125431.46
8	8	2159234.26	2126673.18	32561.08
9	9	2146457.73	2057372.41	89085.32
10	10	2294300.1	2127742.48	166557.62
11	11	2144188.67	2057326.51	86862.16
12	12	2247953.83	2126183.24	121770.59

Business Scenario 2

Analyze the sales performance for Europe and North America together. To merge the data sets,

- alter the data so that the data sets are compatible

- match observations using more than one common variable.

17

Preparing Data for Merging

Often you must manipulate data before you can perform a merge. You might have to

- rename variables

- sort the data.

18

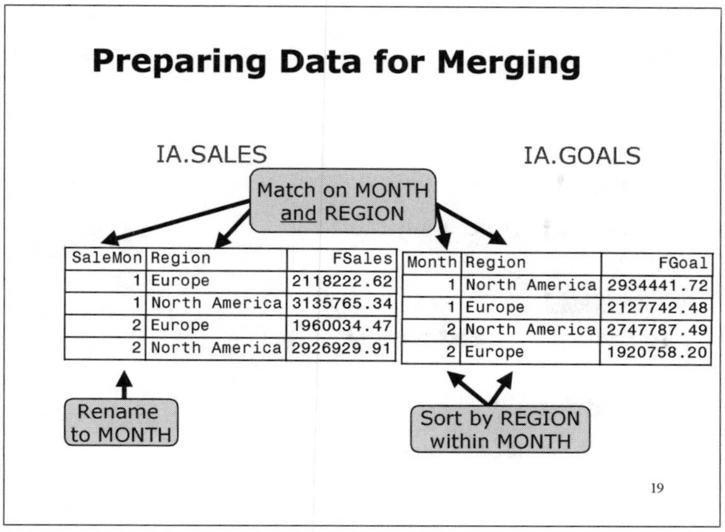
Preparing Data for Merging
IA.SALES
IA.GOALS
Match on MONTH and REGION
SaleMon | Region | FSales
1 | Europe | 2118222.62
1 | North America | 3135765.34
2 | Europe | 1960034.47
2 | North America | 2926929.91
Month | Region | FGoal
1 | North America | 2934441.72
1 | Europe | 2127742.48
2 | North America | 2747787.49
2 | Europe | 1920758.20
Rename to MONTH
Sort by REGION within MONTH
19

1. The matching variables do not have the same name. SALEMON must be renamed to MONTH.

2. The observations need to have matching values for REGION and MONTH. IA.GOALS is not in the correct order. It must be sorted by REGION within each MONTH.

Sorting a SAS Data Set

General form of the PROC SORT step:

```
PROC SORT DATA=input-SAS-data-set
          OUT=output-SAS-data-set;
     BY <DESCENDING> by-variable(s);
RUN;
```

20

Sorting is very time Consuming

If the OUT= option is omitted, the DATA= data set is sorted and the sorted version replaces the original data set.

To sort variables in descending order, use the keyword DESCENDING before the name of each variable in the BY statement whose values you want sorted in descending order.

Sorting a SAS Data Set

The SORT procedure

- rearranges the observations in a SAS data set
- can create a new SAS data set containing the rearranged observations
- can sort on multiple variables
- can sort in ascending (default) or descending order
- does not generate printed output
- treats missing values as the smallest possible value.

21

The missing #s Comes First

Sorting a SAS Data Set

Create a temporary copy of IA.GOALS that is in the order needed to perform a merge.

```
proc sort data=ia.goals out=work.goals;
   by Month Region;
run;
```

22

The RENAME= Data Set Option

You can use a RENAME= data set option to change the name of a variable for the duration of a step.

General form of the RENAME= data set option:

> SAS-data-set(RENAME=(old-name=new-name))

This is to make sure that the columns headings are the same, when you merge 2 data sets.

23

When the RENAME= data set option is used with an input SAS data set, the new name is used in the DATA step program and in the output SAS data set, but it is not changed in the input data set.

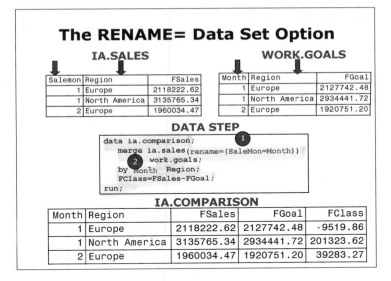

The RENAME= Data Set Option

IA.SALES

Salemon	Region	FSales
1	Europe	2118222.62
1	North America	3135765.34
2	Europe	1960034.47

WORK.GOALS

Month	Region	FGoal
1	Europe	2127742.48
1	North America	2934441.72
2	Europe	1920751.20

DATA STEP

```
data ia.comparison;
   merge ia.sales(rename=(SaleMon=Month))
         work.goals;
   by Month  Region;
   FClass=FSales-FGoal;
run;
```

IA.COMPARISON

Month	Region	FSales	FGoal	FClass
1	Europe	2118222.62	2127742.48	-9519.86
1	North America	3135765.34	2934441.72	201323.62
2	Europe	1960034.47	1920751.20	39283.27

1. Rename the variable SALEMON to MONTH as the data is read in from IA.SALES. Because the name change occurs during the reading of data, the new name, MONTH, is used in the subsequent DATA step code. The structure of IA.SALES is unchanged, which means that SALEMON is still the variable name in the IA.SALES data set.

2. Use the values of the MONTH and REGION variables to match appropriate observations.

Performing a Match MERGE

IA.SALES

SaleMon	Region	FSales
1	Europe	2118222.62
1	North America	3135765.34
2	Europe	1960034.47

WORK.GOALS

Month	Region	FGoal
1	Europe	2127742.48
1	North America	2934441.72
2	Europe	1920751.20

DATA STEP

```
data ia.comparison;
   merge ia.sales(rename=(SaleMon=Month))
         work.goals;
   by Month Region;
   FClass=FSales-FGoal;
run;
```

IA.COMPARISON

Month	Region	FSales	FGoal	FClass
1	Europe	2118222.62	2127742.48	-9519.86
1	North America	3135765.34	2934441.72	201323.62
2	Europe	1960034.47	1920751.20	39283.27

1. The values of MONTH and REGION are compared in both data sets.

2. If the MONTH and REGION values are the same, then the observation is read from each data set to create a composite observation.

3. Once the data is read, the new variable's values are calculated and a new observation is written to IA.COMPARISON.

4. The values of MONTH and REGION are compared in the next observation of both data sets.

Performing a Match Merge

File: c7s2d2.sas

1. Sort the input SAS data set by the common variables. Create an output SAS data set.

```
proc sort data=ia.goals out=work.goals;
   by Month Region;
run;
```

2. Rename SALEMON to MONTH, merge the sorted SAS data sets, create three new variables, and display the new data set.

```
data ia.comparison(keep=Month Region FClass
                        BClass EClass);
   merge ia.sales(rename=(SaleMon=Month))
         work.goals;
   by Month Region;
   FClass=FSales-FGoal;
   BClass=BSales-BGoal;
   EClass=ESales-EGoal;
run;

proc print data=ia.comparison;
   title 'Sales Performance';
run;
```

Partial SAS Output

		Sales Performance			
Obs	Month	Region	FClass	BClass	EClass
1	1	Europe	-9519.86	49696.80	69953.42
2	1	North America	201323.62	55122.24	265783.52
3	2	Europe	39283.27	95708.98	346825.71
4	2	North America	179142.42	117457.44	567062.79
5	3	Europe	-30892.40	78634.66	396138.11
6	3	North America	55779.15	97362.38	349177.00
7	4	Europe	71851.76	69358.33	110510.24
8	4	North America	29880.04	62558.06	615186.80
9	5	Europe	-27530.75	71733.95	499819.92
10	5	North America	127052.96	131867.46	317823.87
11	6	Europe	108494.76	110510.22	177129.48
12	6	North America	175409.32	51533.25	298882.81
13	7	Europe	125431.46	71825.29	303767.41
14	7	North America	95644.19	97077.67	456643.13

Exercises

1. Sorting and Merging Data

The weather in Birmingham, Alabama, on December 15, 1999, might have caused some customers to alter their shipping plans. Investigate how much cargo revenue was lost on all flights out of Birmingham by comparing the budgeted revenue with the actual revenue.

a. Sort the data set IA.BUDGET121999 into a temporary data set called SORTB. Sort by the variable FLIGHTID. Use the WHERE statement to create a subset for Birmingham on December 15, 1999.

```
where Date='15dec1999'd and Origin='BHM';
```

b. Sort the data set IA.SALES121999 into a temporary data set called SORTS. Sort by the variable FLIGHTID. Use the WHERE statement to create a subset for Birmingham on December 15, 1999.

```
where Date='15dec1999'd and Origin='BHM';
```

c. Create a new temporary data set called COMPARE by merging the SORTB and SORTS data sets by the variable FLIGHTID. Subtract CARGOREV from CARGOBUDREV to create a new variable called LOSTCARGOREV.

d. Print the data set COMPARE (all variables except FLIGHTID) and label the LOSTCARGOREV variable. Format the LOSTCARGOREV variable with dollar signs and two decimal digits.

		Scheduled			
Start		Date of	Target Revenue	Revenue from	Lost Cargo
Point	Destination	Flight	from Cargo	Cargo	Revenue
BHM	RDU	15DEC1999	$3,441.00	$3,751.00	$-310.00
BHM	RDU	15DEC1999	$3,441.00	$3,441.00	$0.00
BHM	RDU	15DEC1999	$3,441.00	$2,821.00	$620.00
BHM	RDU	15DEC1999	$3,441.00	$3,751.00	$-310.00
BHM	RDU	15DEC1999	$3,441.00	$2,883.00	$558.00
BHM	RDU	15DEC1999	$3,441.00	$2,945.00	$496.00

Birmingham Flights - Dec 15, 1999

Other Merges (Self-study)

The DATA step merge works with many other kinds of data combinations:

One-to-many	Unique BY values are in one data set and duplicate matching BY values are in the other data set.
Many-to-many	Duplicate matching BY values are in both data sets.
Non-matches	Some BY values in one data set have no matching BY values in the other data set.

28

One-To-Many Merging

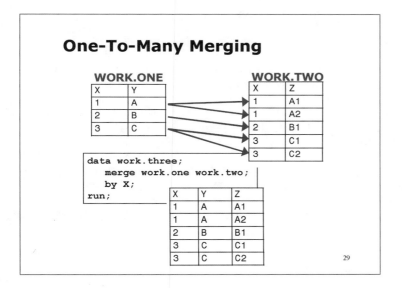

29

A one-to-many merge is common when you are combining a single master observation with multiple transaction observations. The resulting data set contains the master information attached to each transaction.

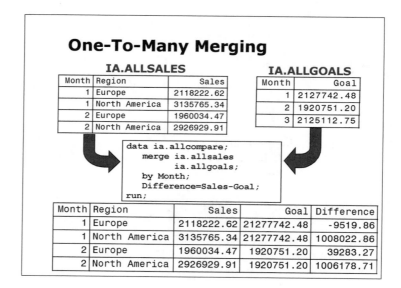

One-To-Many Merging

IA.ALLSALES

Month	Region	Sales
1	Europe	2118222.62
1	North America	3135765.34
2	Europe	1960034.47
2	North America	2926929.91

IA.ALLGOALS

Month	Goal
1	2127742.48
2	1920751.20
3	2125112.75

```
data ia.allcompare;
   merge ia.allsales
         ia.allgoals;
   by Month;
   Difference=Sales-Goal;
run;
```

Month	Region	Sales	Goal	Difference
1	Europe	2118222.62	21277742.48	-9519.86
1	North America	3135765.34	21277742.48	1008022.86
2	Europe	1960034.47	1920751.20	39283.27
2	North America	2926929.91	1920751.20	1006178.71

In a one-to-many merge situation, the single observation is sequentially combined with each of the matching observations.

1. The values of MONTH are compared in both data sets.

2. If the MONTH values are the same, then the observation is read from each data set to create a composite observation.

   If the values are not the same, the DATA step reads the next observation (in this example, from IA.ALLSALES) and combines its data values with the already read values (in this example, from IA.ALLGOALS).

3. Once the data is read, the new variable's values are calculated and a new observation is written to IA.ALLCOMPARE.

4. The values of MONTH are compared in the next observation of both data sets.

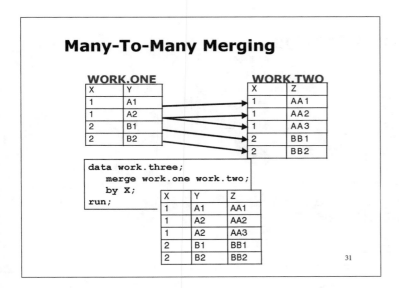

Each matching observation is combined sequentially. If there is an uneven number of matches, then the merge performs a one-to-many merge for the remaining observations.

Caution: This is not a very common form of the DATA step merge. Usually multiple BY variables are used to more specifically match the observations.

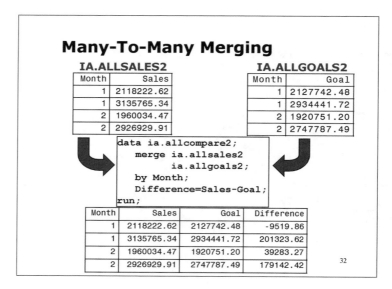

In a many-to-many merge situation, each matching observation is combined sequentially.

1. The values of MONTH are compared in both data sets.

2. If the MONTH values are the same, then the observation is read from each data set to create a composite observation.

3. Once the data is read, the new variable's values are calculated and a new observation is written to IA.ALLCOMPARE2.

4. The values of MONTH are compared in the next observation of both data sets.

 It is important to note that this example requires perfectly matched data to produce the correct result. The merge can be more safely performed if a REGION variable exists and the data is merged by MONTH and REGION.

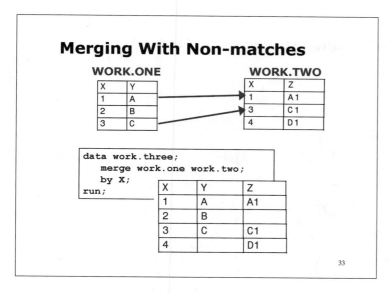

Non-matches occur when you have information for a BY variable in one data set but not in the other. This is common when you merge a master file, which has an observation for each BY value, with a sparse transaction file, that is, there is not an observation for every BY value.

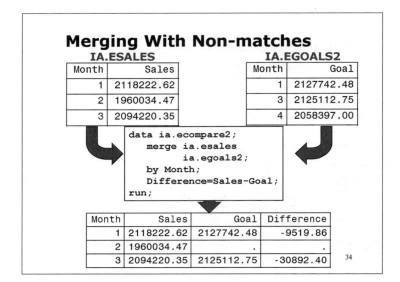

In a non-matching merge situation, matching observations are combined and the observations without matches are present in the result but do not have data for all variables.

1. The values of MONTH are compared in both data sets.

2. If the MONTH values are the same, then the observation is read from each data set to create a composite observation.

   If the values are not the same, the one with the next value in the sort order (in this example, the lower of the two numbers) is read. For the data set that is not read, the read pointer remains at the same observation for the next iteration and the variables unique to that data set have missing values for the DATA step calculations.

3. Once the data is read, the new variable's values are calculated and a new observation is written to IA.ECOMPARE2.

4. The values of MONTH are compared in the next observation of both data sets.

Other Merges

File: c7s2d3.sas

One-To-Many Merge

IA.SALES_ALL contains a sales figure for each month for each region. IA.BUDGET_ALL contains a sales goal for each month. (Each region has the same sales goal for each month.) Merge the data sets and create a listing report that displays the sales performance for each month for each region.

```
data ia.allcompare;
   merge ia.allsales ia.allgoals;
   by Month;
   Difference=Sales-Goal;
run;

proc print data=ia.allcompare;
   title 'Sales Performance';
run;
```

Partial SAS Output

```
                              Sales Performance

Obs          Month  Region               Sales       Goal        Difference

  1             1    Europe          2118222.62   2127742.48       -9519.86
  2             1    North America   3135765.34   2127742.48     1008022.86
  3             2    Europe          1960034.47   1920751.20       39283.27
  4             2    North America   2926929.91   1920751.20     1006178.71
  5             3    Europe          2094220.35   2125112.75      -30892.40
  6             3    North America   3065902.93   2125112.75      940790.18
  7             4    Europe          2130248.76   2058397.00       71851.76
  8             4    North America   3496058.61   2058397.00     1437661.61
  9             5    Europe          2100211.73   2127742.48      -27530.75
 10             5    North America   3135696.04   2127742.48     1007953.56
 11             6    Europe          2164796.68   2056301.92      108494.76
 12             6    North America   3088312.62   2056301.92     1032010.70
```

Many-To-Many Merge

IA.ALLSALES2 contains two observations for each month. (There is one for each region, but there is no REGION variable.) IA.ALLGOALS2 contains two observations for each month (one for each region, but no REGION variable). Merge the data sets and create a listing report that displays the sales performance for each month for each region.

```
data ia.allcompare2;
   merge ia.allsales2 ia.allgoals2;
   by Month;
   Difference=Sales-Goal;
run;

proc print data=ia.allcompare2;
run;
```

Partial SAS Output

Sales Performance				
Obs	Month	Sales	Goal	Difference
1	1	2118222.62	2127742.48	-9519.86
2	1	3135765.34	2934441.72	201323.62
3	2	1960034.47	1920751.20	39283.27
4	2	2926929.91	2747787.49	179142.42
5	3	2094220.35	2125112.75	-30892.40
6	3	3065902.93	3010123.78	55779.15
7	4	2130248.76	2058397.00	71851.76
8	4	3496058.61	3466178.57	29880.04
9	5	2100211.73	2127742.48	-27530.75
10	5	3135696.04	3008643.08	127052.96
11	6	2164796.68	2056301.92	108494.76
12	6	3088312.62	2912903.30	175409.32

    It is important to note that this example requires perfectly matched data to produce the correct result. The merge can be more safely performed if a REGION variable exists and the data is merged by MONTH and REGION.

Merging with Non-matches

IA.ESALES contains one observation for each month. IA.EGOALS2 contains one observation for each month except February. Merge the data sets and create a listing report that displays the sales performance for each month.

```
data ia.ecompare2;
   merge ia.esales ia.egoals2;
   by Month;
   Difference=Sales-Goal;
run;

proc print data=ia.ecompare2;
   title 'Sales Performance';
run;
```

SAS Output

```
                              Sales Performance

      Obs         Month           Sales          Goal        Difference

       1             1        2118222.62     2127742.48        -9519.86
       2             2        1960034.47          .                .
       3             3        2094220.35     2125112.75       -30892.40
       4             4        2130248.76     2058397.00        71851.76
       5             5        2100211.73     2127742.48       -27530.75
       6             6        2164796.68     2056301.92       108494.76
       7             7        2252662.24     2127230.78       125431.46
       8             8        2159234.26     2126673.18        32561.08
       9             9        2146457.73     2057372.41        89085.32
      10            10        2294300.1      2127742.48       166557.62
      11            11        2144188.67     2057326.51        86862.16
      12            12        2247953.83     2126183.24       121770.59
```

7.3 Creating HTML Reports

Objectives

- Create HTML reports using the Output Delivery System (ODS).

37

Business Scenario

International Airlines is examining how its sales compared to its goals. The information will be presented as HTML reports.

HTML List Report

Month	Region	First Class	Business Class	Economy Class
1	Europe	$-9,519.86	$49,696.80	$69,953.42
1	North America	$201,323.62	$55,122.24	$265,783.52
2	Europe	$39,283.27	$95,708.98	$346,825.71
2	North America	$179,142.42	$117,457.44	$567,062.79
3	Europe	$-30,892.40	$78,634.66	$396,138.11
3	North America	$55,779.15	$97,362.38	$349,177.00
4	Europe	$71,851.76	$69,358.33	$110,510.24
4	North America	$29,880.04	$62,558.06	$615,186.80
5	Europe	$-27,530.75	$71,733.95	$499,819.92
5	North America	$127,052.96	$131,867.46	$317,823.87

8

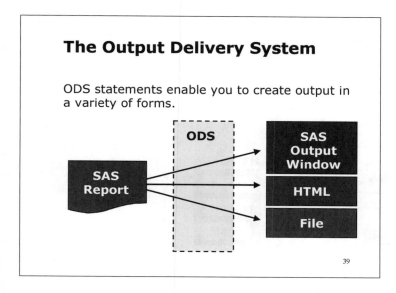

The Output Delivery System

ODS statements enable you to create output in a variety of forms.

39

Generating HTML Files

The ODS HTML statement opens, closes, or manages the HTML destination.

General form of the ODS statement to create an HTML file:

```
ODS HTML FILE='HTML-file-specification'
    <options>;
SAS code generating output
ODS HTML CLOSE;
```

40

Additional ODS HTML statement options are available that enable you to organize your HTML output for easy and efficient access and viewing.

CONTENTS=*'filename'*   contains links to the individual pieces of output contained in the HTML body file.

PAGE=*'filename'*   contains links to the individual pages of output contained in the HTML body file.

FRAME=*'filename'*   integrates the table of contents, the page contents, and the HTML body file.

If you specify the FRAME= option, you must also specify the CONTENTS= option, PAGE= option, or both.

Generating HTML Files

Output is directed to the specified HTML file until you

- close the HTML destination
- specify another destination file.

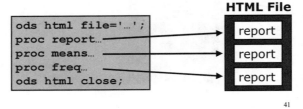

```
ods html file='…';
proc report…
proc means…
proc freq…
ods html close;
```

HTML File

report

report

report

41

Creating an HTML Report

Indicate that you want to create HTML output.

```
ods html
```

Identify where to store the HTML file.

```
ods html file='listing.html';
```

42

Creating an HTML Report

Create a report.

```
ods html file='listing.html';
proc report data=ia.comparison nowd;
    column Month …;
    define Month /…;
    other statements
run;
```

43

Creating an HTML Report

Close the HTML destination.

```
ods html file='listing.html';
proc report data=ia.comparison nowd;
    column Month …;
    define Month /…;
    other statements
run;
ods html close;
```

44

If you are not able to view HTML files in your operating environment, you can create the HTML files and FTP them to another platform for viewing. Consult your SAS and operating environment documentation for more information.

Creating HTML Reports

File: c7s3d1.sas

1. Use ODS statements and PROC REPORT to create an HTML list report.

    ```
    ods html file='listing.html';

    proc report data=ia.comparison nowd;
       column Month Region FClass BClass EClass;
       define Month  / display center;
       define Region / display center;
       define FClass / display format=dollar12.2
                       'First Class' center;
       define BClass / display format=dollar12.2
                       'Business Class' center;
       define EClass / display format=dollar12.2
                       'Economy Class' center;
       title 'HTML List Report';
    run;

    ods html close;
    ```

SAS HTML Output

HTML List Report

Month	Region	First Class	Business Class	Economy Class
1	Europe	$-9,519.86	$49,696.80	$69,953.42
1	North America	$201,323.62	$55,122.24	$265,783.52
2	Europe	$39,283.27	$95,708.98	$346,825.71
2	North America	$179,142.42	$117,457.44	$567,062.79
3	Europe	$-30,892.40	$78,634.66	$396,138.11
3	North America	$55,779.15	$97,362.38	$349,177.00
4	Europe	$71,851.76	$69,358.33	$110,510.24
4	North America	$29,880.04	$62,558.06	$615,186.80
5	Europe	$-27,530.75	$71,733.95	$499,819.92
5	North America	$127,052.96	$131,867.46	$317,823.87
6	Europe	$108,494.76	$110,510.22	$177,129.48
6	North America	$175,409.32	$51,533.25	$298,882.81
7	Europe	$125,431.46	$71,825.29	$303,767.41
7	North America	$95,644.19	$97,077.67	$456,643.13
8	Europe	$32,561.08	$12,629.60	$53,446.11
8	North America	$104,742.02	$60,261.91	$-2,344.89
9	Europe	$89,085.32	$-17,217.58	$341,705.55
9	North America	$-48,800.93	$126,105.99	$351,911.03
10	Europe	$166,557.62	$54,914.96	$85,309.59
10	North America	$40,897.79	$69,109.17	$159,570.92
11	Europe	$86,862.16	$2,866.45	$273,995.20
11	North America	$30,321.88	$121,264.80	$170,704.99
12	Europe	$121,770.59	$49,416.88	$545,034.05
12	North America	$144,144.67	$147,364.03	$732,236.65

2. Use ODS statements and PROC REPORT to create an HTML summary report.

```
ods html file='summary.html';

proc report data=ia.comparison nowd;
   column Region FClass BClass EClass;
   define Region / group;
   define FClass / sum format=dollar16.2 'First Class';
   define BClass / sum format=dollar16.2 'Business Class';
   define EClass / sum format=dollar16.2 'Economy Class';
   rbreak after  / summarize dol;
   title 'HTML Summary Report';
run;

ods html close;
```

> The RBREAK statement with the SUMMARIZE option displays a summary line in your report. AFTER indicates to place the summary line at the end of the report. DOL indicates to draw a double overline.

SAS HTML Output

HTML Summary Report

Region	First Class	Business Class	Economy Class
Europe	$773,955.01	$650,078.54	$3,203,634.79
North America	$1,135,537.13	$1,137,084.40	$4,282,638.62
	$1,909,492.14	$1,787,162.94	$7,486,273.41

Exercises

2. Creating HTML Reports

a. Recall the program from a previous exercise that created the lost cargo revenue report for Birmingham on December 15, 1999.

```
proc print data=work.compare noobs label;
   var Origin Destination Date CargoBudRev
      CargoRev LostCargoRev;
   format LostCargoRev dollar12.2;
   label LostCargoRev='Lost Cargo Revenue';
   title 'Birmingham Flights - Dec 15, 1999';
run;
```

You can include the BKUP72 file if you need a starting point.

Directory-based   `include 'bkup72.sas'`

OS/390   `include '.prog1.sascode(bkup72)'`

Alter the program so that it creates a Web-publishable HTML file called RANGE.

Directory-based   range.html

OS/390   *userid*.PROG1.SASCODE(RANGE)

HTML Output

Birmingham Flights - Dec 15, 1999

Start Point	Destination	Scheduled Date of Flight	Target Revenue from Cargo	Revenue from Cargo	Lost Cargo Revenue
BHM	RDU	15DEC1999	$3,441.00	$3,751.00	$-310.00
BHM	RDU	15DEC1999	$3,441.00	$3,441.00	$0.00
BHM	RDU	15DEC1999	$3,441.00	$2,821.00	$620.00
BHM	RDU	15DEC1999	$3,441.00	$3,751.00	$-310.00
BHM	RDU	15DEC1999	$3,441.00	$2,883.00	$558.00
BHM	RDU	15DEC1999	$3,441.00	$2,945.00	$496.00

b. Use the FREQ procedure on the data set IA.AIRCRAFT to generate a report displaying frequency counts and percentages for the long-range aircraft models. Use the variable MODEL and use a WHERE statement to subset only those models that have a range greater than 2500.

SAS Output

```
                              Long Range Aircraft

                              The FREQ Procedure

                                                Cumulative    Cumulative
Model                 Frequency     Percent     Frequency      Percent

JetCruise LF5200              9       29.03             9       29.03
JetCruise MF6000             22       70.97            31      100.00
```

c. After the report program is debugged, send the output to an HTML file called FREQ.

Directory-based   freq.html

OS/390   *userid*.PROG1.SASCODE(FREQ)

HTML Output

Long Range Aircraft

The FREQ Procedure

Model	Frequency	Percent	Cumulative Frequency	Cumulative Percent
JetCruise LF5200	9	29.03	9	29.03
JetCruise MF6000	22	70.97	31	100.00

7.4   Using the SQL Procedure (Optional)

Objectives

- Understand how SQL is used in SAS.
- Join SAS data sets and create a report.
- Join SAS data sets and create a new SAS data set.

48

Business Scenario 1

International Airlines compares monthly sales performance to monthly goals.

Sales and goal information is stored in two SAS data sets.

49

What Is SQL?

The SQL procedure uses Structured Query Language to
- retrieve and manipulate SAS data sets
- create and delete SAS data sets
- generate reports
- add or modify values in a SAS data set
- add, modify, or drop columns in a SAS data set.

50

Structured Query Language, or SQL, is a standardized language.

Creating a Report Using PROC SQL

General form of a PROC SQL query to generate output:

```
PROC SQL;
    SELECT variables
        FROM SAS-data-set;
```

51

The SELECT statement

- retrieves the data by evaluating the query
- optionally formats the selected data into a report
- displays the report in the OUTPUT destination.

Creating a Report Using PROC SQL

Create a listing report of IA.ESALES.

Invoke PROC SQL.

```
proc sql;
```

Identify the variables to display on the report.

```
proc sql;
    select Month, Sales
```

52

Creating a Report Using PROC SQL

Identify the input data set.

```
proc sql;
   select Month, Sales
      from ia.esales;
```

53

Creating a Report Using PROC SQL

Partial SAS Output

Month	Sales
1	2118222.62
2	1960034.47
3	2094220.35
4	2130248.76
5	2100211.73

54

Joining Data Sets Using PROC SQL

General form of a PROC SQL join to generate output:

```
PROC SQL;
   SELECT variables
      FROM SAS-data-set1 AS a,
           SAS-data-set2 AS b
      WHERE a.variable=b.variable;
```

55

Joining Data Sets Using PROC SQL

Create a listing report by joining IA.EGOALS and IA.ESALES by MONTH. Create a DIFFERENCE variable.

Invoke PROC SQL and list the variables to display.

```
proc sql;
    select Month, Sales, Goal,
```

56

Joining Data Sets Using PROC SQL

Create a new variable named DIFFERENCE by subtracting GOAL from SALES.

```
proc sql;
    select Month, Sales, Goal,
           Sales-Goal as Difference
```

57

Joining Data Sets Using PROC SQL

Identify the data sets to join and provide an alias for each.

```
proc sql;
    select Month, Sales, Goal,
           Sales-Goal as Difference
        from ia.esales as a,
             ia.egoals as b
```

58

Joining Data Sets Using PROC SQL

State the condition on which observations are matched.

Because MONTH exists in both data sets, identify which MONTH variable to use in each situation.

```
proc sql;
   select a.Month, Sales, Goal,
          Sales-Goal as Difference
       from ia.esales as a,
            ia.egoals as b
      where a.Month=b.Month;
```

59

Creating a Report Using PROC SQL

Partial SAS Output

Month	Sales	Goal	Difference
1	2118222.62	2127742	-9519.86
2	1960034.47	1920751	39283.27
3	2094220.35	2125113	-30892.4
4	2130248.76	2058397	71851.76
5	2100211.73	2127742	-27530.8

60

In this example, the PROC SQL join produces the same result as the DATA step merge. Because the internal process for an SQL join is different from the internal process for a merge, you see different results when

- each key value does not have a match in both data sets
- a many-to-many match occurs.

Creating a SAS Data Set

General form of a PROC SQL query to create a
SAS data set:

```
PROC SQL;
    CREATE TABLE SAS-data-set AS
        SELECT ...
        other SQL clauses;
```

61

The CREATE TABLE statement enables you to store the results of any query
in a SAS data set instead of displaying the query results in the OUTPUT
window.

Creating a SAS Data Set

Join IA.EGOALS and IA.ESALES to create a new
data set.

```
proc sql;
    create table ia.ecompare as
        select a.Month, Sales, Goal,
                Sales-Goal as Difference
            from ia.esales as a,
                ia.egoals as b
            where a.Month=b.Month;
```

62

Joining SAS Data Sets Using the SQL Procedure

File: c7s4d1.sas

1. Use PROC SQL to join two SAS data sets and create a listing report.

```
title 'Sales Performance';
proc sql;
   select a.Month, Sales, Goal,
          Sales-Goal as Difference
      from ia.esales as a,
           ia.egoals as b
      where a.Month=b.Month;
quit;
```

SAS Output

Sales Performance			
Month	Sales	Goal	Difference
1	2118222.62	2127742	-9519.86
2	1960034.47	1920751	39283.27
3	2094220.35	2125113	-30892.4
4	2130248.76	2058397	71851.76
5	2100211.73	2127742	-27530.8
6	2164796.68	2056302	108494.8
7	2252662.24	2127231	125431.5
8	2159234.26	2126673	32561.08
9	2146457.73	2057372	89085.32
10	2294300.1	2127742	166557.6
11	2144188.67	2057327	86862.16
12	2247953.83	2126183	121770.6

2. Use PROC SQL to join two SAS data sets and create a SAS data set.

```
proc sql;
   create table ia.ecompare as
      select a.Month, Sales, Goal,
             Sales-Goal as Difference
         from ia.esales as a,
              ia.egoals as b
         where a.Month=b.Month;
quit;
```

Join Features

SQL joins

- do not require sorted data
- can be performed on up to 32 data sets at one time
- allow complex matching criteria using the WHERE clause.

64

Business Scenario 2

Analyze the sales performance for Europe and North America together. To join the data sets, you must

- alter the data so that the data sets are compatible
- match observations using more than one common variable.

65

Joining Data Sets

List the desired variables.

```
proc sql;
    select Month, Region,
           FSales-FGoal as FClass,
           BSales-BGoal as BClass,
           ESales-EGoal as EClass
```

66

Joining Data Sets

Identify the contributing data sets and provide aliases.

```
proc sql;
   select Month, Region,
          FSales-FGoal as FClass,
          BSales-BGoal as BClass,
          ESales-EGoal as EClass
      from ia.sales as a,
           ia.goals as b
```

67

Joining Data Sets

Identify the matching criteria and use aliases to identify overlapping variables.

```
proc sql;
   select Month, a.Region,
          FSales-FGoal as FClass,
          BSales-BGoal as BClass,
          ESales-EGoal as EClass
      from ia.sales as a,
           ia.goals as b
      where SaleMon=Month and
            a.Region=b.Region;
```

68

Joining SAS Data Sets Using the SQL Procedure

File: c7s4d2.sas

1. Use PROC SQL to join two SAS data sets and create a listing report.

```
title 'Sales Performance';
proc sql;
   select Month, a.Region,
          FSales-FGoal as FClass,
          BSales-BGoal as BClass,
          ESales-EGoal as EClass
      from ia.sales as a,
           ia.goals as b
      where SaleMon=Month and
            a.Region=b.Region;
quit;
```

SAS Output

Sales Performance				
Month	Region	FClass	BClass	EClass
1	Europe	-9519.86	49696.8	69953.42
1	North America	201323.6	55122.24	265783.5
2	Europe	39283.27	95708.98	346825.7
2	North America	179142.4	117457.4	567062.8
3	Europe	-30892.4	78634.66	396138.1
3	North America	55779.15	97362.38	349177
4	Europe	71851.76	69358.33	110510.2
4	North America	29880.04	62558.06	615186.8
5	Europe	-27530.8	71733.95	499819.9
5	North America	127053	131867.5	317823.9
6	Europe	108494.8	110510.2	177129.5
6	North America	175409.3	51533.25	298882.8
7	Europe	125431.5	71825.29	303767.4
7	North America	95644.19	97077.67	456643.1
8	Europe	32561.08	12629.6	53446.11
8	North America	104742	60261.91	-2344.89
9	Europe	89085.32	-17217.6	341705.5
9	North America	-48800.9	126106	351911
10	Europe	166557.6	54914.96	85309.59
10	North America	40897.79	69109.17	159570.9
11	Europe	86862.16	2866.45	273995.2
11	North America	30321.88	121264.8	170705
12	Europe	121770.6	49416.88	545034
12	North America	144144.7	147364	732236.7

2.   Use PROC SQL to join two SAS data sets and create a SAS data set.

```
proc sql;
   create table ia.comparison as
      select Month, a.Region,
             FSales-FGoal as FClass,
             BSales-BGoal as BClass,
             ESales-EGoal as EClass
        from ia.sales as a,
             ia.goals as b
        where SaleMon=Month and
              a.Region=b.Region;
quit;
```

Additional SQL Features

PROC SQL enables you to

- customize column headings
- format values
- use ODS statements to create HTML reports
- summarize data.

70

Enhancing SQL Reports

General form of a PROC SQL query to use labels and formats:

```
PROC SQL;
    SELECT variable LABEL='column-head'
                    FORMAT=format.
        FROM SAS-data-set;
```

71

Enhancing SQL Reports

Enhance the previous report.

```
proc sql;
    select Month, a.Region,
            FSales-FGoal as FClass
                label='First Class'
                format=dollar12.2,
            BSales-BGoal as BClass
                label='Business Class'
                format=dollar12.2,
            ESales-EGoal as EClass
                label='Economy Class'
                format=dollar12.2
        other SQL clauses
```

72

Creating an HTML Report

Use ODS statements to create an HTML report.

```
ods html file='listing.html';
proc sql;
    select Month, a.Region,
            FSales-FGoal as FClass
                label='First Class'
                format=dollar12.2,
            BSales-BGoal as BClass
                label='Business Class'
                format=dollar12.2,
            ESales-EGoal as EClass
                label='Economy Class'
                format=dollar12.2
        other SQL clauses
ods html close;
```

73

Creating a Custom HTML Report

File: c7s4d3.sas

1. Customize an HTML listing report.

```
ods html file='listing.html';

title 'Sales Performance';
proc sql;
   select Month, a.Region,
          FSales-FGoal as FClass
             label='First Class' format=dollar12.2,
          BSales-BGoal as BClass
             label='Business Class' format=dollar12.2,
          ESales-EGoal as EClass
             label='Economy Class' format=dollar12.2
      from ia.sales as a,
           ia.goals as b
      where SaleMon=Month and
            a.Region=b.Region;
quit;

ods html close;
```

SAS HTML Output

Sales Performance				
Month	Region	First Class	Business Class	Economy Class
1	Europe	$-9,519.86	$49,696.80	$69,953.42
1	North America	$201,323.62	$55,122.24	$265,783.52
2	Europe	$39,283.27	$95,708.98	$346,825.71
2	North America	$179,142.42	$117,457.44	$567,062.79
3	Europe	$-30,892.40	$78,634.66	$396,138.11
3	North America	$55,779.15	$97,362.38	$349,177.00
4	Europe	$71,851.76	$69,358.33	$110,510.24
4	North America	$29,880.04	$62,558.06	$615,186.80
5	Europe	$-27,530.75	$71,733.95	$499,819.92
5	North America	$127,052.96	$131,867.46	$317,823.87
6	Europe	$108,494.76	$110,510.22	$177,129.48
6	North America	$175,409.32	$51,533.25	$298,882.81
7	Europe	$125,431.46	$71,825.29	$303,767.41
7	North America	$95,644.19	$97,077.67	$456,643.13
8	Europe	$32,561.08	$12,629.60	$53,446.11
8	North America	$104,742.02	$60,261.91	$-2,344.89
9	Europe	$89,085.32	$-17,217.58	$341,705.55
9	North America	$-48,800.93	$126,105.99	$351,911.03
10	Europe	$166,557.62	$54,914.96	$85,309.59
10	North America	$40,897.79	$69,109.17	$159,570.92
11	Europe	$86,862.16	$2,866.45	$273,995.20
11	North America	$30,321.88	$121,264.80	$170,704.99
12	Europe	$121,770.59	$49,416.88	$545,034.05
12	North America	$144,144.67	$147,364.03	$732,236.65

Creating Summary SQL Reports

General form of a PROC SQL query to generate summary output:

```
PROC SQL;
    SELECT group-variable,
            SUM(analysis-variable)
        FROM SAS-data-set
        GROUP BY group-variable;
```

75

Creating Summary SQL Reports

Identify the variables to display, the input data sets, and the matching criteria.

```
proc sql;
   select a.Region,
          sum(FSales-FGoal)...
      from ia.sales as a, ia.goals as b
      where SaleMon=Month and
            a.Region=b.Region
```

76

Creating Summary SQL Reports

Identify the grouping variable.

```
proc sql;
   select a.Region,
          sum(FSales-Fgoal)...
      from ia.sales as a,
           ia.goals as b
      where SaleMon=Month and
            a.Region=b.Region
      group by a.Region;
```

77

Creating Summary SQL Reports

File: c7s4d4.sas

1. Create an HTML summary report.

```
ods html file='summary.html';

proc sql;
   select a.Region,
          sum(FSales-FGoal) label='First Class'
                            format=dollar16.2,
          sum(BSales-BGoal) label='Business Class'
                            format=dollar16.2,
          sum(ESales-EGoal) label='Economy Class'
                            format=dollar16.2
      from ia.sales as a,
           ia.goals as b
      where SaleMon=Month and
            a.Region=b.Region
      group by a.Region;
quit;

ods html close;
```

SAS HTML Output

Sales Performance

Region	First Class	Business Class	Economy Clas
Europe	$773,955.01	$650,078.54	$3,203,634.7
North America	$1,135,537.13	$1,137,084.40	$4,282,638.6

Exercises

3. Using the SQL Procedure

The weather in Birmingham, Alabama, on December 15, 1999, may have caused some passengers to cancel their shipping. Investigate how much revenue was lost from the cargo on all flights out of Birmingham on that date.

a. Use PROC SQL and the IA.SALES121999 data set to create a report listing the cargo revenue for Birmingham for December 15, 1999. Display the variables ORIGIN, DESTINATION, DATE, and CARGOREV. Use the following WHERE clause to subset the data:

```
where Origin='BHM' and Date='15dec1999'd;
```

PROC SQL Output

```
                  Birmingham Flights - Dec 15, 1999

                              Scheduled
        Start                  Date of      Revenue from
        Point   Destination     Flight          Cargo
        ────────────────────────────────────────────────
        BHM       RDU         15DEC1999        $3,751.00
        BHM       RDU         15DEC1999        $3,441.00
        BHM       RDU         15DEC1999        $2,821.00
        BHM       RDU         15DEC1999        $3,751.00
        BHM       RDU         15DEC1999        $2,883.00
        BHM       RDU         15DEC1999        $2,945.00
```

b. Display a report that calculates the difference between the actual revenue and the budgeted revenue by joining the IA.BUDGET121999 and IA.SALES121999. Use the previous program as a starting point.

- Add CARGOBUDREV to your SELECT list

- Format CARGOREV and CARGOBUDREV using DOLLAR10.2

- Subtract CARGOREV from CARGOBUDREV to create a new variable called LOSTCARGOREV. Format the new variable using DOLLAR8.2 and add a label.

- Add IA.BUDGET121999 to the FROM clause. Specify aliases for each table.

- Alter the WHERE clause to include the matching criteria (this example assumes IA.SALES121999 is aliased to A and IA.BUDGET121999 is aliased to B).

```
where a.Origin='BHM' and
      a.Date='15dec1999'd and
      a.FlightID=b.FlightID and
      a.date=b.date
```

- Add the appropriate aliases to variables in the query which exist in both data sets.

PROC SQL Output

```
                      Birmingham Flights - Dec 15, 1999

                              Scheduled                 Target      Lost
              Start           Date of      Revenue     Revenue     Cargo
              Point  Destination  Flight  from Cargo  from Cargo   Revenue

              BHM    RDU      15DEC1999   $3,751.00   $3,441.00   $-310.00
              BHM    RDU      15DEC1999   $3,441.00   $3,441.00     $0.00
              BHM    RDU      15DEC1999   $2,821.00   $3,441.00   $620.00
              BHM    RDU      15DEC1999   $3,751.00   $3,441.00   $-310.00
              BHM    RDU      15DEC1999   $2,883.00   $3,441.00   $558.00
              BHM    RDU      15DEC1999   $2,945.00   $3,441.00   $496.00
```

c. Recall the previous program and alter it so that the query results are used to create a new data set called WORK.COMPARE.

4. Using PROC SQL to Create Summary HTML Reports (Optional)

a. Use PROC SQL and the IA.SALES121999 data set to create a summary report displaying the total passenger revenues for each point of origin. Specify ORIGIN as the group variable and sum the values of FCLASSREV, BCLASSREV, and ECLASSREV.

PROC SQL Output

```
                        Revenue Summary By Origin

        Start       Total First      Total Business     Total Economy
        Point       Class Revenue    Class Revenue      Class Revenue

        BHM          $392,000.00                .        $1,466,697.00
        LHR        $6,944,189.00      $5,632,402.00     $20,291,538.00
```

b. Recall the previous program and alter it to use ODS to create an HTML file called ORIGIN

Directory-based   origin.html

OS/390   *userid*.prog1.sascode(origin)

HTML Output

Revenue Summary By Origin

Start Point	Total First Class Revenue	Total Business Class Revenue	Total Economy Class Revenue
BHM	$392,000.00	.	$1,466,697.00
LHR	$6,944,189.00	$5,632,402.00	$20,291,538.00

7.5 Chapter Summary

You can use a MERGE statement in a DATA step to combine two or more SAS data sets horizontally. You merge data sets when you would like to combine the variables from each data set into one composite observation in the resulting data set. The most common merge is a match merge where you identify one or more matching variables. The matching variable must have the same value in each data set for the observations to be combined. The matching variable(s) is identified in the BY statement. Each data set to be merged must be sorted or indexed by the BY (matching) variable(s).

You can use a RENAME= data set option to change the name of variables before the merge occurs. This is most helpful when there are variables in each data set that have related values, but are not named the same.

By default, any output produced from your SAS session is sent to the standard SAS output location. The Output window is the destination for an interactive SAS session. You can use the Output Delivery System to easily create output in other forms. By using the ODS HTML statement, you can route your SAS output to an HTML file that you can view using a Web browser. All output produced by your program once the ODS HTML statement is issued is sent to the HTML file specified. To stop producing HTML output, submit an ODS HTML CLOSE statement. To route the HTML output to another file, submit an ODS HTML statement that specifies a different HTML file.

The SQL procedure is another tool you can use to query data, produce reports, and combine data sets. PROC SQL enables you to use ANSI standard Structured Query Language (SQL) in your SAS programs. You use the SELECT statement to query a data set. The SELECT statement includes a list of the variables you want to display and can include new variables that you calculate. The FROM clause specifies the data set that contains the variables. If you wish to combine data sets, you can list two or more data sets on the FROM clause separated by a comma. This is known as an SQL join. Use the WHERE clause to indicate the matching condition(s).

If you want to create a SAS data set from the result of your SQL query, use the CREATE TABLE statement. PROC SQL provides many other statements and clauses to enable you to further manipulate the data and result. For example, you can summarize the data by using a GROUP BY clause to identify a grouping variable(s).

General form of a DATA step match-merge:

> **DATA** *SAS-data-set*;
>   **MERGE** *SAS-data-sets*;
>   **BY** *by-variable(s)*;
>   *other statements*
> **RUN**;

General form of the PROC SORT step:

> **PROC SORT** DATA=*input-SAS-data-set*
>   OUT=*output-SAS-data-set*;
>   **BY** <DESCENDING> *by-variables*;
> **RUN**;

General form of the RENAME= data set option:

> *SAS-data-set*(**RENAME=(***old-name=new-name***))**

General form of the ODS statement to create an HTML file:

> **ODS** HTML FILE='*HTML-file-specification*' <options>;
> *S*AS *code generating output*
> **ODS** HTML CLOSE;

General form of a PROC SQL query to generate output:

> **PROC SQL**;
>   **SELECT** *variables*
>   **FROM** *SAS-data-set;*

General form of a PROC SQL join to generate output:

> **PROC SQL**;
>   **SELECT** *variables*
>   **FROM** *SAS-data-set1* **AS** *a,*
>   *SAS-data-set2* **AS** *b*
>   **WHERE** *a.variable=b.variable*;

General form of a PROC SQL query to create a SAS data set:

> **PROC SQL**;
>   **CREATE TABLE** *SAS-data-set* **AS**
>   **SELECT**
>   ... *other SQL clauses;*

General form of a PROC SQL query to use labels and formats:

```
PROC SQL;
     SELECT variable LABEL='column-head'
                     FORMAT=format.
     FROM SAS-data-set;
```

General form of a PROC SQL query to generate summary output:

```
PROC SQL;
     SELECT group-variable,
            SUM(analysis-variable)
     FROM SAS-data-set
     GROUP BY group-variable;
```

7.6 Solutions

1. **Sorting and Merging Data**

    a.

    ```
    proc sort data=ia.budget121999 out=work.sortb;
       by FlightID;
       where Date='15dec1999'd and Origin='BHM';
    run;
    ```

    b.

    ```
    proc sort data=ia.sales121999 out=work.sorts;
       by FlightID;
       where Date='15dec1999'd and Origin='BHM';
    run;
    ```

    c.

    ```
    data work.compare;
       merge work.sortb work.sorts;
       by FlightID;
       LostCargoRev=CargoBudRev-CargoRev;
    run;
    ```

    d.

    ```
    proc print data=work.compare noobs label;
       var Origin Destination Date CargoBudRev
           CargoRev LostCargoRev;
       format LostCargoRev dollar12.2;
       label LostCargoRev='Lost Cargo Revenue';
       title 'Birmingham Flights - Dec 15, 1999';
    run;
    ```

2. **Creating HTML Reports**

    a.

    ```
    ods html file='range.html';
      /* ods html file='.prog1.sascode(range)'; */

    proc print data=work.compare noobs label;
       var Origin Destination Date CargoBudRev
           CargoRev LostCargoRev;
       format LostCargoRev dollar12.2;
       label LostCargoRev='Lost Cargo Revenue';
       title 'Birmingham Flights - Dec 15, 1999';
    run;

    ods html close;
    ```

b.

```
proc freq data = ia.airplanes;
   tables Model;
   where Range gt 2500;
   title 'Long Range Aircraft';
run;
```

c.

```
ods html file='freq.html';
  /* ods html file='.prog1.sascode(freq)'; */

proc freq data = ia.airplanes;
   tables Model;
   where Range gt 2500;
   title 'Long Range Aircraft';
run;

ods html close;
```

3.   **Using the SQL Procedure**

a.

```
title 'Birmingham Flights - Dec 15, 1999';
proc sql;
   select Origin, Destination,
          Date, CargoRev
      from ia.sales121999
      where Origin='BHM' and
            Date='15dec1999'd;
quit;
```

b.

```
proc sql;
   select a.Origin, a.Destination, a.Date,
          CargoRev format=dollar10.2,
          CargoBudRev format=dollar10.2,
          CargoBudRev-CargoRev as LostCargoRev
             format=dollar8.2
             label='Lost Cargo Revenue'
      from ia.sales121999 as a,
           ia.budget121999 as b
      where a.Origin='BHM' and
            a.Date='15dec1999'd and
            a.FlightID=b.FlightID and
            a.date=b.date;
quit;
```

c.

```
proc sql;
   create table work.compare as
      select a.Origin, a.Destination, a.Date,
            CargoRev format=dollar10.2,
            CargoBudRev format=dollar10.2,
            CargoBudRev-CargoRev as LostCargoRev
               format=dollar8.2
               label='Lost Cargo Revenue'
         from ia.sales121999 as a,
            ia.budget121999 as b
         where a.Origin='BHM' and
            a.Date='15dec1999'd and
            a.FlightID=b.FlightID and
            a.date=b.date;
   quit;
```

4. **Using PROC SQL to Create Summary HTML Reports (Optional)**

   a.

```
title 'Revenue Summary By Origin';
proc sql;
   select Origin,
         sum(FClassRev) format=dollar15.2
            label='Total First Class Revenue',
         sum(BClassRev) format=dollar15.2
            label='Total Business Class Revenue',
         sum(EClassRev) format=dollar15.2
            label='Total Economy Class Revenue'
      from ia.sales121999
      group by Origin;
   quit;
```

   b.

```
ods html file='origin.html';
  /* ods html file='.prog1.sascode(origin)'; */

proc sql;
   select Origin,
         sum(FClassRev) format=dollar15.2
            label='Total First Class Revenue',
         sum(BClassRev) format=dollar15.2
            label='Total Business Class Revenue',
         sum(EClassRev) format=dollar15.2
            label='Total Economy Class Revenue'
      from ia.sales121999
      group by Origin;
   quit;

ods html close;
```

Chapter 8   Learning More

8.1 Where Do I Go From Here?

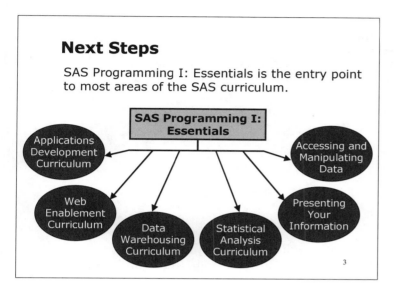

SAS Institute offers a variety of comprehensive training curricula. Courses are available to address all aspects of the SAS System:

- data access
- data analysis
- data presentation
- data warehousing
- applications development.

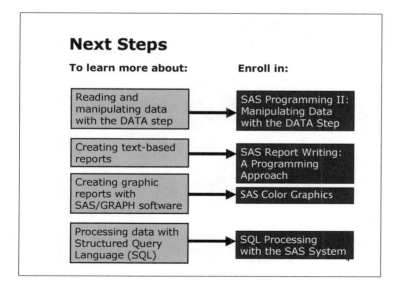

Next Steps

Refer to the SAS Training Web site at
www.sas.com/service/edu/certify/intro.html
for more information on these classes and the
broad curriculum of courses available from SAS
Institute Inc.

5

You can register for a course through the SAS Training Web site
(www.sas.com/service/edu/intro.html) or by calling **1-800-333-7660.**

Next Steps

Consider taking a certification exam to assess
your knowledge of SAS software. For a current
listing of certification exams and registration
information, visit
www.sas.com/service/edu/certify/intro.html.

6

8.2 SAS Institute Resources

SAS Services

SAS is a full-service company that
provides

Consulting   short- or long-term consulting
                  services to meet business needs

Training   instructor-based and online training
                  options

Certification   global certification program to
                  assess knowledge of SAS software
                  and earn industry-recognized
                  credentials.

8

SAS Services

SAS is a full-service company that
provides

Online Help   a comprehensive online
                  Help system to address many
                  information needs

Documentation   extensive online and hardcopy
                  reference information

Technical Support specialists for all SAS software
                  products and supported
                  operating systems.

9

SAS Services

Access the SAS Web site at **www.sas.com** to learn more about available software, support, and services and to take advantage of these offerings.

10

You can use the SAS Web site to

- read about software, either by application or by industry
- learn about upcoming worldwide events, such as industry trade shows
- report problems to the Technical Support Division
- learn about consulting services
- identify the most appropriate learning path and register for courses online
- review the list of certification exams designed to assess knowledge of SAS software; identify test preparation options; and register online for a certification exam
- browse and order from the online version of the *SAS® Publications Catalog*
- access online versions of SAS publications.

Consulting Services

SAS offers flexible consulting options to meet short- or long-term business needs. Services such as installation, needs assessment, project scoping, prototyping, or short-term technical assistance help you reap the benefits of SAS software as quickly as possible.

Consultants provide expertise in areas such as

- data warehousing
- data mining
- business intelligence
- Web-enablement tasks
- e-intelligence
- analytical solutions
- business solutions
- custom applications
- client/server technology
- systems-related issues.

Training Services

SAS offers training services and a certification program to help you achieve business and professional goals. Whether you are a beginning or an accomplished SAS software user, training services are available to help you increase your skills and expand your knowledge.

Instructor-based Training offers both public and on-site courses that encompass the breadth of SAS software including

- the SAS programming language
- report writing
- applications development
- data warehousing
- client/server strategies
- structured query language (SQL)
- financial consolidation and reporting
- database access
- statistical analysis.

Seminars led by industry experts are also available through the Business Knowledge Series to provide you with expertise in the latest business developments.

Online Training combines the instructional quality of SAS courses with the benefits of self-paced training.

SAS OnlineTutor for Version 8: SAS Programming is the latest online training product. With thirty-five comprehensive, highly interactive lessons and also quizzes and exercises to test your comprehension, SAS OnlineTutor provides fifty to sixty hours of instruction.

The content is relevant to both novice and intermediate SAS software users. The lessons range from how to use the new features in the Version 8 SAS environment to how to write programming code to access, manage, analyze, and present your data.

For more information about training services, visit the Web at www.sas.com/training and order the complimentary *SAS Training*™ catalog, published biannually.

The **SAS Certified Professional Program** provides SAS software users with the opportunity to earn globally recognized credentials that signify their knowledge of SAS software.

How does certification benefit you? The SAS Certified Professional credentials inform current or prospective employers of your proficiency with SAS software and distinguish you as a leading technical professional. The SAS Certified Professional Program represents an opportunity for you to

- assess your knowledge of SAS software
- enhance your credibility as a technical professional
- earn industry recognition for your knowledge
- increase your career opportunities and marketability to employers.

For Version 6 of SAS software, four exams comprise the core program and assess knowledge in various areas of SAS programming, including data management, business intelligence reporting, and application development.

Version 8 certification exams are projected to be available in beta form throughout the third and fourth quarter, 2000, and first quarter, 2001. These exams include

- SAS Core Concepts V8 Exam (Level I)
- Data Management V8 Exam
- Data Warehousing V8 Exam
- Application Development (Traditional/Frame) V8 Exam
- Application Development (Integrated Technologies) V8 Exam
- Web Java-Based V8 Exam
- Web Non-Java V8 Exam
- Report Writing V8 Exam.

Individuals certified in Version 6 of SAS software will not be required to take a Version 8 exam to maintain Version 6 certification. Version 8 exams provide previously certified candidates with the opportunity to upgrade their certification status to be current with Version 8 of SAS software.

For more information on the SAS Certified Professional Program, please visit www.sas.com/certification.

Online Help and Documentation

SAS features an extensive online Help system.

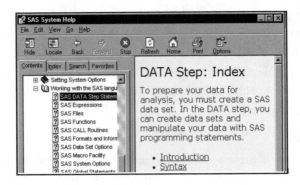

Online Help and Documentation

You can also access SAS OnlineDoc, which provides you with SAS System reference documentation.

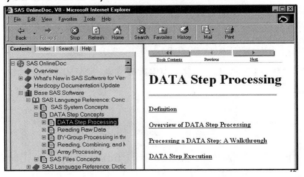

SAS Documentation

SAS documentation is also available in hardcopy. Some useful references are

- *SAS® Language Reference: Concepts, Version 8* (order # Q57375)
- *SAS® Language Reference: Dictionary, Version 8, Volumes 1 and 2* (order # Q57239)
- *SAS® Procedures Guide, Version 8* (order # Q57238)

continued...

13

SAS Documentation

- *The Complete Guide to the SAS® Output Delivery System, Version 8* (order # Q57241)
- *SAS/GRAPH® Software: Reference, Version 8* (order # Q57263)
- *SAS® SQL Query Window User's Guide, Version 8* (order # Q57280).

14

Publications Services

For a complete list of documentation available in online and hardcopy form, access the SAS Publications Web site at www.sas.com/pubs.

 You can order documentation using the Publications Catalog through the SAS Publications Web site or by calling **1-800-727-3228**.

SAS also publishes a number of magazines and newsletters. To view these periodicals, access the SAS Publications Web site.

SAS also offers **SelecText**, a service for U.S. colleges and universities. The SelecText service allows instructors to create custom course textbooks for teaching students to use SAS software. Access the SelecText Web site at www.sas.com/selectext or send email to selectext@sas.com.

Technical Support Services

Technical Support provides you with the resources to answer any questions or solve any problems that you encounter when you use SAS software. You have access to a variety of tools to solve problems on your own and a variety of ways to contact Technical Support when you need help.

- **Free, Unlimited Support**

  Free technical support is available to all sites that license software from SAS. This includes unlimited telephone support for customers in North America by calling **1-919-677-8008**. Customers outside North America can contact their local SAS Institute office. There is also an electronic mail interface and FTP site.

- **Reported Problems**

  Although SAS software is recognized as a leader in reliability, SAS realizes that no software is problem-free. We do our best to let you know about bugs or problems that have been reported to Technical Support. Information about reported problems is available in the SAS Notes and SAS/C Compiler Usage Notes, which are distributed with the software, and can also be searched via the Web interface. We also inform you about more serious problems through Alert Notes and the TSNEWS-L list server.

- **Local Support at Your Site**

  To provide the most effective response to your questions and problems, one or more people at your site are designated as local SAS Support personnel. These are knowledgeable SAS users who are provided with additional resources to assist all SAS users at your site. You can often get a quick answer to your SAS questions by contacting your local SAS consultant before calling SAS Technical Support.

Index